Standard Grade | General | Credit

Geography

General Level 2003

Credit Level 2003

General Level 2004

Credit Level 2004

General Level 2005

Credit Level 2005

General Level 2006

Credit Level 2006

General Level 2007

Credit Level 2007

Leckie × Leckie

First exam published in 2003.
Published by Leckie & Leckie Ltd, 3rd Floor, 4 Queen Street, Edinburgh EH2 1JE
tel: 0131 220 6831 fax: 0131 225 9987 enquiries@leckieandleckie.co.uk www.leckieandleckie.co.uk

ISBN 978-1-84372-512-1

A CIP Catalogue record for this book is available from the British Library.

Printed in Scotland by Scotprint.

Leckie & Leckie is a division of Huveaux plc.

Leckie & Leckie is grateful to the copyright holders, as credited at the back of the book, for permission to use their material. Every effort has been made to trace the copyright holders and to obtain their permission for the use of copyright material. Leckie & Leckie will gladly receive information enabling them to rectify any error or omission in subsequent editions.

2003 | General

[BLANK PAGE]

FOR OFFICIAL USE

G

KU	ES

Total Marks

1260/403

NATIONAL QUALIFICATIONS 2003

THURSDAY, 15 MAY
10.25 AM–11.50 AM

GEOGRAPHY
STANDARD GRADE
General Level

Fill in these boxes and read what is printed below.

Full name of centre

Town

Forename(s)

Surname

Date of birth
Day Month Year

Scottish candidate number

Number of seat

1 Read the whole of each question carefully before you answer it.

2 Write in the spaces provided.

3 Where boxes like this ☐ are provided, put a tick ✓ in the box beside the answer you think is correct.

4 Try all the questions.

5 Do not give up the first time you get stuck: you may be able to answer later questions.

6 Extra paper may be obtained from the invigilator, if required.

7 Before leaving the examination room you must give this book to the invigilator. If you do not, you may lose all the marks for this paper.

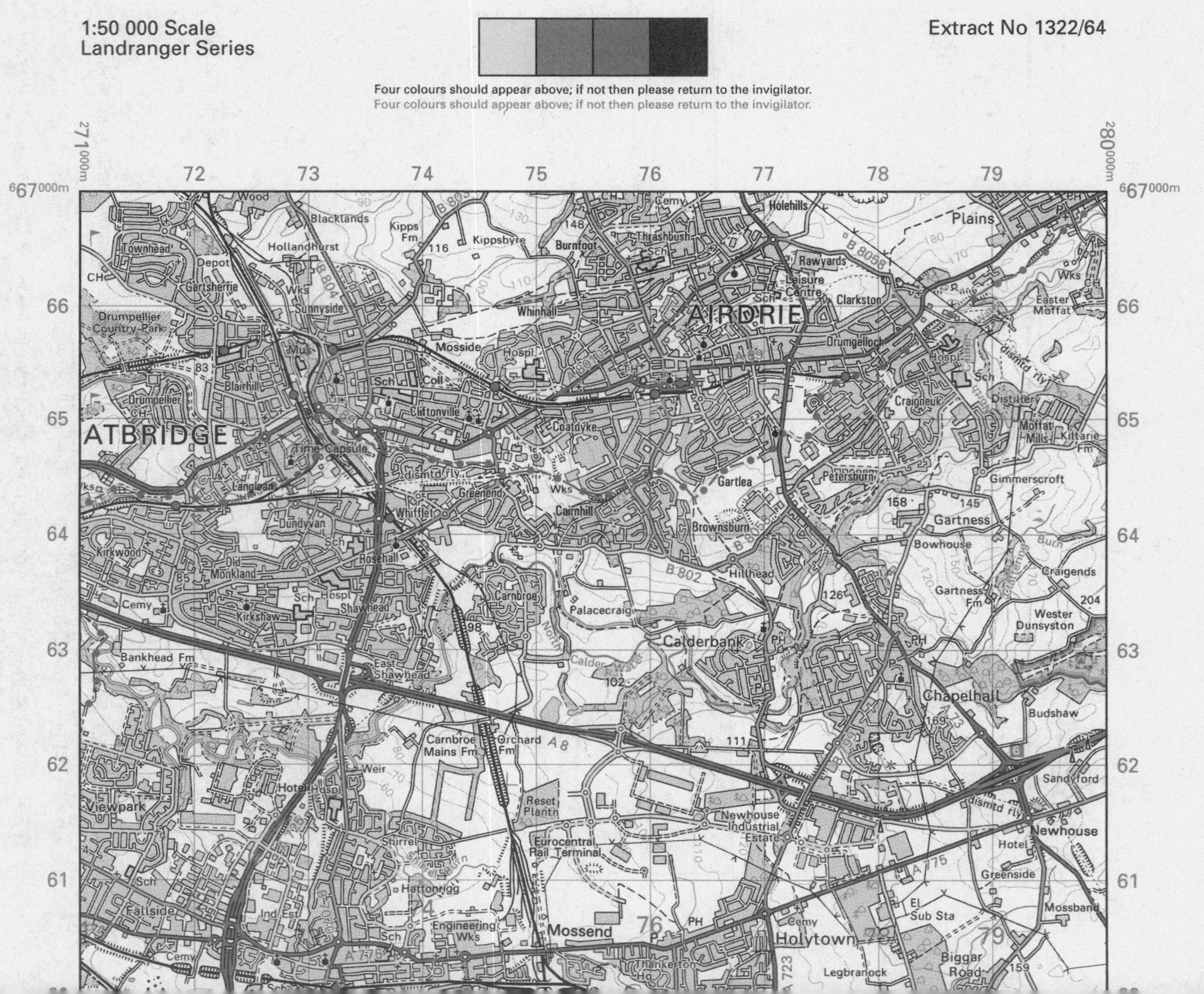
1:50 000 Scale
Landranger Series
Extract No 1322/64
Four colours should appear above; if not then please return to the invigilator.
AIRDRIE
ATBRIDGE
Chapelhall
Calderbank
Holytown
Mossend
Newhouse
Plains
Eurocentral Rail Terminal
Newhouse Industrial Estate
Drumpellier Country Park
Viewpark
Gartness
Petersburn
Gartlea
Coatdyke
Whinhall
Clarkston
271000m
280000m
667000m

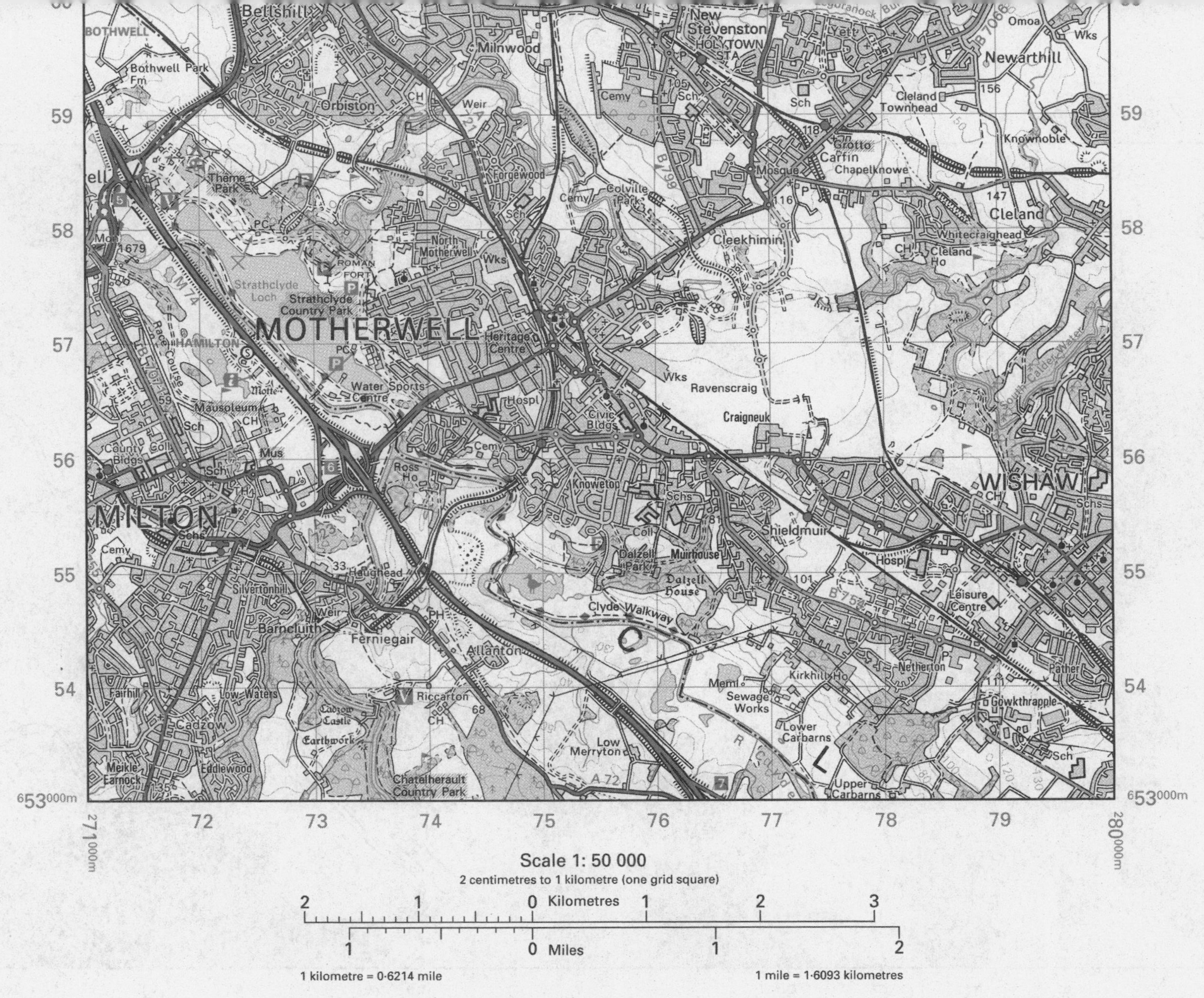
MOTHERWELL
WISHAW
MILTON
HAMILTON
Strathclyde Country Park
Strathclyde Loch
Water Sports Centre
Heritage Centre
Clyde Walkway
Dalzell House
Dalzell Park
Chatelherault Country Park
Cadzow Castle
New Stevenston
Newarthill
Cleland
Carfin
Craigneuk
Ravenscraig
Cleekhimin
Shieldmuir
Netherton
Orbiston
Bothwell Park Fm
Milnwood
North Motherwell
Knowetop
Muirhouse
Ferniegair
Barncluith
Allanton
Riccarton
Low Merryton
Lower Carbarns
Upper Carbarns
Gowkthrapple
Scale 1: 50 000
2 centimetres to 1 kilometre (one grid square)
Kilometres
Miles
1 kilometre = 0·6214 mile
1 mile = 1·6093 kilometres

1. **Reference Diagram Q1A**

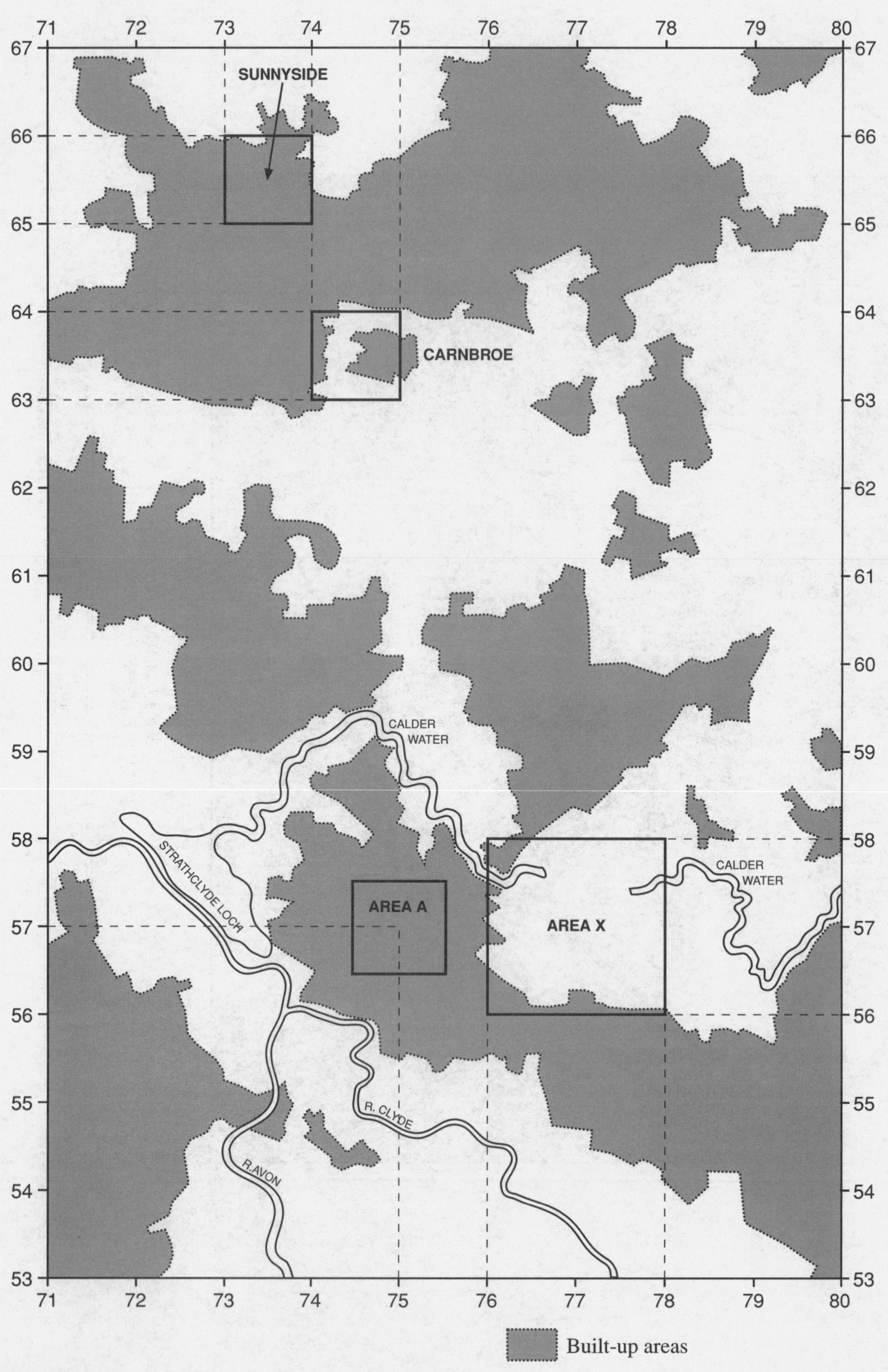

DO NOT WRITE IN THIS MARGIN

KU ES

Marks

1. (continued)

Look at the Ordnance Survey Map Extract (No 1322/64) and at Reference Diagram Q1A on *Page two*.

(*a*) Give map evidence to show that the CBD of Motherwell is in Area A. **3**

(*b*) Two residential areas of Coatbridge are found in squares 7365 (Sunnyside) and 7463 (Carnbroe).

Describe the differences between these areas, referring to map evidence. **4**

(*c*) Find Bankhead Farm at 713630.

Using map evidence, describe the advantages **and** disadvantages of its location. **4**

[Turn over

DO NOT WRITE IN THIS MARGIN

KU	ES

Marks

1. (continued)

Reference Diagram Q1B: An old Ordnance Survey Map of part of Motherwell (1950 edition)

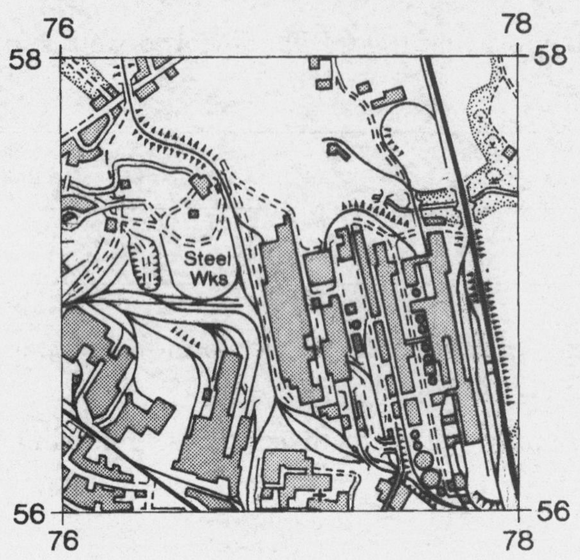

(*d*) (i) The area shown on the diagram above is identified as Area X on Reference Diagram Q1A.

Look at the Ordnance Survey Extract **and** the old Ordnance Survey Map above.

Describe the changes which have taken place between 1950 and the present day.

____

____

____

______________________________ 3

(ii) Comparing old and new maps is one technique for gathering data on land use.

State **two other** techniques that local pupils could use to gather information about land use change in this industrial area.

Give reasons for your choice.

Technique one ______________________________

Technique two ______________________________

Reasons ______________________________

____

____

______________________________ 4

DO NOT WRITE IN THIS MARGIN

KU	ES

Marks

1. (continued)

(*e*) Strathclyde Country Park is centred on Strathclyde Loch.

Using map evidence, describe the attractions which this park has for visitors.

3

(*f*) Describe the **physical** features of the River Clyde **and** its valley between 774530 and 737560.

4

[Turn over

2. **Reference Diagram Q2: Landscapes of the Tay Valley**

Q2A: Upper Course of the River Tay

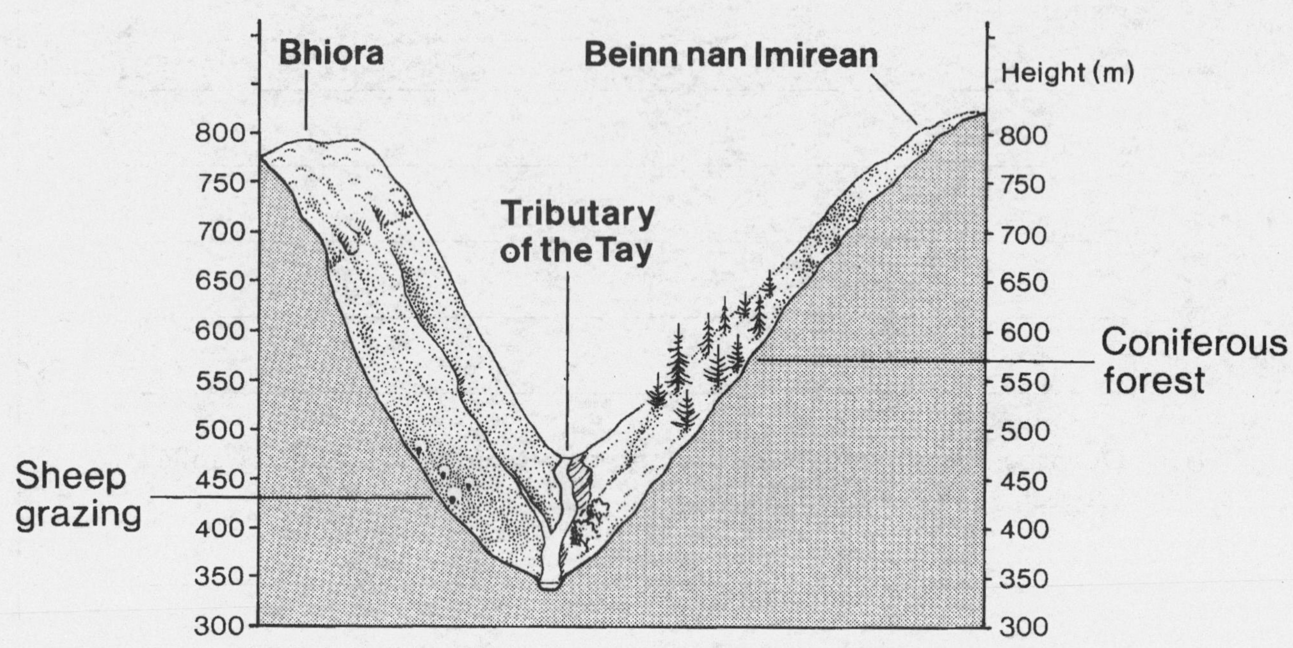

Q2B: Lower Course of the River Tay

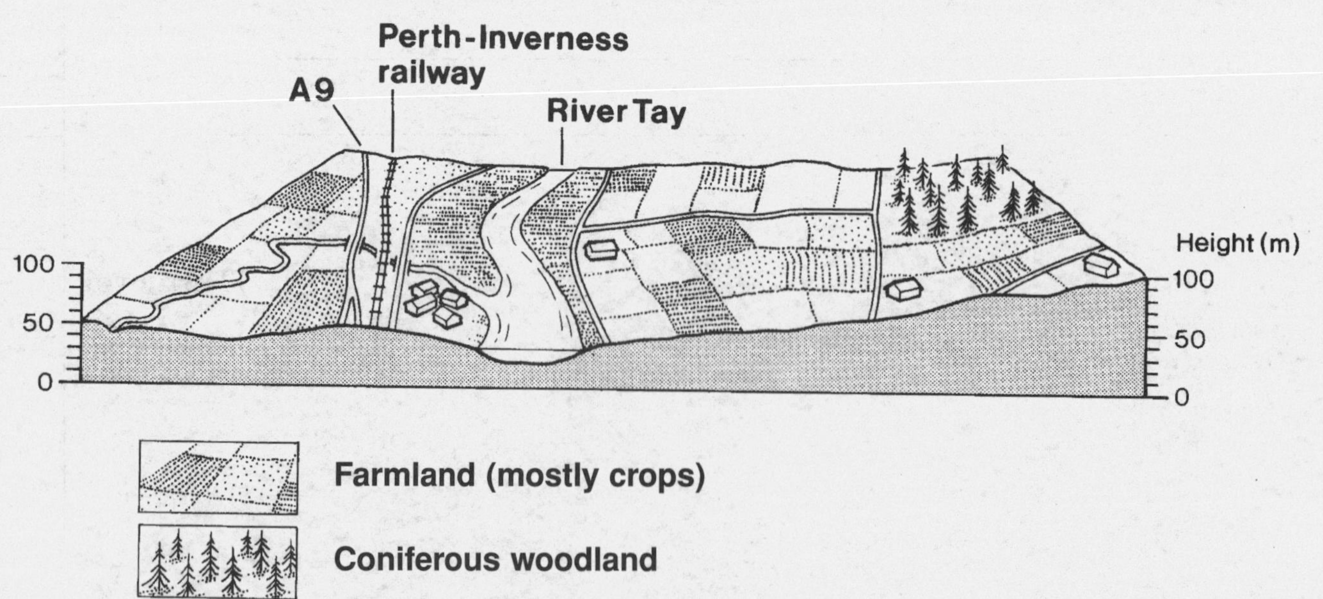

DO NOT WRITE IN THIS MARGIN

KU ES

Marks

2. (continued)

(*a*) Look at the landscapes shown in the Reference Diagram opposite.

Compare the **physical** features of the River Tay and its valley in the two diagrams.

4

(*b*) **Explain** why land use along the River Tay is different in the two diagrams.

4

[Turn over

DO NOT WRITE IN THIS MARGIN

KU | ES

Marks

3. Reference Diagram Q3A: Features of a Stevenson Screen

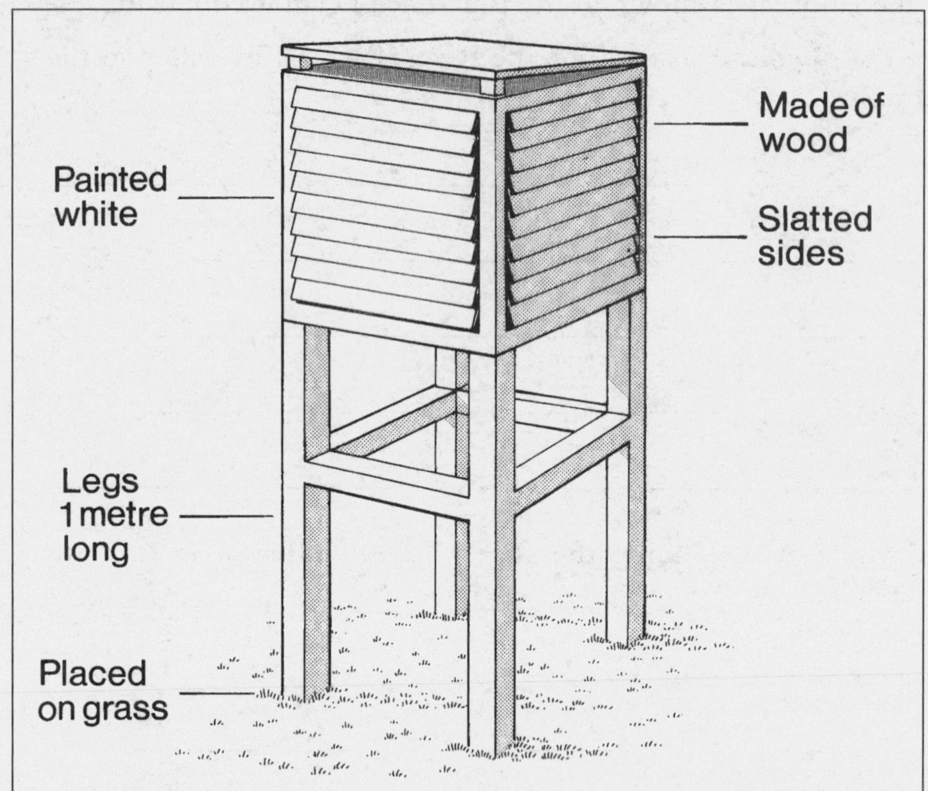

(*a*) Look at Reference Diagram Q3A which shows some design features of a Stevenson Screen which is used to house thermometers.

Choose **three** of these features and for each **explain** why it is necessary.

First Feature Chosen ____________________

Explanation ____________________

____

Second Feature Chosen ____________________

Explanation ____________________

____

Third Feature Chosen ____________________

Explanation ____________________

____________________ **3**

DO NOT WRITE IN THIS MARGIN

KU	ES

Marks

3. (continued)

Reference Diagram Q3B: Weather Map of Mainland Scotland on 25 November 2001

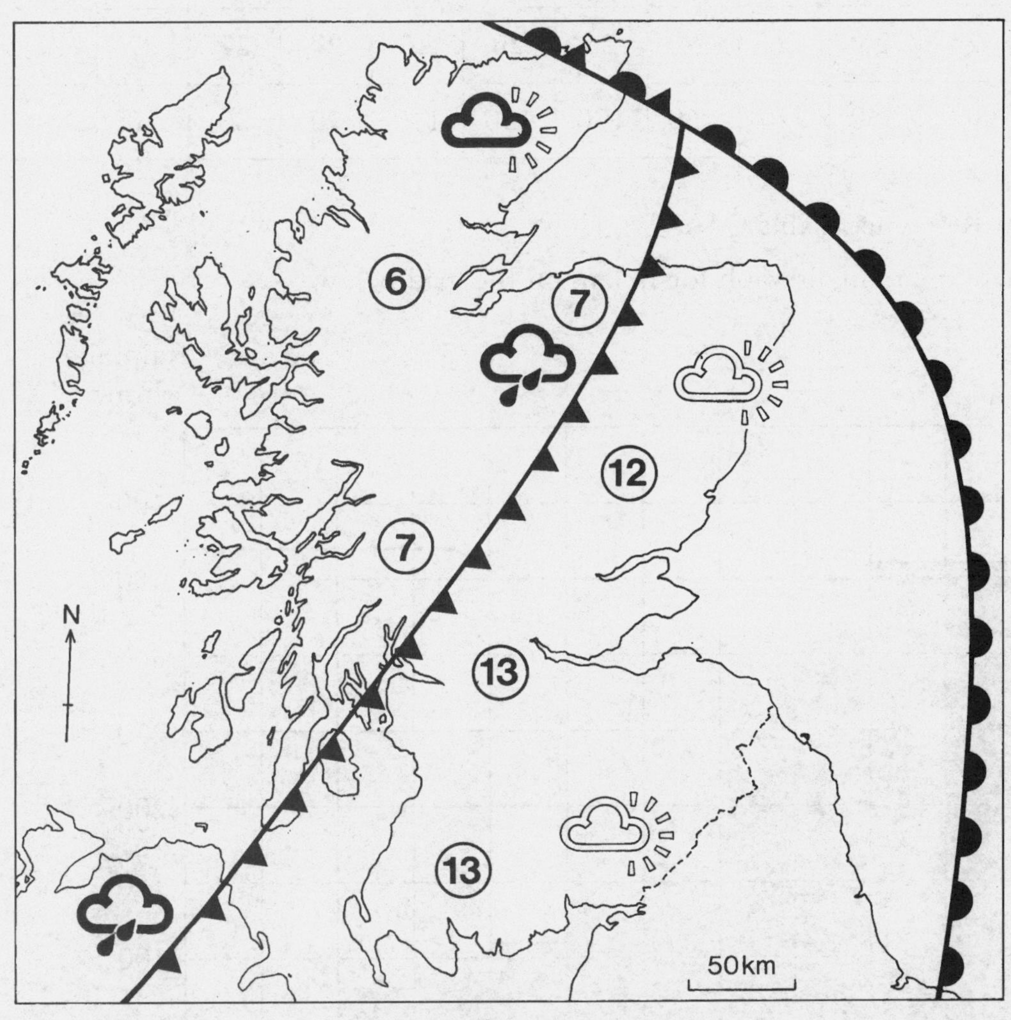

(*b*) Look at Reference Diagram Q3B.

Give reasons for the variations in temperatures throughout Scotland on 25 November.

____

____

____

____

____

____ **3**

DO NOT WRITE IN THIS MARGIN

KU | ES

Marks

4. Reference Table Q4A: Climate Statistics for Belem, Brazil

	J	F	M	A	M	J	J	A	S	O	N	D
Temperature (°C)	27	26	26	26	26	26	26	26	27	27	27	27
Rainfall (mm)	320	360	360	320	260	170	150	110	90	80	70	160

(*a*) Look at Reference Table Q4A.

Complete the rainfall graph for Belem on the grid below.

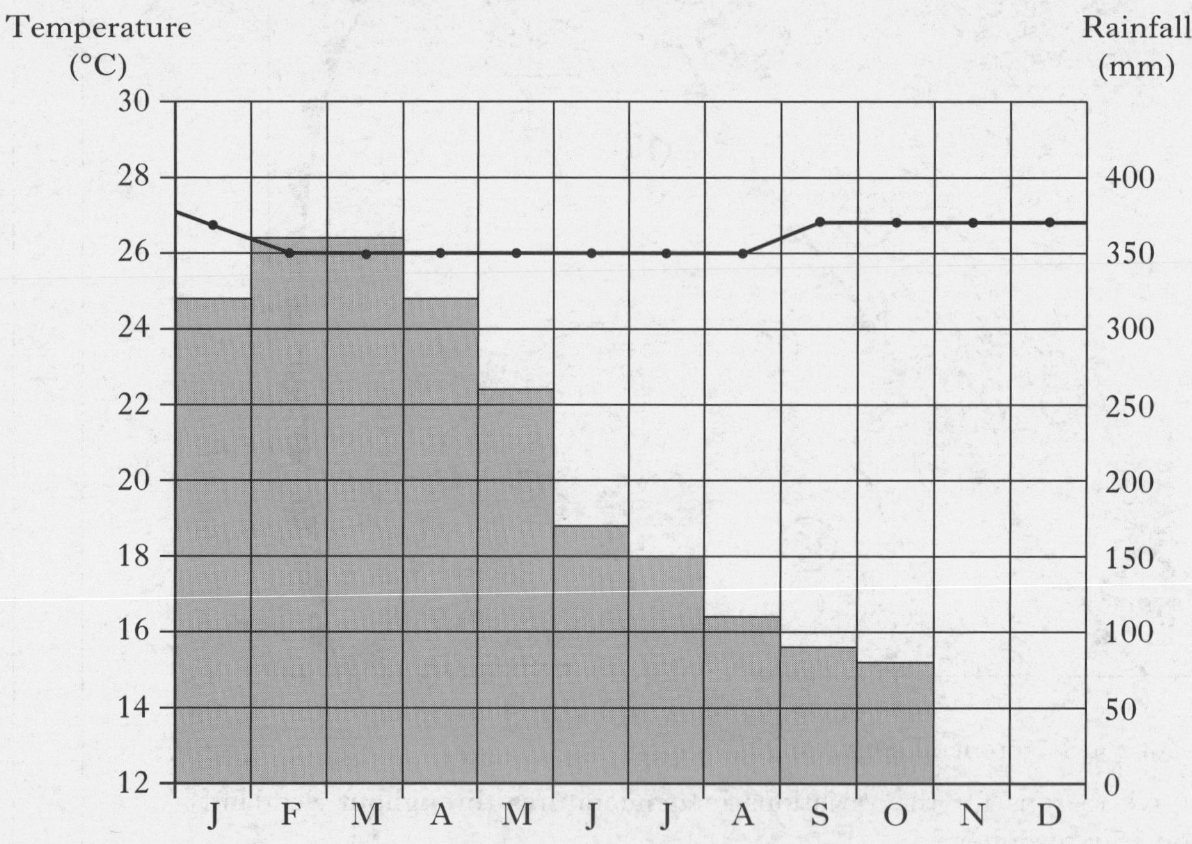

2

(*b*) Describe in detail the climate of Belem.

4

4. (continued)

Reference Diagram Q4B: Causes of Deforestation in Brazil

Trans Amazon Highway

Cattle Ranching

Open-Cast Iron Ore Mine

DO NOT WRITE IN THIS MARGIN

	KU	ES

Marks

(*c*) Look at Reference Diagram Q4B above.

Describe the effects of the activities shown in the diagram on the environment **and** people of Brazil's rainforest.

____

____

____

____

____

____ 4

[Turn over

5. **Reference Diagram Q5A: Needs for a Modern Port**

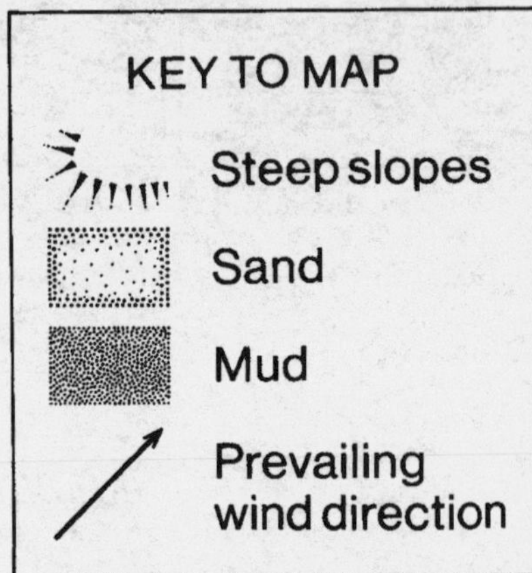

Reference Diagram Q5B: Potential Sites for a Modern Port

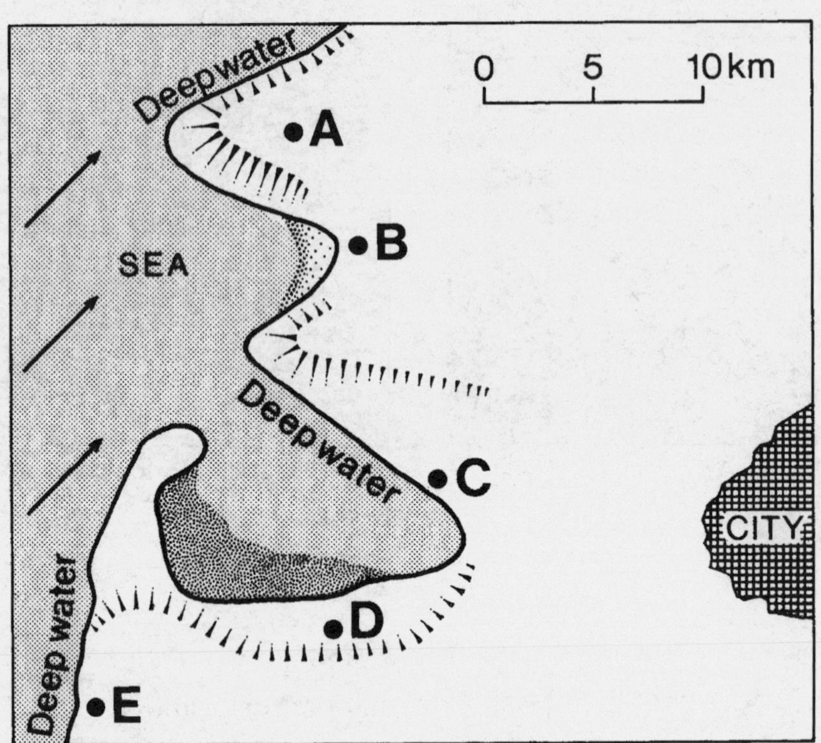

DO NOT WRITE IN THIS MARGIN

	KU	ES

Marks

Look at Reference Diagrams Q5A and Q5B.

Which site—**A**, **B**, **C**, **D** or **E**—is the best for a modern port?

Choice __________

Give reasons for your answer.

____

____

____

____

____ **4**

DO NOT WRITE IN THIS MARGIN

KU	ES

Marks

6. Reference Diagram Q6A: Migration from Rural Areas in Developing Countries

(*a*) Look at Reference Diagram Q6A.

People living in rural areas in developing countries can face many problems which may encourage them to migrate to cities.

Describe the type of problems found in such rural areas.

____

____

____

____

____ **4**

[Turn over

6. (continued)

Reference Diagram Q6B: Migrants' View of Life in a Developing City

DO NOT WRITE IN THIS MARGIN

	KU	ES

Marks

(*b*) Look at Reference Diagram Q6B.

Do you think people benefit by moving from the countryside to the city?

Explain your answer.

4

DO NOT WRITE IN THIS MARGIN

KU	ES

Marks

7. Reference Diagram Q7: Headquarters of the World's 100 Largest Companies

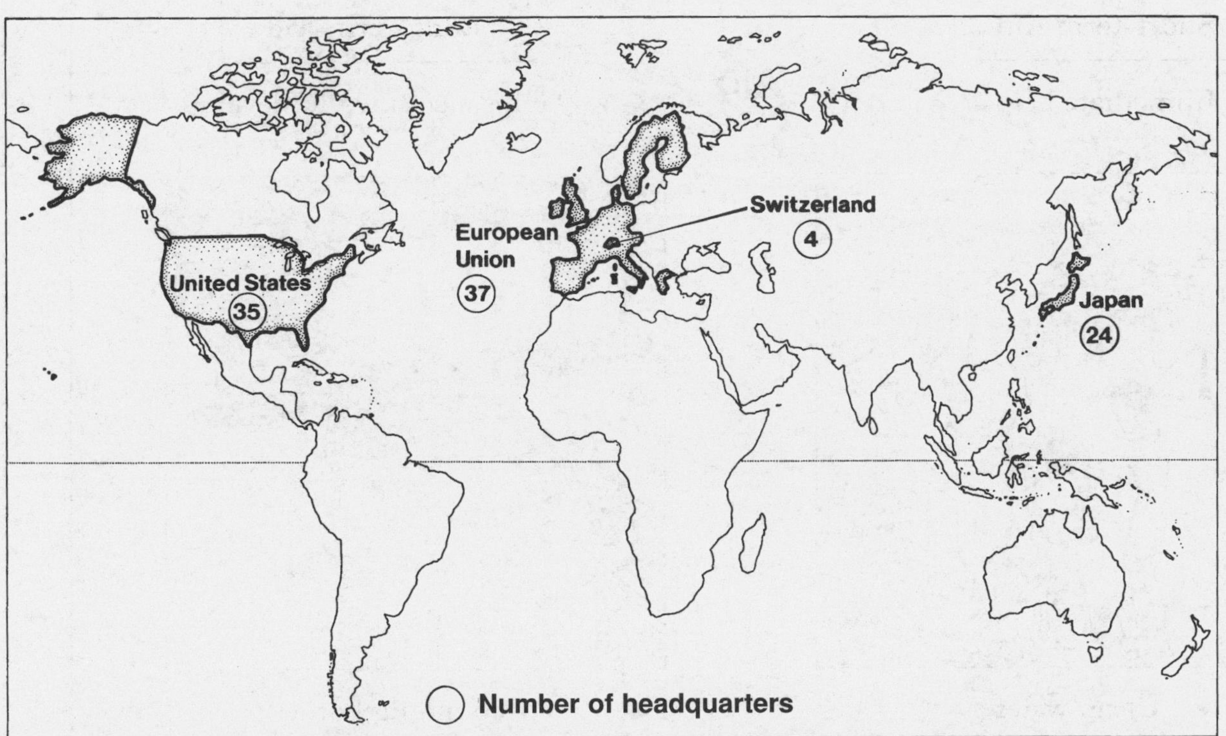

Look at Reference Diagram Q7 above.

(*a*) Give reasons for the location of the world's 100 largest companies. **3**

(*b*) Give **one other** technique that could be used to process the information shown on the map.

Give reasons for your choice. **3**

 [Turn over for Question 8 on *Page sixteen*

DO NOT WRITE IN THIS MARGIN

KU | ES

Marks

8. **Reference Diagram Q8: Aid to Developing Countries**

Short-term Aid	Long-term Aid
Immediate help	Helps a country to develop

- Clean water
- Food
- Emergency shelter
- Medicines

- Rebuilding homes
- Road building
- Electricity network
- Building hospitals

Look at Reference Diagram Q8.

Which type of aid, short-term or long-term, would be most useful to a **developing** country after an earthquake?

Give reasons for your answer.

____

____

____

____

____ 4

[*END OF QUESTION PAPER*]

[BLANK PAGE]

C

1260/405

NATIONAL QUALIFICATIONS 2003

THURSDAY, 15 MAY
1.00 PM – 3.00 PM

GEOGRAPHY
STANDARD GRADE
Credit Level

All questions should be attempted.

Candidates should read the questions carefully. Answers should be clearly expressed and relevant.

Credit will always be given for appropriate sketch-maps and diagrams.

Write legibly and neatly, and leave a space of about one cm between the lines.

Marks may be deducted for bad spelling and bad punctuation, and for writing that is difficult to read.

All maps and diagrams in this paper have been printed in black only: no other colours have been used.

THB 1260/405 6/3/20170

Extract No 1323/36/43

Four colours should appear above; if not then please return to the invigilator.

Four colours should appear above; if not then please return to the invigilator.

1:50 000 Scale
Landranger Series

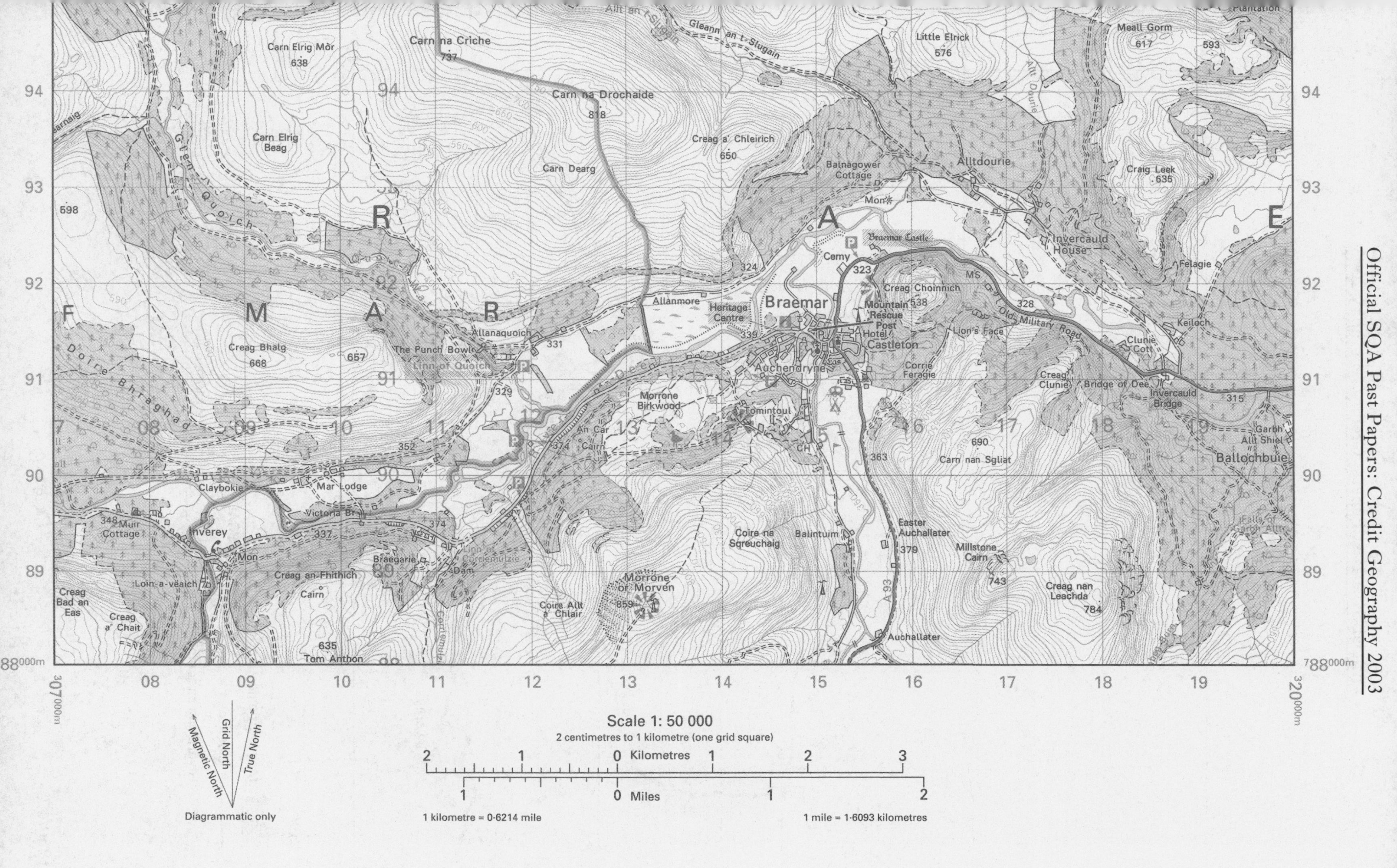
Carn Elrig Mòr
638
Carn na Criche
737
Gleann an t-Slugain
Little Elrick
576
Meall Gorm
617
593
Carn na Drochaide
818
Carn Elrig Beag
Glen Quoich
Creag a' Chleirich
650
Carn Dearg
Balnagower Cottage
Alltdourie
Craig Leek
635
598
R
A
E
Braemar Castle
Invercauld House
Cemy
323
324
Felagie
F
M
A
R
Allanmore
Heritage Centre
Braemar
Creag Choinnich
Mountain Rescue Post
538
MS
Old Military Road
328
Keiloch
Allanaquoich
The Punch Bowl
Linn of Quoich
331
339
Hotel
Castleton
Lion's Face
Clunie Cott
Creag Bhalg
668
657
Doire Bhraghad
Auchendryne
Corrie Feragie
329
Morrone Birkwood
Tomintoul
Creag Clunie
Bridge of Dee
Invercauld Bridge
315
An Car
374
Cairn
352
CH
690
Carn nan Sgliat
363
Garbh Allt Shiel
Ballochbuie
Claybokie
Mar Lodge
Victoria Br
348
Muir Cottage
Inverey
337
374
Coire na Sgreuchaig
Balintuim
Easter Auchallater
379
Millstone Cairn
Falls of Garbh Allt
Mon
Braegarie
Linn of Corriemulzie
Dam
Loin-a-veaich
Creag an Fhithich
Cairn
Morrone or Morven
859
743
Creag nan Leachda
784
Creag Bad an Eas
Creag a' Chait
Coire Allt a' Chlair
A 93
635
Tom Anthon
Auchallater
Corriemulzie
307000m
320000m
788000m
Scale 1: 50 000
2 centimetres to 1 kilometre (one grid square)
Kilometres
Miles
1 kilometre = 0·6214 mile
1 mile = 1·6093 kilometres
Grid North
True North
Magnetic North
Diagrammatic only

1. **Reference Diagram Q1A**

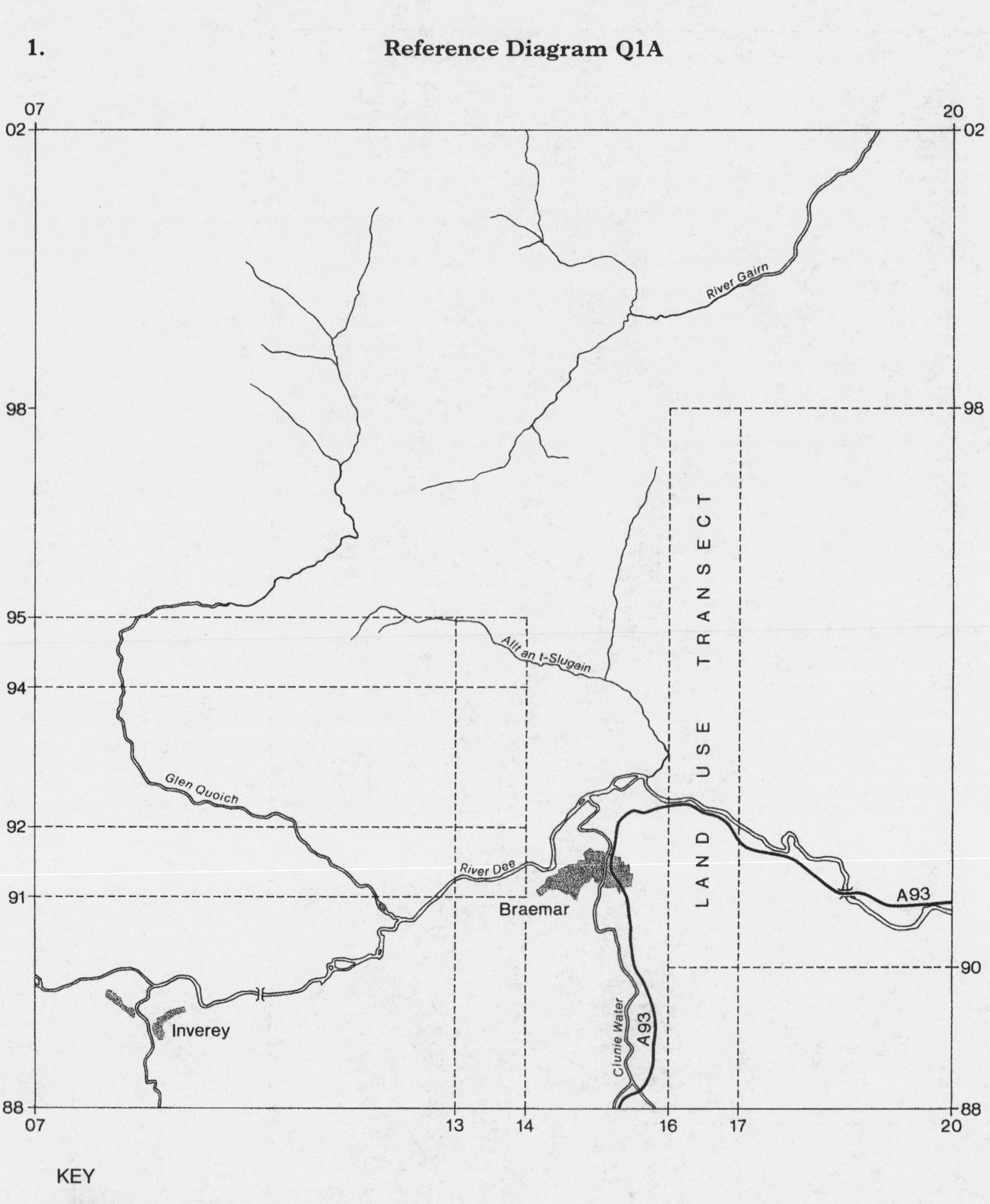

Marks KU ES

1. (continued)

This question refers to the OS Map Extract (No 1323/36/43) of the Braemar Area and the Reference Diagram Q1A on *Page two*.

(*a*) (i) Match each of the features named below with the correct grid reference.

Features: hanging valley; truncated spur; corrie; U shaped valley.

Choose from grid references: 094992, 134996, 155993, 146980. **3**

(ii) **Explain** how **one** of these features listed in (*a*)(i) was formed.

You may use diagrams to illustrate your answer. **4**

Reference Diagram Q1B: Requirements for National Park Status

High quality landscape	*Variety of plant and animal habitats*
Recreation and tourist value	*Historic features*

Reference Diagram Q1C: Main Land Uses in the Braemar Area

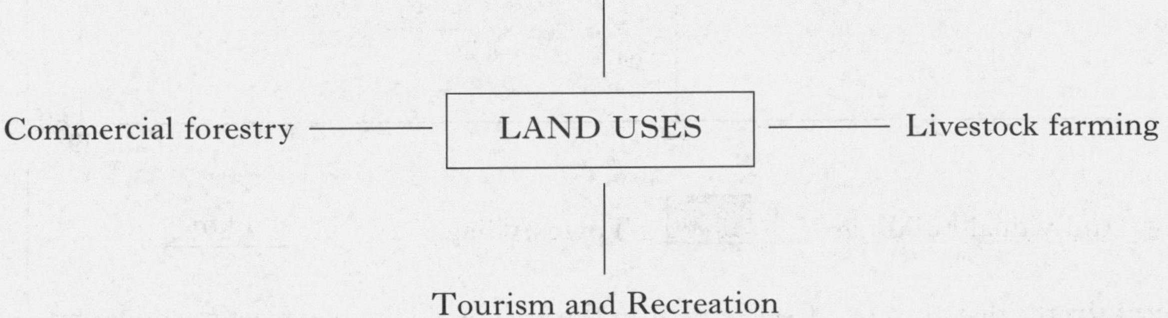

(*b*) Look at Reference Diagrams Q1B and Q1C.

The whole of the area covered by the OS map extract is within the recently designated Cairngorm National Park.

Describe the advantages **and** disadvantages this area has for a national park.

Use map evidence to support your answer. **6**

[Turn over

Marks | KU |

1. (continued)

(*c*) Study Reference Diagram Q1A and the OS map extract.

The Rivers Dee (1391) and Allt an t-Slugain (1394) and their valleys are very different.

Describe these differences **in detail**.

Reference Diagram Q1D: Settlement Pattern around Braemar

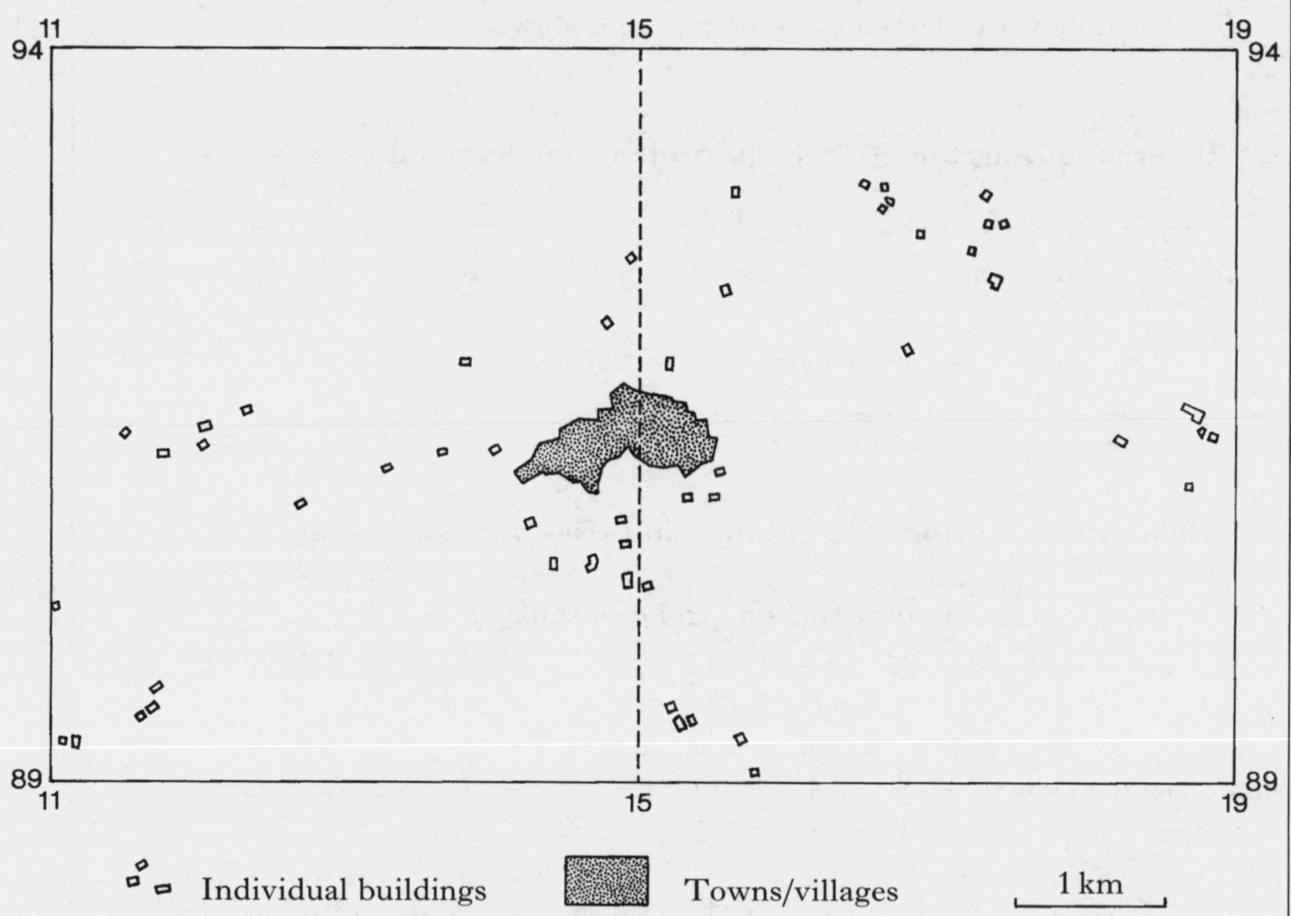

(*d*) **Explain** the distribution of settlement in the area of the map extract as shown by Reference Diagram Q1D.

Marks

KU	ES

1. (continued)

Reference Diagram Q1E: Land Use Transect

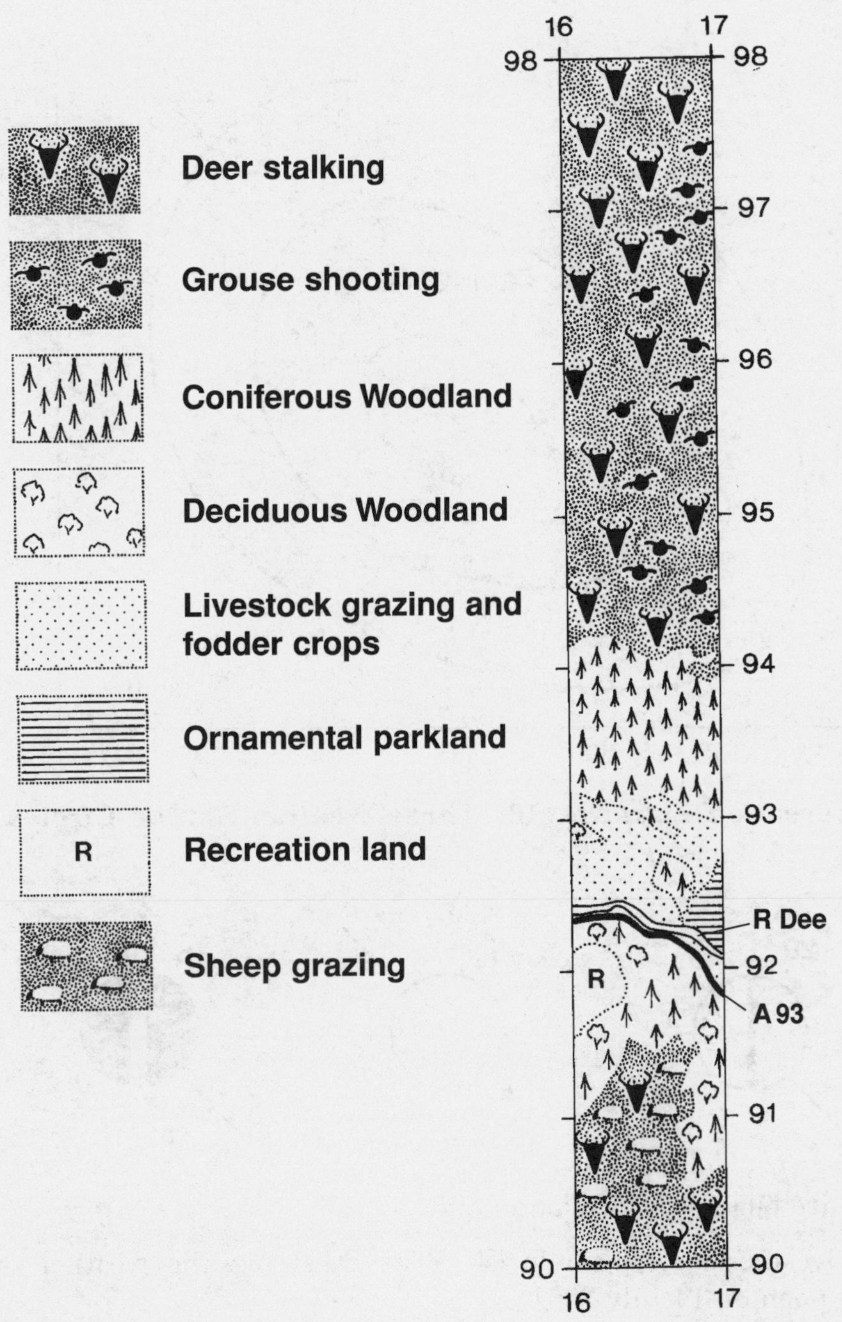

(*e*) Look at Reference Diagram Q1E, Reference Diagram Q1A and the OS map.

Give reasons for the pattern of land use which is shown on the transect. **6**

[Turn over

Marks
KU

2. Reference Diagram Q2A: European Synoptic Chart for Noon, 14 July 2001

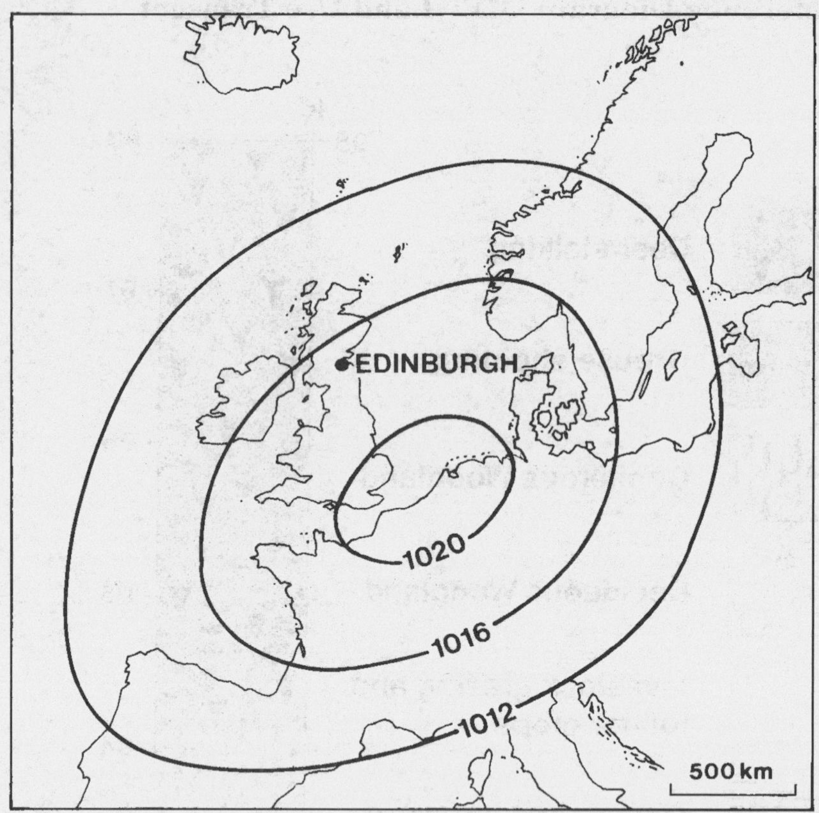

Reference Diagram Q2B: Three Weather Station Circles

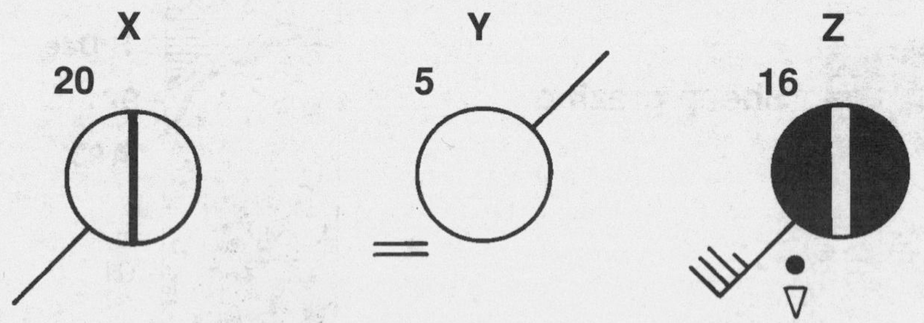

Study Reference Diagrams Q2A and Q2B.

State which weather station circle (**X**, **Y** or **Z**) shows the weather conditions at Edinburgh at noon on 14 July 2001.

Explain your choice **in detail**. 5

3. **Reference Diagram Q3: Changing Landscape in West Africa**

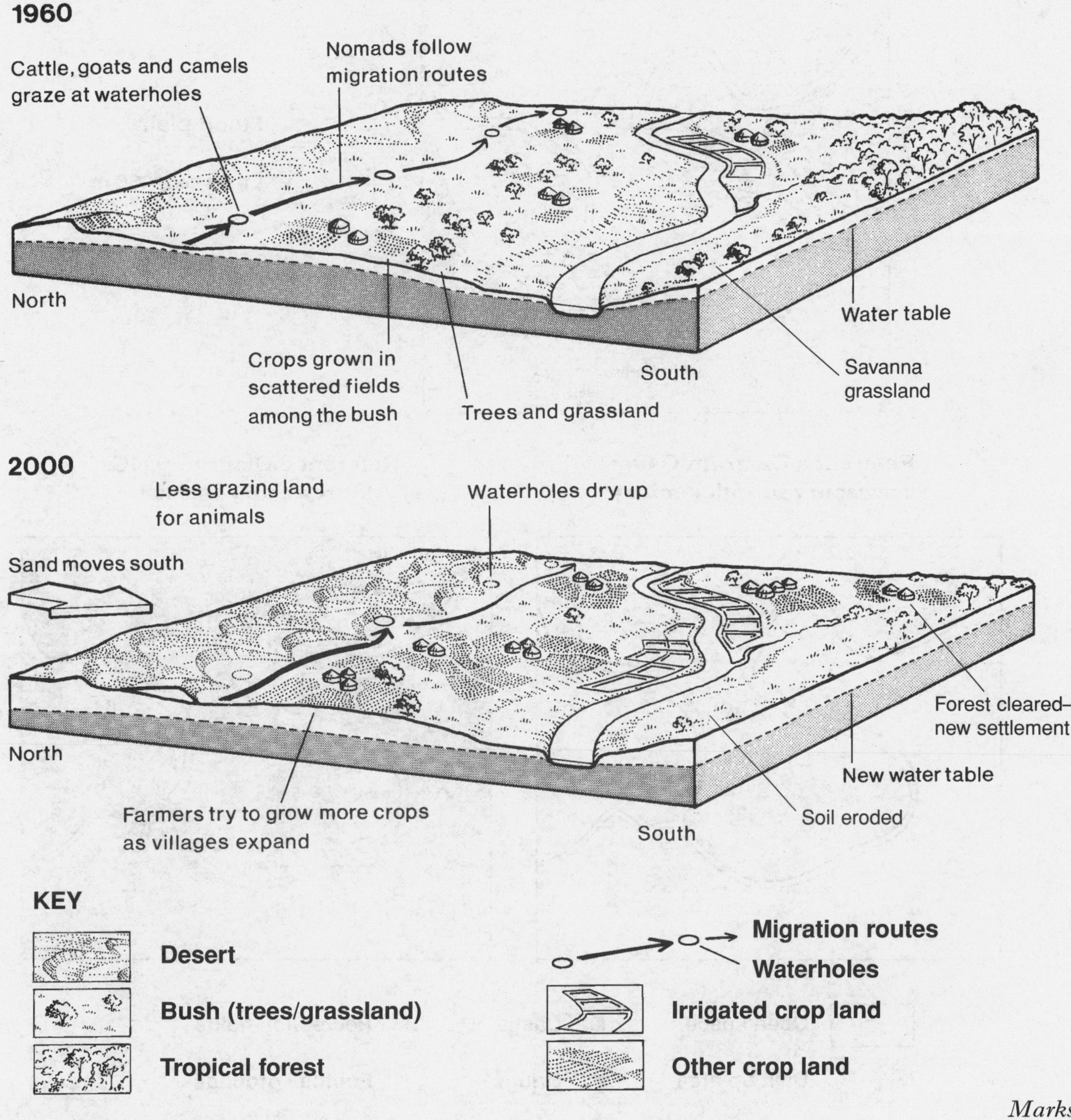

	Marks KU	ES
Look at Reference Diagram Q3. Give reasons for the changes in the landscapes of West Africa.	6	

4. Reference Diagram Q4A: Site of Shrewsbury

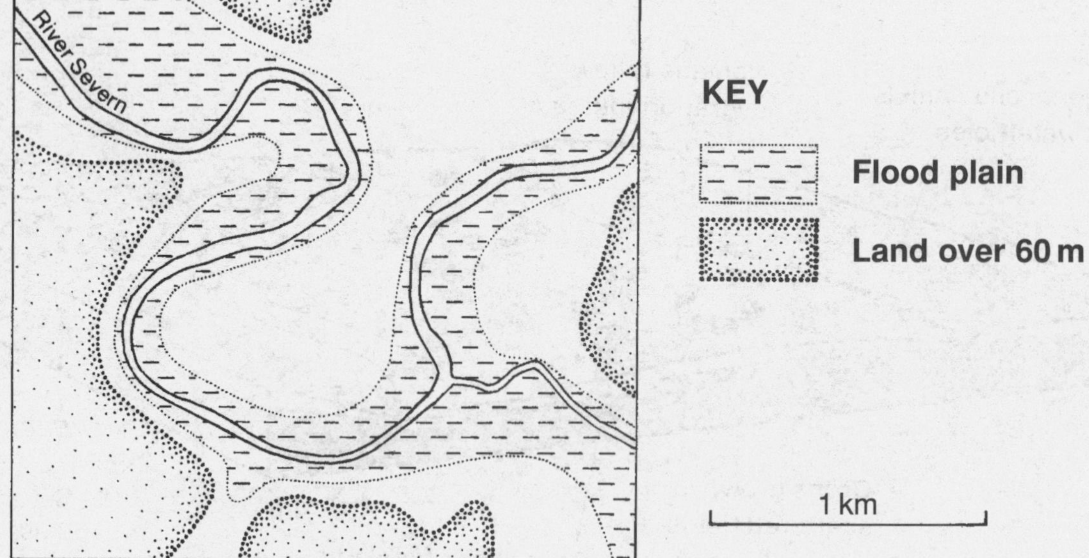

Reference Diagram Q4B: Shrewsbury in 16th century

Reference Diagram Q4C: Shrewsbury in 2000

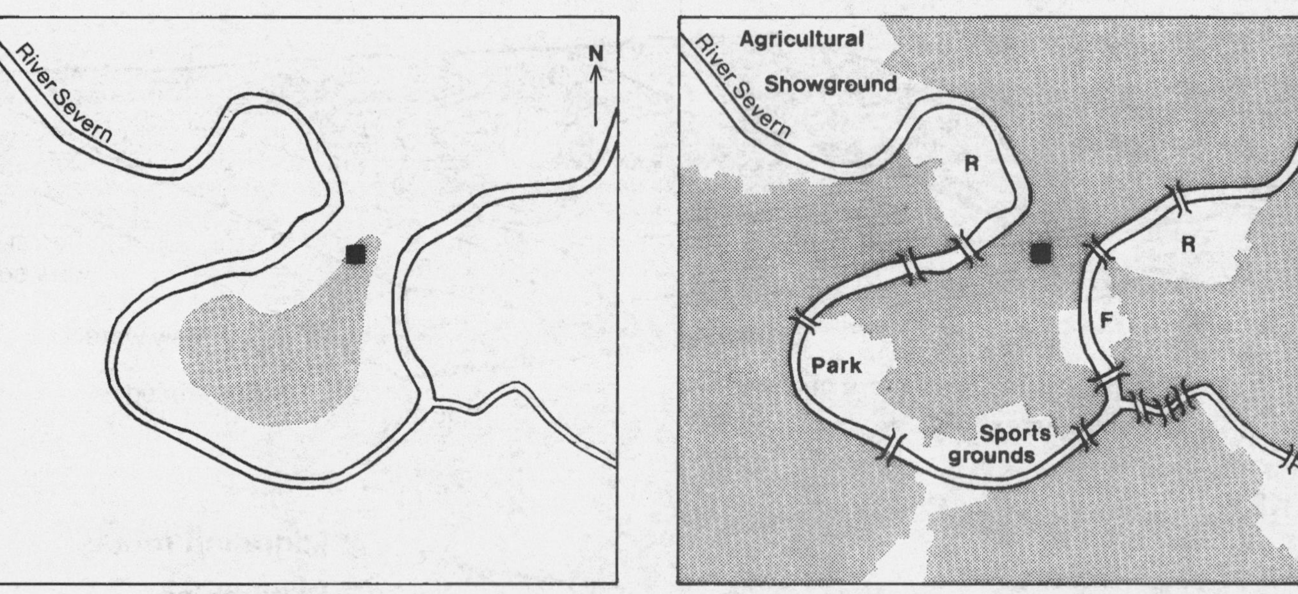

KEY

Open space	■ Castle	R Recreation fields
Built up area	Bridge	F Football grounds

Marks

KU	E

Look at Reference Diagrams Q4A, Q4B and Q4C.

Explain the ways in which the River Severn has influenced Shrewsbury in terms of its site, growth and land use.

	Marks KU	Marks ES

5. **Reference Diagram Q5: Sketch of Keilor Farm**

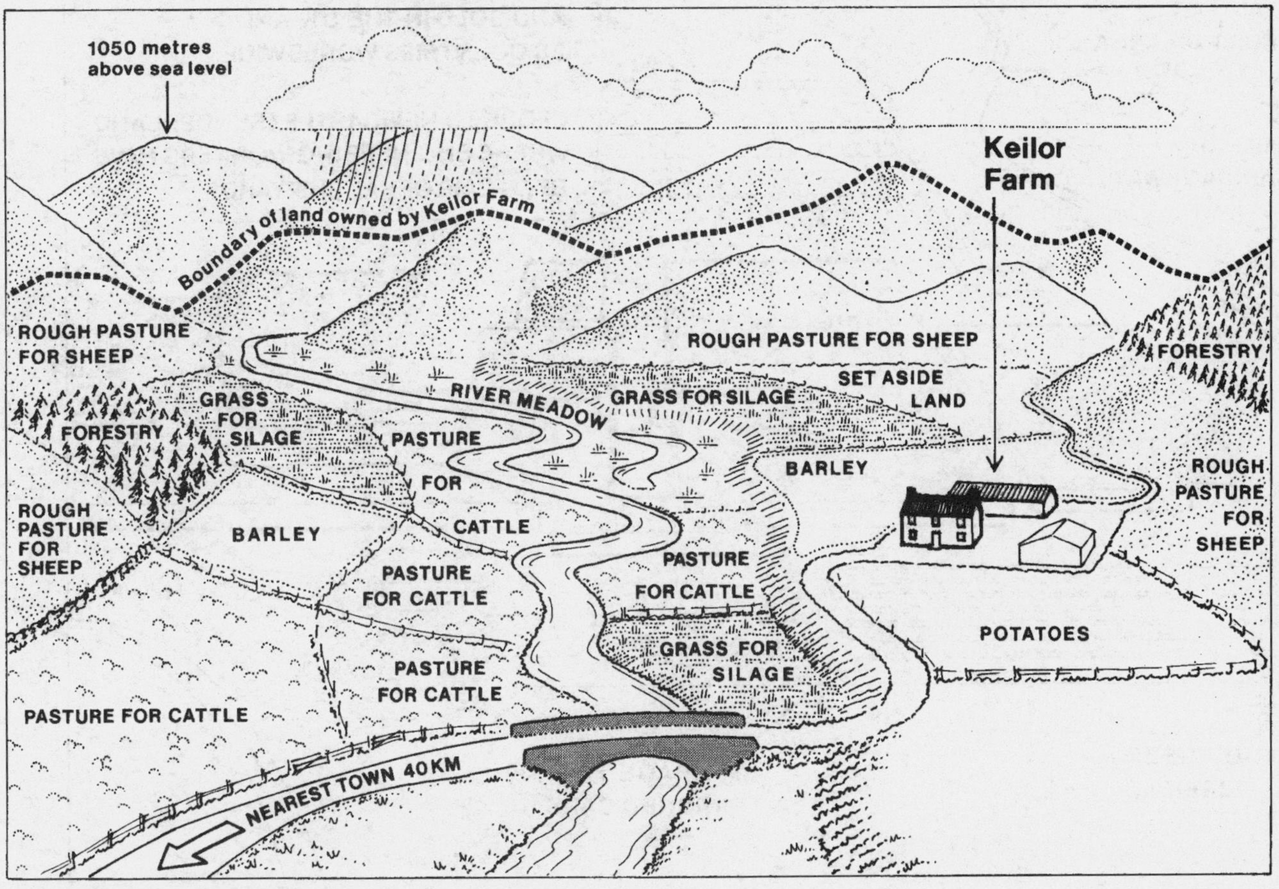

Study Reference Diagram Q5.

Keilor farm is a hill farm producing mainly beef cattle and sheep.

Explain the links between land use and the physical and human factors affecting the farm. 6

[Turn over

6. Reference Diagram Q6A: Nissan Car Factory, Washington (View looking South)

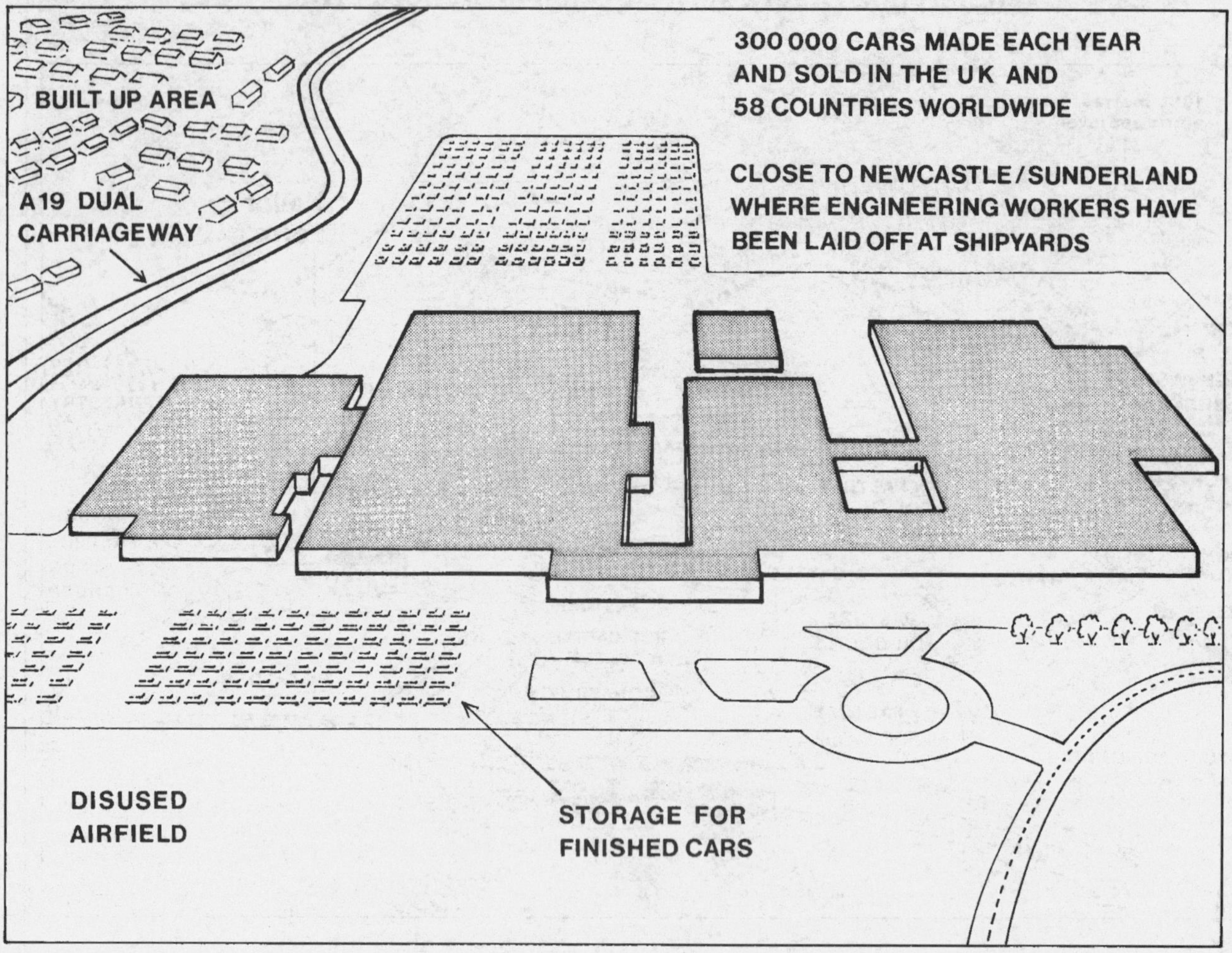

300 000 CARS MADE EACH YEAR
AND SOLD IN THE UK AND
58 COUNTRIES WORLDWIDE
CLOSE TO NEWCASTLE / SUNDERLAND
WHERE ENGINEERING WORKERS HAVE
BEEN LAID OFF AT SHIPYARDS
BUILT UP AREA
A19 DUAL
CARRIAGEWAY
DISUSED
AIRFIELD
STORAGE FOR
FINISHED CARS

Marks

KU	E

Reference Diagram Q6B: Location of Nissan Car Factory

NORTH SEA
A1
R Tyne
Newcastle
NISSAN
CAR FACTORY
Sunderland
Washington
A1231
A1(M)
A19
5 km
KEY
Docks and closed
shipyards
Built up areas

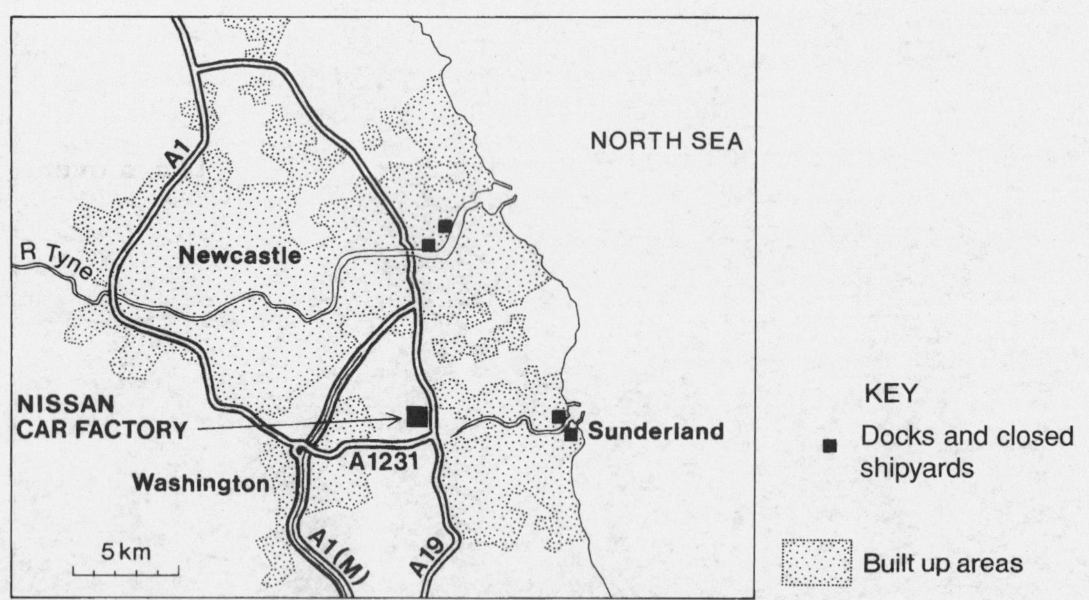

Study Reference Diagrams Q6A and Q6B.

Suggest reasons why Nissan chose to locate their car manufacturing plant at this site in Washington, NE England.

7. **Reference Diagram Q7: The Millennium Link Canal Project**

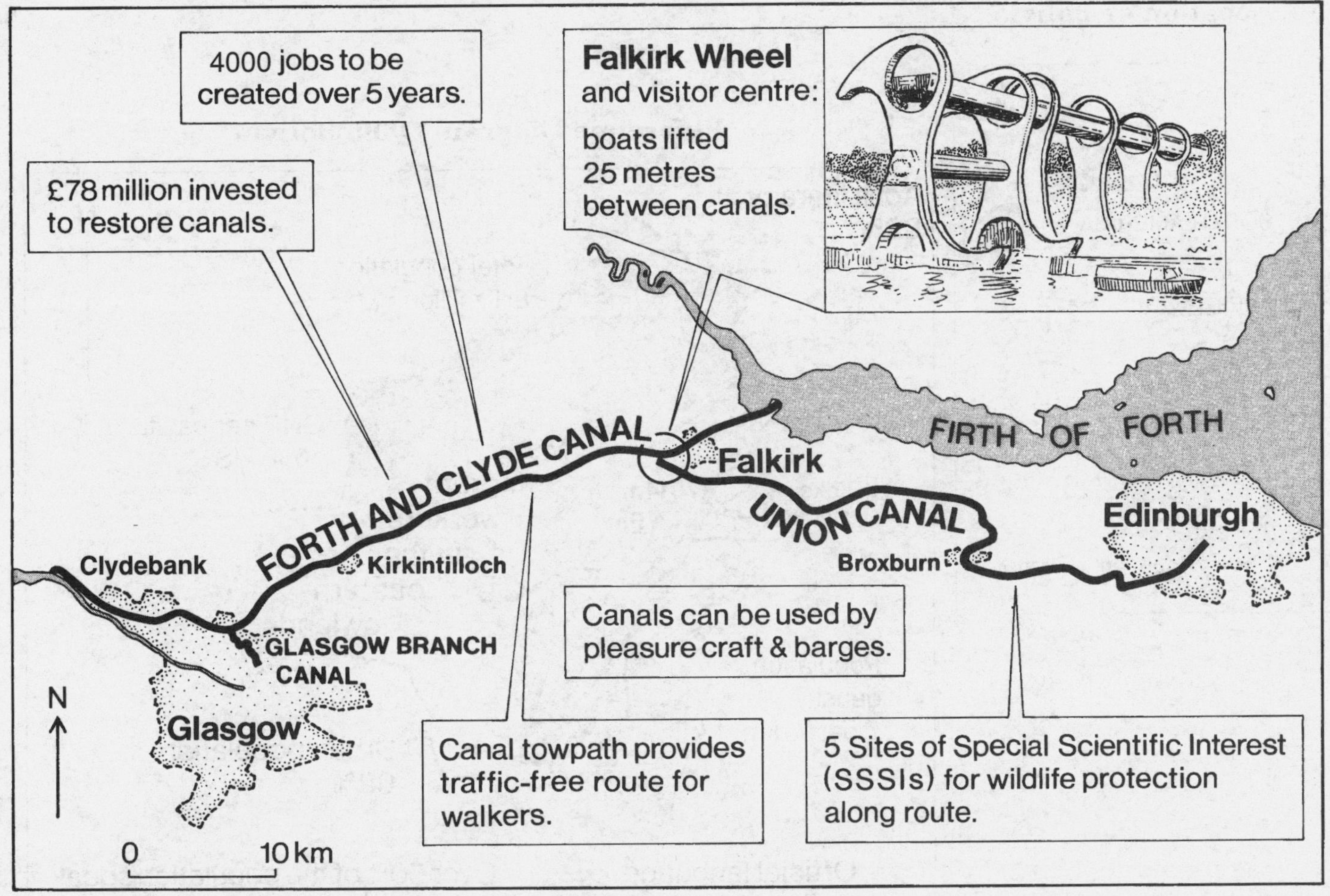

	Marks	
	KU	ES
(*a*) Look at Reference Diagram Q7. The Millennium Link has restored the Forth and Clyde Canal and the Union Canal in Central Scotland. It links the estuaries of the Rivers Forth and Clyde together as well as the cities of Edinburgh and Glasgow. Describe the benefits which the opening of the Millennium Link will have for the economy and environment of the areas around it.		5
(*b*) A group of geography students is researching the effects of the opening of the Millennium Link on the communities along its route. Describe **two** gathering techniques they could use to do this. Give reasons for your choices.		5

[Turn over

8.

Reference Diagram Q8A: Location of Bolivia

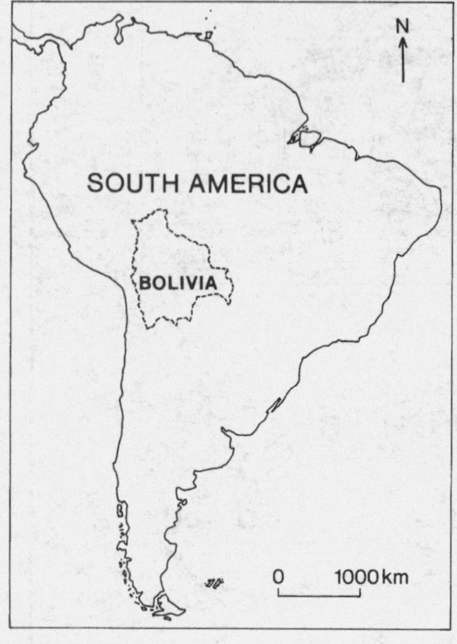

Reference Diagram Q8B: Bolivia

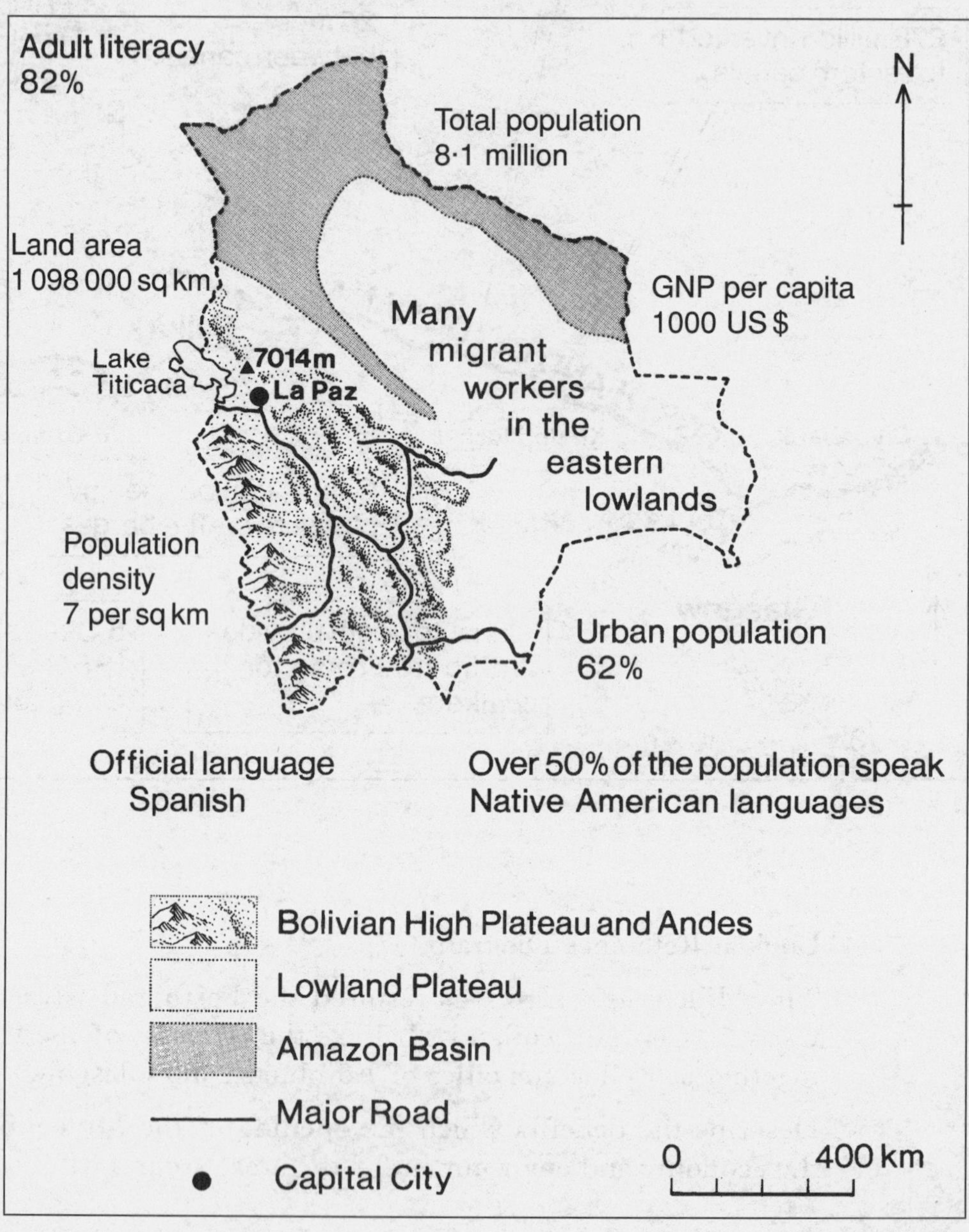

Marks | KU | E

Look at Reference Diagrams Q8A and Q8B.

(*a*) Give reasons why it may be difficult to take an accurate census in **a developing** country such as Bolivia. **5**

(*b*) What use could the Government of **a developing** country make of population census data? **4**

Marks

KU	ES

9. **Reference Table Q9: Key Mineral Exports of South Africa**

Mineral	Percentage of World Reserves	World Rank	Percentage of World Production	World Rank
Chrome	68%	1	44%	1
Vermiculite	40%	2	46%	1
Gold	39%	1	21%	1
Titanium	31%	1	27%	2
Manganese	81%	1	14%	3
Uranium	7%	5	4%	9

Look at Reference Table Q9.

Identify other **techniques** that could be used to **process** the data shown above.

Give reasons for your choices. 5

[*END OF QUESTION PAPER*]

[BLANK PAGE]

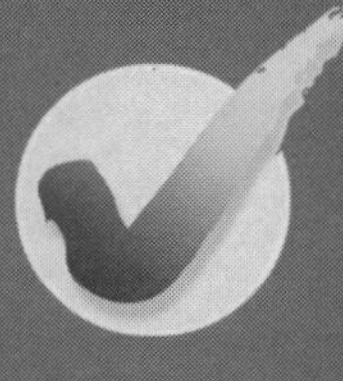

2004 | General

[BLANK PAGE]

FOR OFFICIAL USE

G

KU	ES

Total Marks

1260/403

NATIONAL QUALIFICATIONS 2004

MONDAY, 17 MAY
10.25 AM–11.50 AM

GEOGRAPHY
STANDARD GRADE
General Level

Fill in these boxes and read what is printed below.

Full name of centre

Town

Forename(s)

Surname

Date of birth
Day Month Year

Scottish candidate number

Number of seat

1 Read the whole of each question carefully before you answer it.

2 Write in the spaces provided.

3 Where boxes like this ☐ are provided, put a tick ✓ in the box beside the answer you think is correct.

4 Try all the questions.

5 Do not give up the first time you get stuck: you may be able to answer later questions.

6 Extra paper may be obtained from the invigilator, if required.

7 Before leaving the examination room you must give this book to the invigilator. If you do not, you may lose all the marks for this paper.

THB 1260/403 6/29420

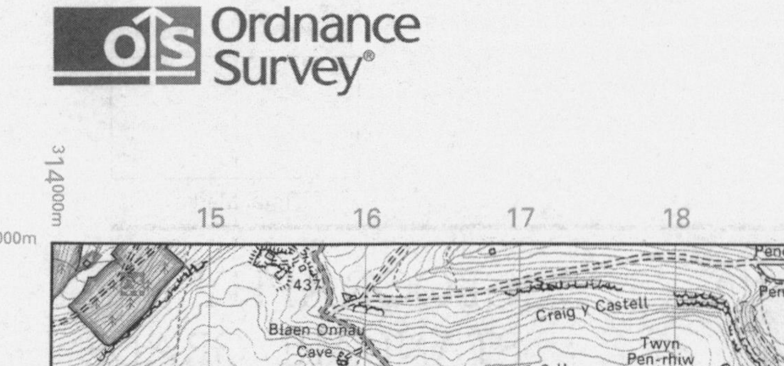

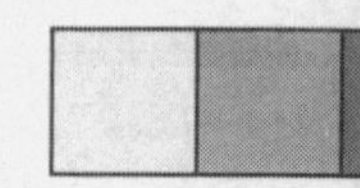

Four colours should appear above; if not

Four colours should appear above; if not

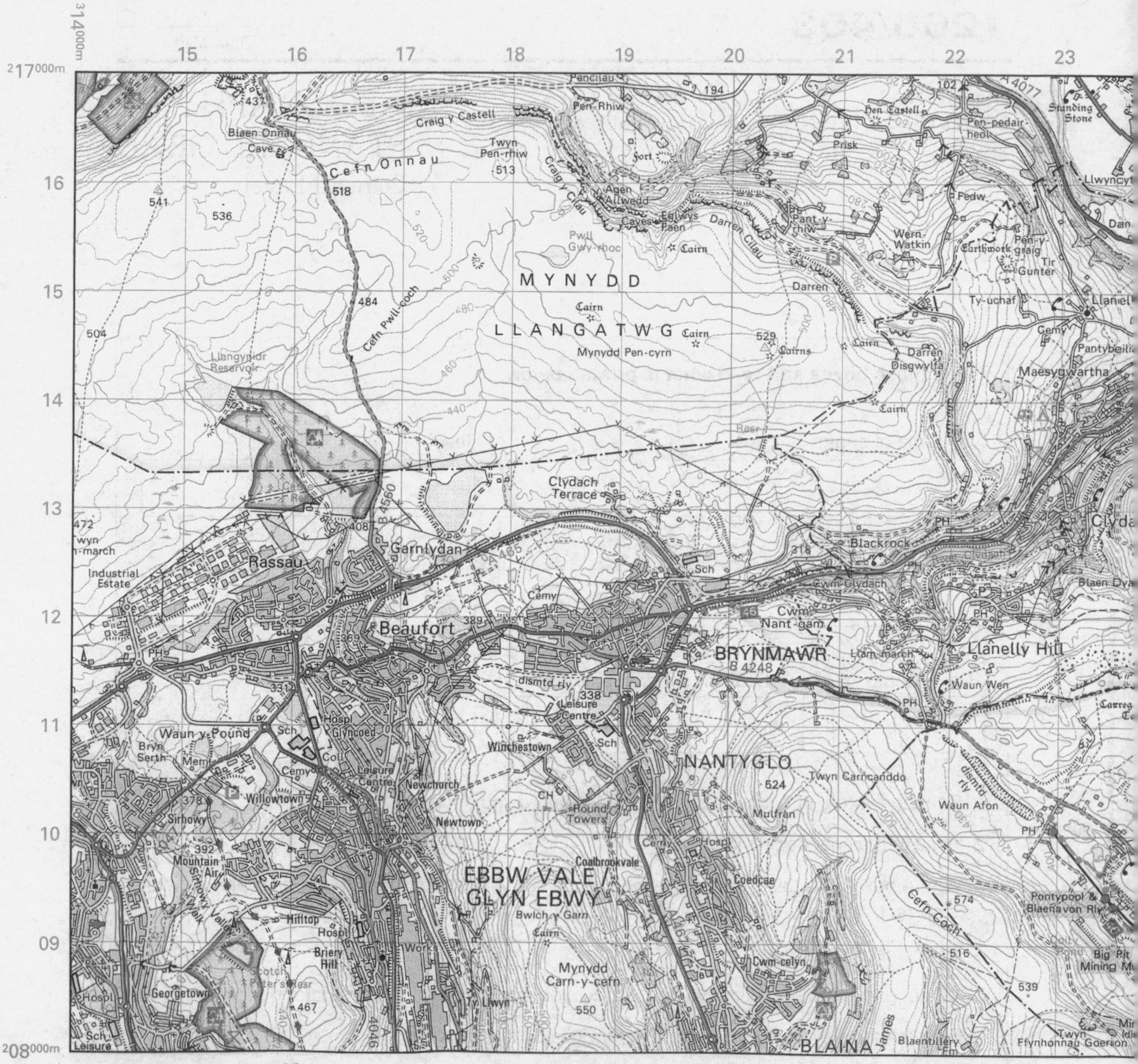

314000m

15 16 17 18 19 20 21 22 23

217000m

16

15

14

13

12

11

10

09

208000m

Cefn Onnau
Craig y Castell
Twyn Pen-rhiw
Pen-Rhiw
Pencilau
Agen Allwedd
Eglwys Faen
Darren Cilau
Pwll Gwy-rhoc
MYNYDD LLANGATWG
Mynydd Pen-cyrn
Cefn Pwll-coch
Llangynidr Reservoir
Blaen Onnau
Hen Castell
Prisk
Pant-y-rhiw
Wern-Watkin
Pen-pedair-heol
Standing Stone
Llwyncyf
Fedw
Pen-y-graig
Tir Gunter
Darren
Ty-uchaf
Darren Disgwylfa
Maesygwartha
Pantybeili
Clydach Terrace
Blackrock
Cwm Clydach
Garnlydan
Rassau
Industrial Estate
Beaufort
BRYNMAWR
Cwm Nant-gam
Llam-march
Llanelly Hill
Waun Wen
Waun-y-Pound
Bryn Serth
Willowtown
Sirhowy
Mountain Air
Glyncoed
Newchurch
Newtown
Winchestown
Leisure Centre
Round Towers
NANTYGLO
Twyn Carncanddo
Mulfran
Waun Afon
Coalbrookvale
EBBW VALE / GLYN EBWY
Bwlch-y-Garn
Coedcae
Cefn Coch
Pontypool & Blaenavon Rly
Big Pit Mining Museum
Hilltop
Briery Hill
Georgetown
Scotch Peter's Resr
Ty Llwyn
Mynydd Carn-y-cefn
Cwm-celyn
BLAINA
Blaentillery
Twyn Ffynhonnau Goerion

15 16 17 18 19 20 21 22 23

314000m

then please return to the invigilator.

then please return to the invigilator.

Extract No 1348/161

1:50 000 Scale
Landranger Series

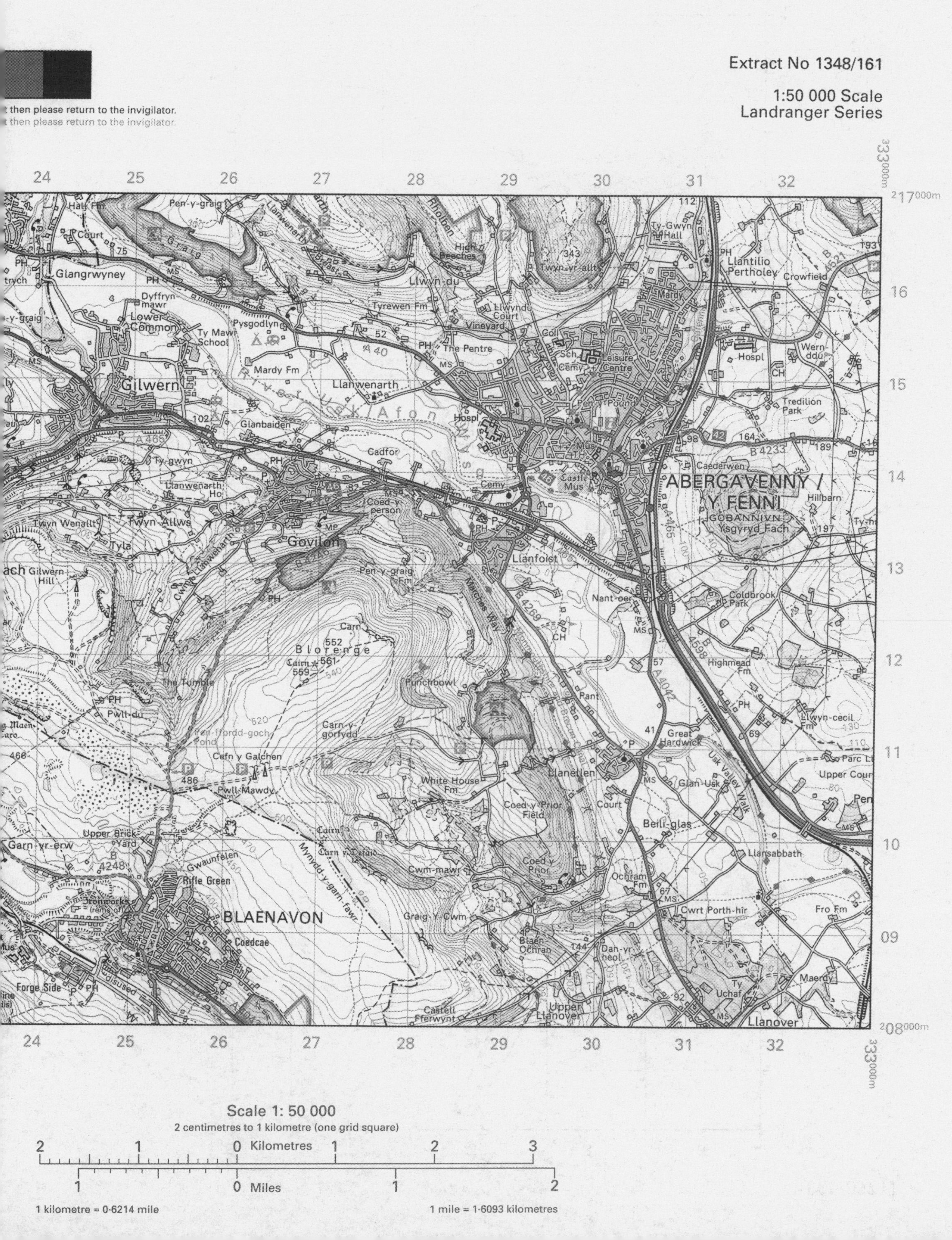

Scale 1: 50 000

2 centimetres to 1 kilometre (one grid square)

2 1 0 Kilometres 1 2 3

1 0 Miles 1 2

1 kilometre = 0·6214 mile

1 mile = 1·6093 kilometres

1. **Reference Diagram Q1A**

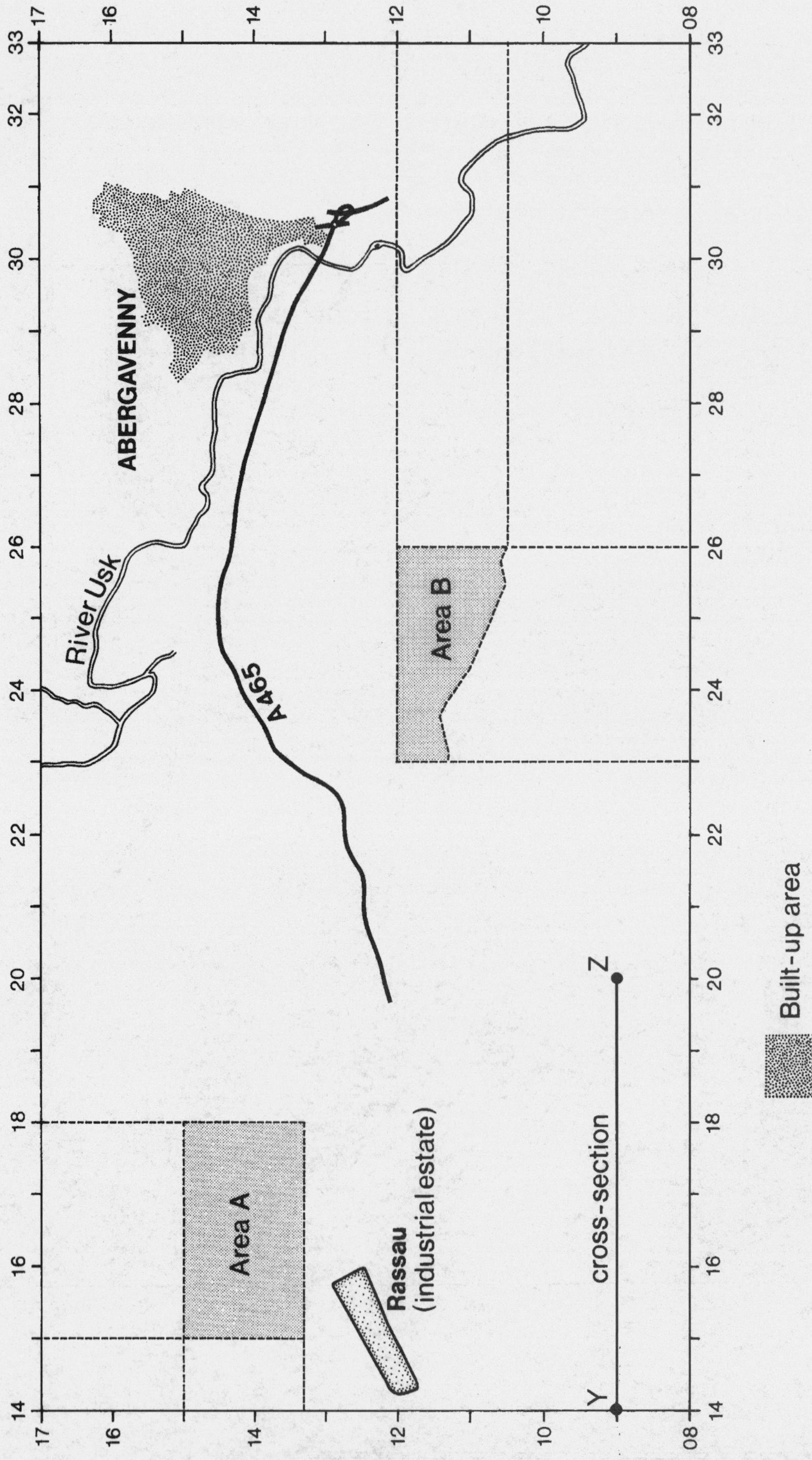

DO NOT WRITE IN THIS MARGIN

KU | ES

Marks

1. (continued)

Look at the Ordnance Survey Map Extract (No 1348/161) of the Ebbw Vale/Abergavenny area and Reference Diagram Q1A on *Page two*.

(*a*) Complete the table below by matching the physical features to the correct grid references.

Choose from the following grid squares.

1814 2316 2112 1808

Physical Feature	Grid Square
Deep narrow valley	
Ridge between two valleys, over 500 metres	
Broad flood plain	
Part of gentle slope, facing south west	

3

[Turn over

DO NOT WRITE IN THIS MARGIN

KU	ES

Marks

1. (continued)

Reference Diagram Q1B: Cross-section YZ from 140090 to 200090

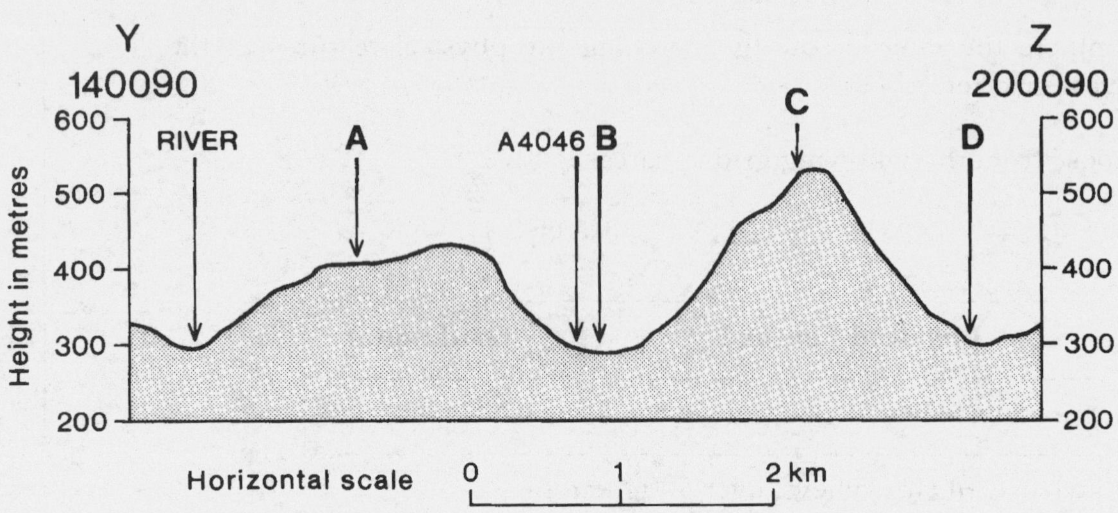

(*b*) Look at Reference Diagram Q1B. Find this cross-section on the Ordnance Survey map.

Match the features (A, B, C and D) on the cross-section YZ with the correct descriptions in the table below.

Feature	Letter
Works	
A467	
Cairn	
Scotch Peter's Reservoir	

3

(*c*) In what ways has the **physical** landscape created problems for engineers in building the A465 road from grid square 1912 to grid square 3012?

4

DO NOT WRITE IN THIS MARGIN

KU	ES

Marks

1. (continued)

(*d*) What is the main function of the town of Abergavenny?

Tick (✓) your choice.

Tourist resort ☐ Market town ☐

Give reasons for your choice.

____

____

____

____

____ 4

(*e*) **Reference Diagram Q1C: Selected Aims of National Parks**

* preserve the beauty of the countryside
* conserve the local wildlife
* provide good access and facilities for public open air enjoyment
* maintain established farming

Areas A and B on Reference Diagram Q1A are in the Brecon Beacons National Park. Find them on the map extract.

For each area, **explain** how land use is in conflict with the aims shown above.

Area A ____

____

____

Area B ____

____

____ 4

[Turn over

DO NOT WRITE IN THIS MARGIN

KU	ES

Marks

1. (continued)

(*f*) There is an industrial estate at Rassau, grid squares 1412/1512.

What are the advantages **and** disadvantages of this location for an industrial estate?

Advantages ____________________

____

____

____

Disadvantages ____________________

____

____

____________________ **4**

DO NOT WRITE IN THIS MARGIN

		KU	ES
	Marks		

2. **Reference Diagram Q2: How a Waterfall develops**

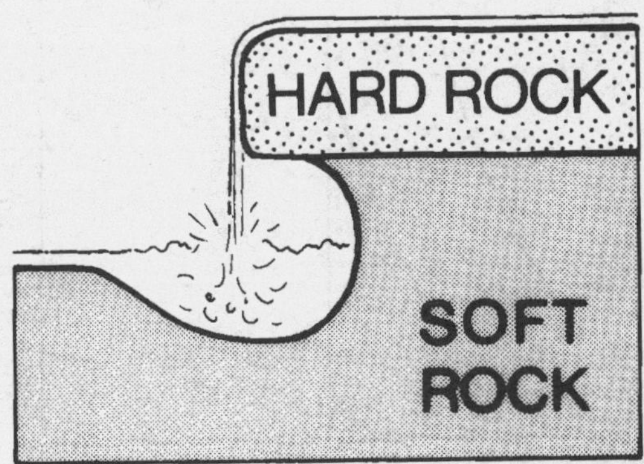

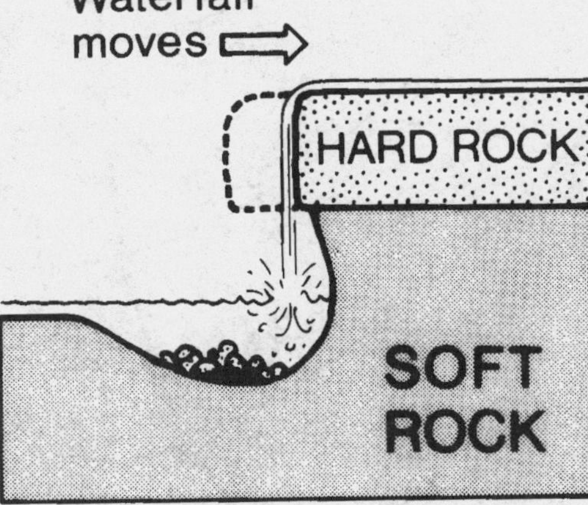

Study Reference Diagram Q2.

Explain, in detail, why a waterfall moves upstream from its original position.

____

____

____

____

______________________________ 3

[Turn over

DO NOT WRITE IN THIS MARGIN

KU	ES

Marks

3. Reference Diagram Q3: Synoptic Chart, 12 December 0600 hours

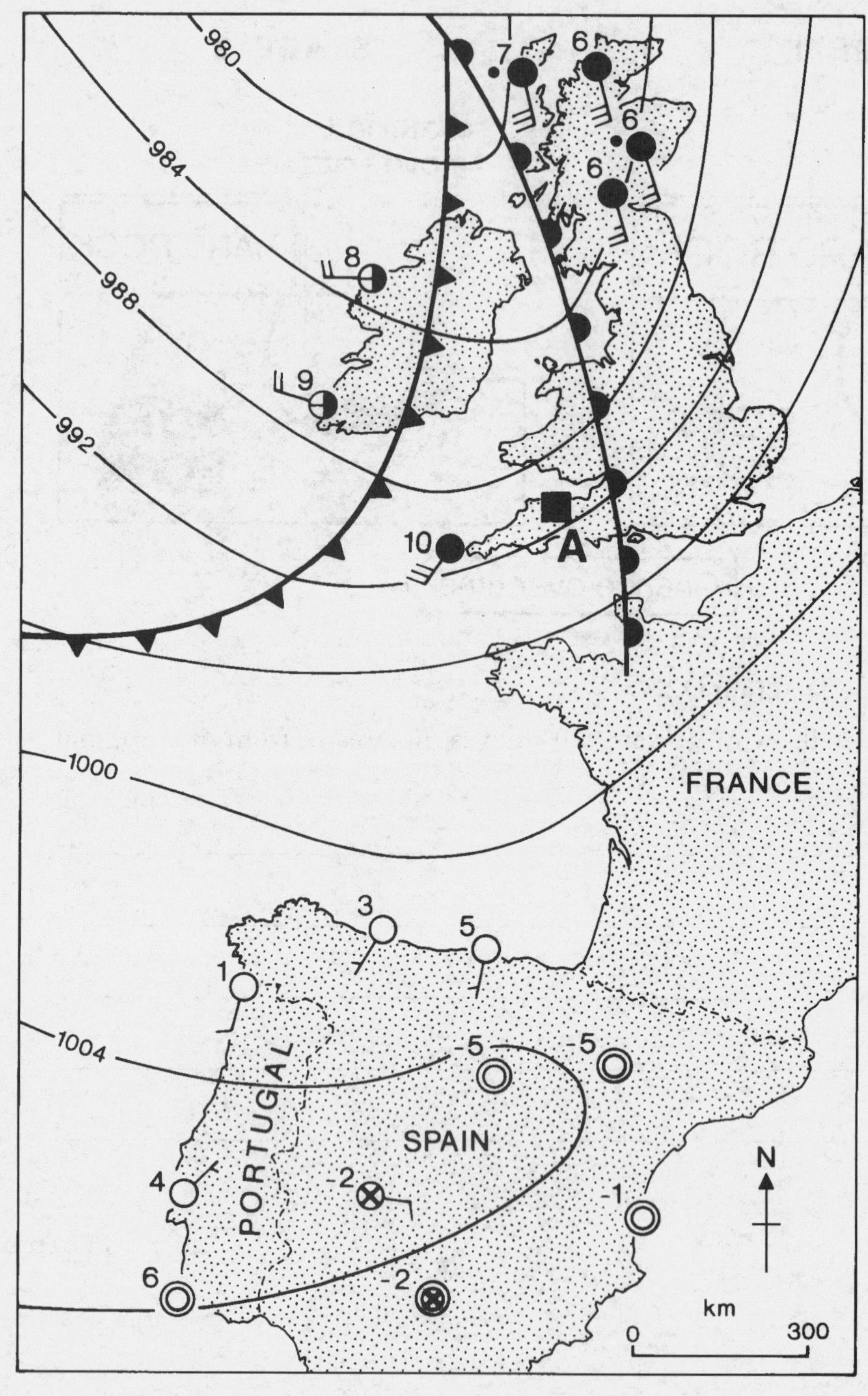

DO NOT WRITE IN THIS MARGIN

KU | ES

Marks

3. (continued)

(*a*) Complete the station circle below to show the weather conditions at **A** on Reference Diagram Q3.

Weather conditions at A

Wind from South West

Cloud cover: 7 oktas

Rain

Wind speed: 15 knots

9

3

(*b*) Study Reference Diagram Q3.

Match the weather systems to the locations given in the table.

Choose from: Anticyclone Depression

Location	Weather System
British Isles	
Spain	

Give reasons for your answer.

4

[Turn over

DO NOT WRITE IN THIS MARGIN

KU | ES

Marks

4. **Reference Diagram Q4A: Tropical Rainforest Climate**

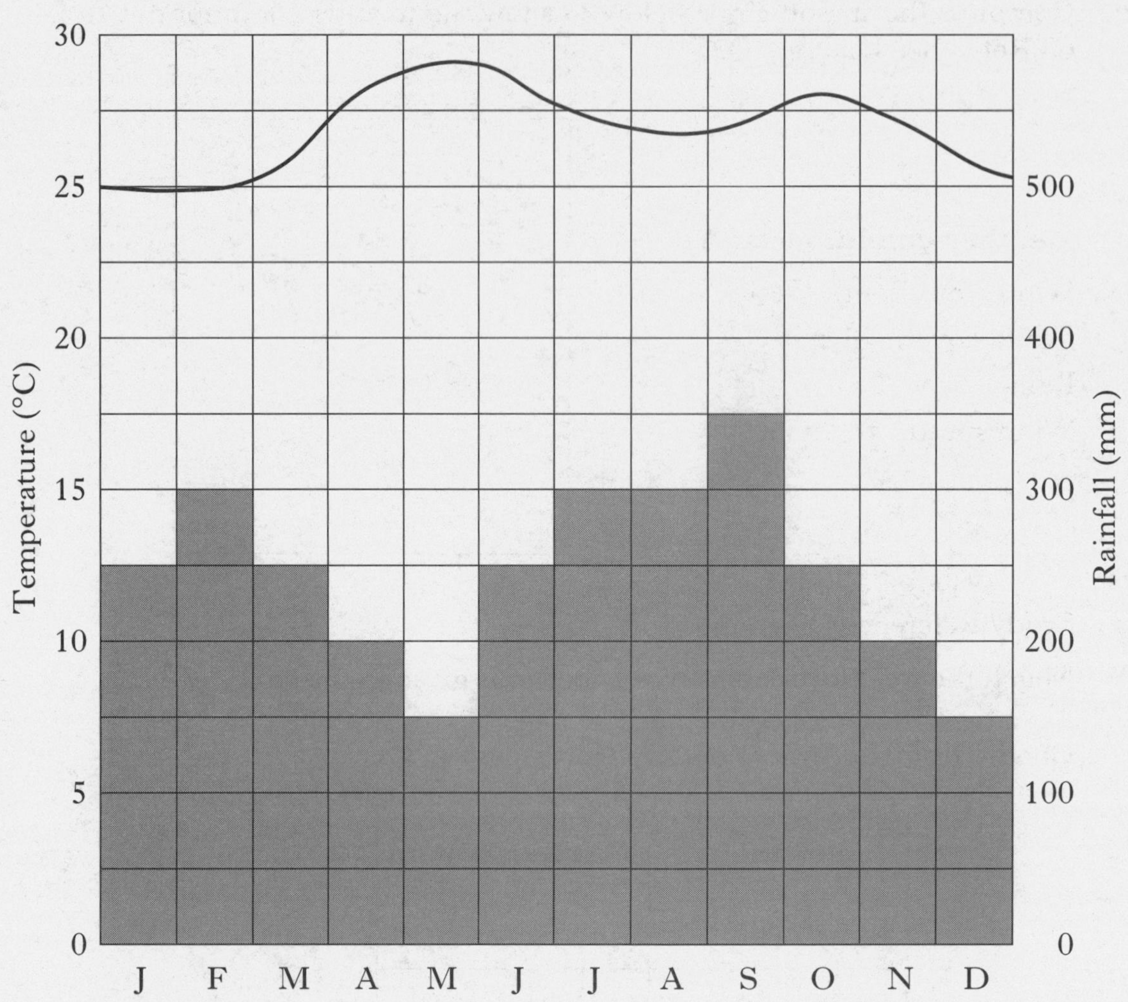

(*a*) Look at Reference Diagram Q4A.

Describe, **in detail**, the climate of the tropical rainforest. **3**

DO NOT WRITE IN THIS MARGIN

KU	ES

Marks

4. (continued)

Reference Diagram Q4B: Tropical Rainforest Landscape Before Deforestation

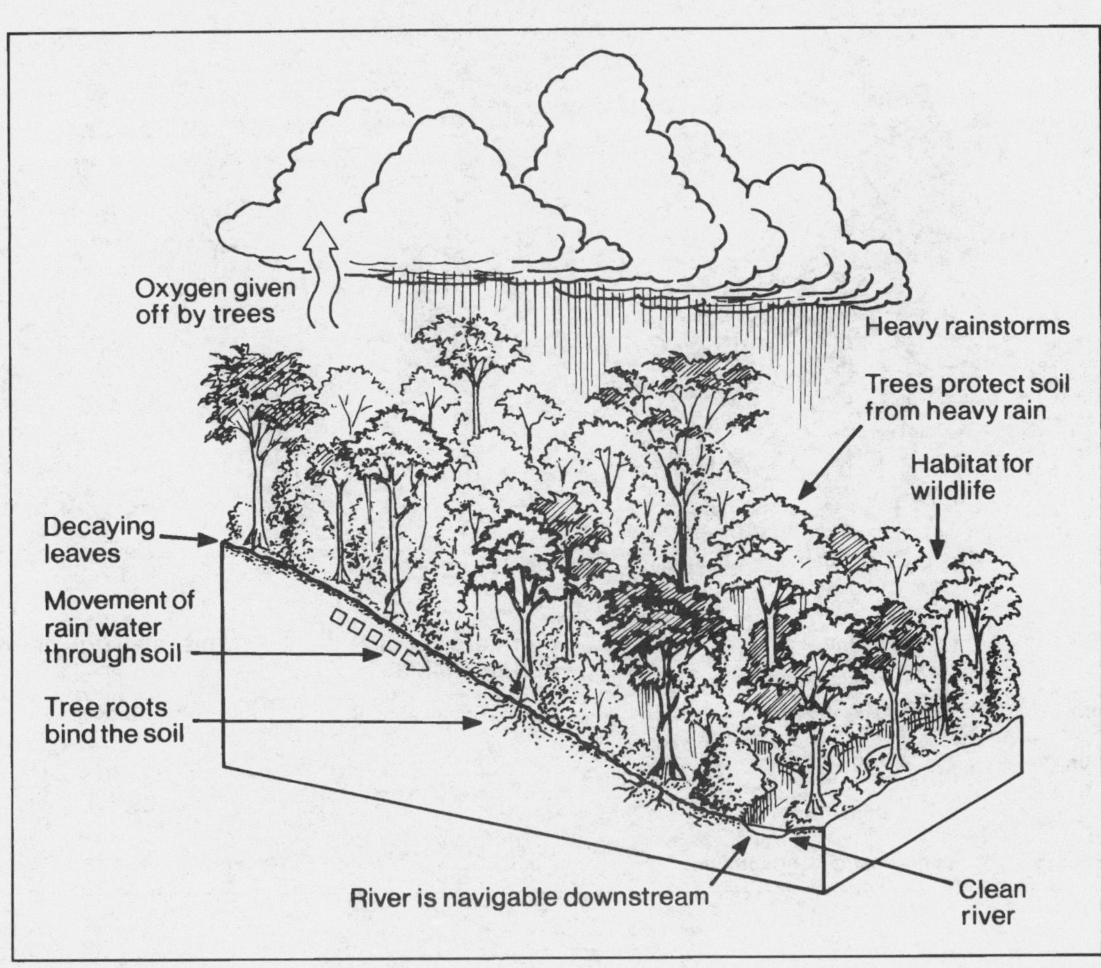

(*b*) Look at Reference Diagram Q4B.

Explain problems caused by deforestation in the Tropical Rainforest.

____

____

____

____

____

____ 4

[Turn over

5. Reference Diagram Q5: Relief, Climate and Selected Land Uses

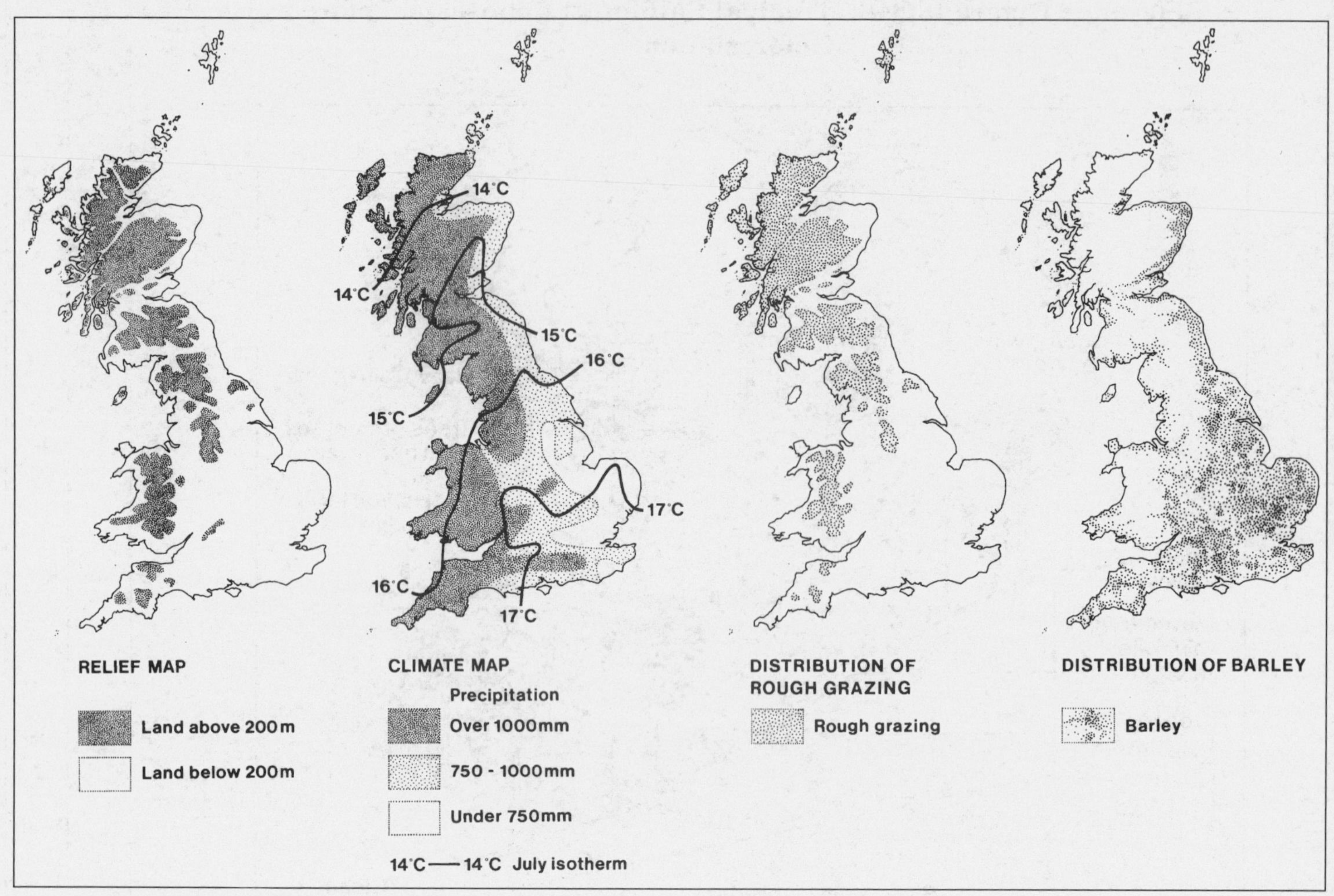

DO NOT WRITE IN THIS MARGIN

KU | ES

Look at Reference Diagram Q5.

Marks

What influence do relief and climate have on the distribution of rough grazing and barley?

____

____

____

____

____ **4**

[Turn over for Question 6 on *Page fourteen*

6. **Reference Diagram Q6A: The Inverfirth Estuary in 1974**

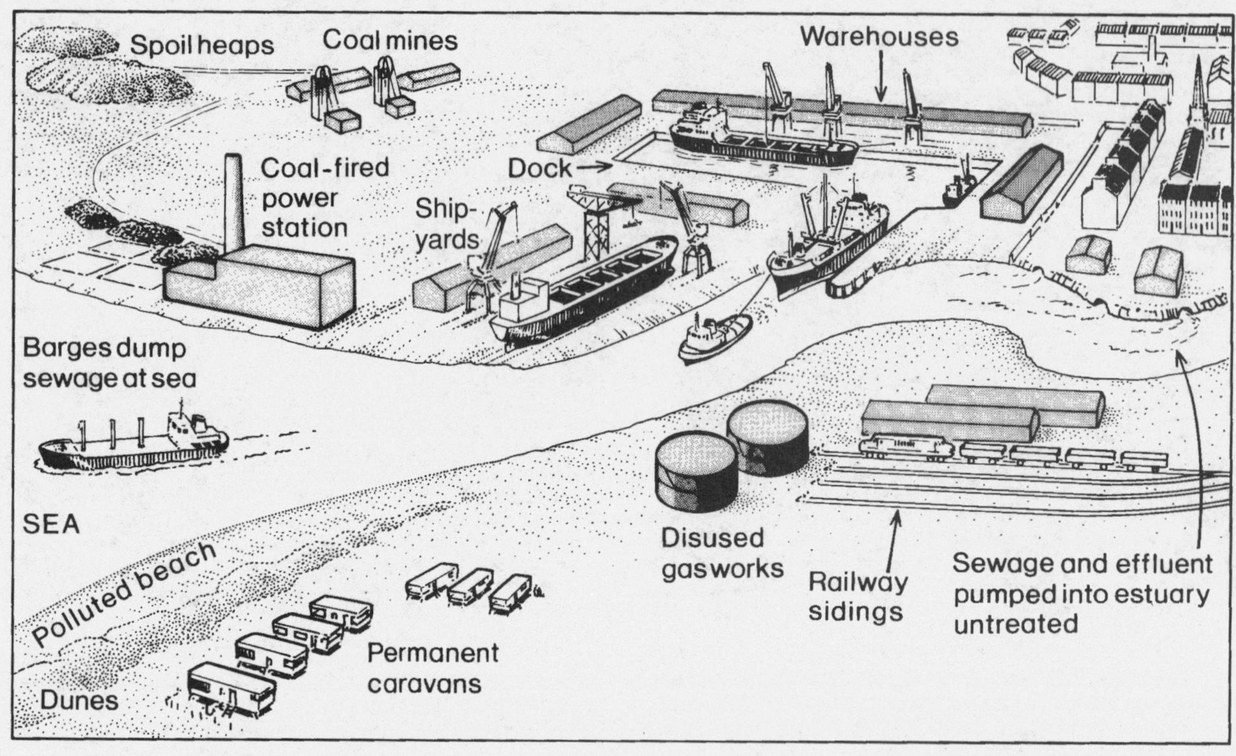

Reference Diagram Q6B: The Inverfirth Estuary in 2004

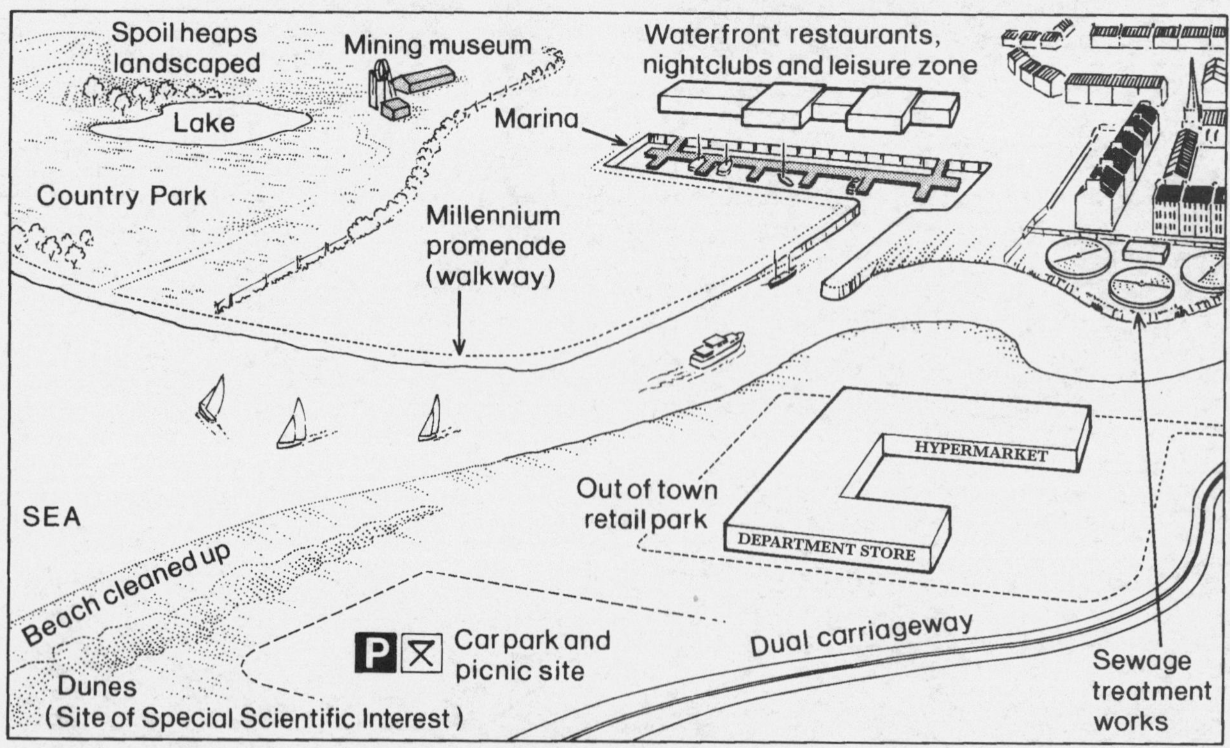

DO NOT WRITE IN THIS MARGIN

KU	ES

Marks

6. (continued)

(*a*) Study Reference Diagrams Q6A and Q6B.

What techniques could pupils have used to gather the information shown on Reference Diagrams Q6A and Q6B?

Give reasons for your choice of techniques.

Techniques ______________________________

____

____

Reasons ______________________________

____

____

____

______________________________ 4

(*b*) Do you think the changes that have taken place between 1974 and 2004 have improved the area?

Give reasons for your answer.

____

____

____

____

____

______________________________ 4

[Turn over

DO NOT WRITE IN THIS MARGIN

KU ES

Marks

7. Reference Diagram Q7A: Shopping Centres in a large Town

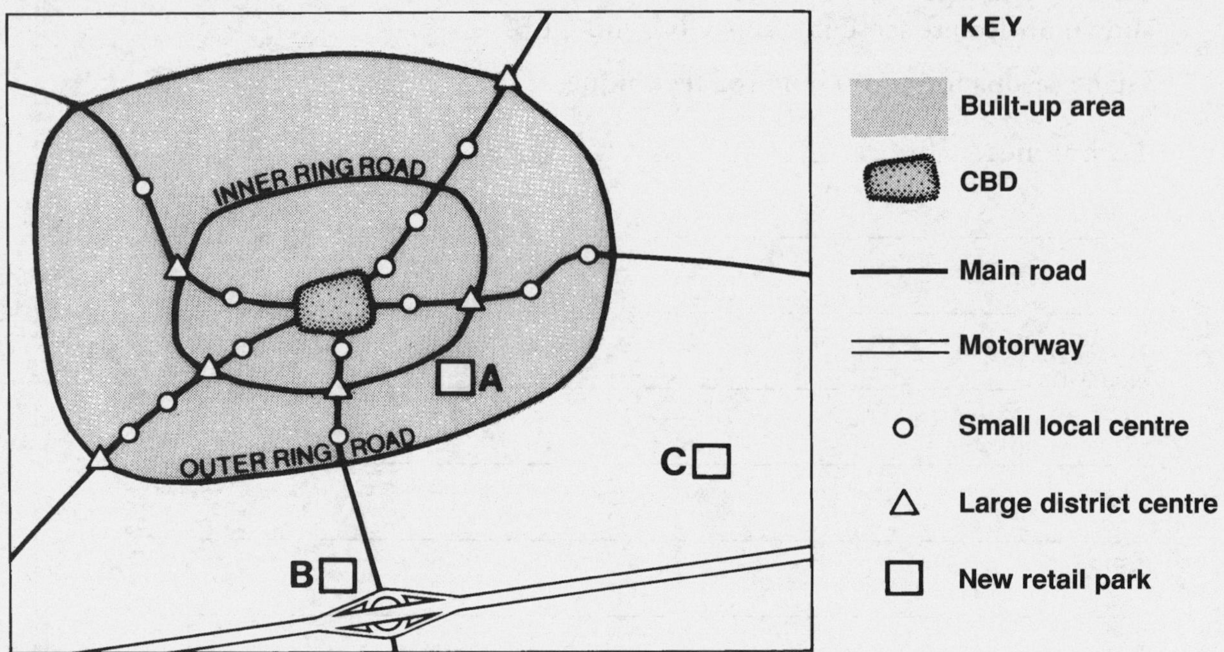

(*a*) Look at Reference Diagram Q7A above.

A, B and C are proposed sites for the development of a large retail park.

Which site do you think is best for this development? Give reasons for your choice.

Site ____________________

Reasons ____

____

____

____

____ 4

DO NOT WRITE IN THIS MARGIN

KU | ES

Marks

7. (continued)

Reference Diagram Q7B: Employment Changes in the UK

		1980	**1990**	**2000**
Sectors of Industry (numbers in millions)	Primary	0·6	0·6	0·5
	Secondary	6·7	5·3	4·3
	Tertiary	16·8	20·1	22·3
	Total	24·1	26·0	27·1

(*b*) Give **two** processing techniques which could be used to present the information shown in Reference Diagram Q7B.

Give reasons for your choices.

Technique 1 ______________________

Reason ______________________

____

____

Technique 2 ______________________

Reason ______________________

____

______________________ 4

[Turn over

DO NOT WRITE IN THIS MARGIN

KU	ES

Marks

8. Reference Diagram Q8: Population Pyramids

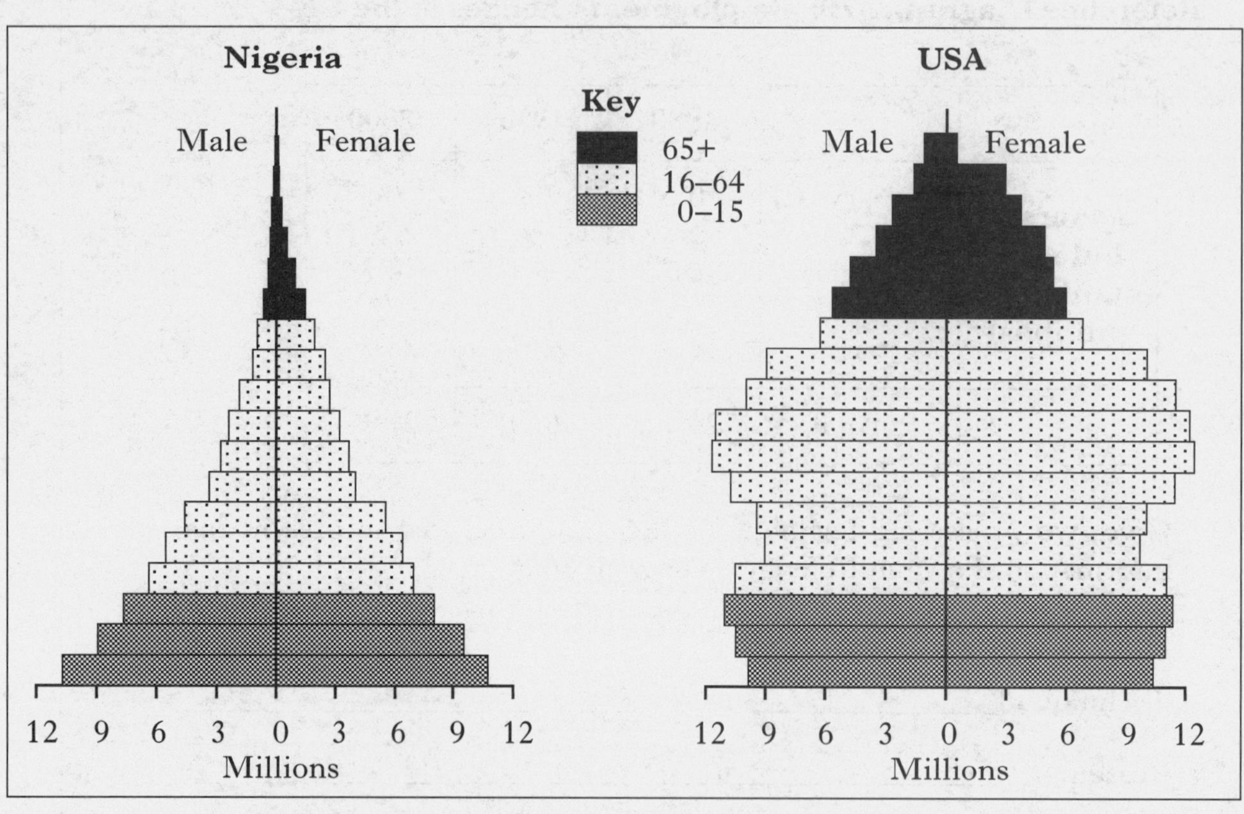

(*a*) Look at Reference Diagram Q8.

Describe three differences between the population pyramids of Nigeria and the United States of America.

____

____

____

______________________________ **3**

DO NOT WRITE IN THIS MARGIN

KU | ES

8. (continued) *Marks*

(*b*) (i) **Describe** two problems which the population structure of Nigeria may cause.

(ii) **Describe** two problems which the population structure of the United States may cause. **4**

[Turn over for Question 9 on *Page twenty*

DO NOT WRITE IN THIS MARGIN

KU	ES

Marks

9. Reference Diagram Q9A: Factors Affecting Sugar Production in the EU

* high subsidies to farmers to produce beet sugar in the EU
* EU buys sugar in bulk from Mozambique
* import tariffs protect EU farmers from foreign competition
* good climate for growing sugar beet

Reference Diagram Q9B: Factors Affecting Sugar Production in Mozambique

* lowest production costs in the world
* Mozambique has to sell sugar to EU at low prices
* cannot sell processed (refined) sugar to EU because of high import tariffs on processed food
* good growing conditions for sugar cane

Give reasons why sugar producers in Mozambique are at a **disadvantage** compared with sugar producers in the EU.

____

____

____

____

____ 4

[*END OF QUESTION PAPER*]

[BLANK PAGE]

C

1260/405

NATIONAL QUALIFICATIONS 2004

MONDAY, 17 MAY
1.00 PM – 3.00 PM

GEOGRAPHY
STANDARD GRADE
Credit Level

All questions should be attempted.

Candidates should read the questions carefully. Answers should be clearly expressed and relevant.

Credit will always be given for appropriate sketch-maps and diagrams.

Write legibly and neatly, and leave a space of about one cm between the lines.

Marks may be deducted for bad spelling and bad punctuation, and for writing that is difficult to read.

All maps and diagrams in this paper have been printed in black only: no other colours have been used.

THB 1260/405 6/19920

Extract No 1349/EXP272

1:25 000 Scale
Explorer Series

Four colours should appear above; if not then please return to the invigilator.

CANWICK CP
Canwick
Bracebridge Heath
BRACEBRIDGE HEATH
South Common
Boultham
Bracebridge
Boultham Moor
Swallow Beck
Hartsholme
Hartsholme Country Park
Bracebridge Low Fields
River Witham
Viking Way
Grantham Road
Sewage Works
Industrial Estate
Swanholme Lakes
Scale 1: 25 000
4 centimetres to 1 kilometre (one grid square)
Kilometres
Miles
1 kilometre = 0·6214 mile
1 Mile =1·6093 kilometres
Magnetic North
Grid North
True North
Diagrammatic only

1.

Reference Diagram Q1A

94 95 96 97 98 99 00

75 74 73 72 71 70 69 68 67 66 65

AREA A

AREA B

AREA C

R. WITHAM

R. WITHAM

BUILT-UP AREA

	Marks KU	ES

1. (continued)

This question refers to the OS Map Extract (No 1349/EXP272) of Lincoln and the Reference Diagram Q1A on *Page two*.

(*a*) Give the Grid Reference of the square which contains the CBD of Lincoln. Support your answer with map evidence. — ES 3

Look at Reference Diagram Q1A.

(*b*) Referring to map evidence, describe the differences between the residential environments of Area A and Area B. — KU 4

(*c*)

> **"A dormitory settlement is a community where most of the residents travel to work in a larger settlement."**

Pupils from a local high school want to find out if Bracebridge Heath (9767–9867) is a dormitory settlement for Lincoln. What techniques could they use to gather relevant information?

Explain the choice of techniques. — ES 5

(*d*) Give reasons for the differences between the leisure activities located in square 9771 and those located in squares 9468 and 9469. — KU 4

(*e*) Suggest the type of farming found at Canwick Manor Farm (993677).

Give reasons for your choice. — ES 4

(*f*) Referring to map evidence, explain how physical landscape features (relief and drainage) have affected land use in Area C. — ES 6

[Turn over

Marks | KU | ES

2. **Reference Diagram Q2A: Glaciated Upland**

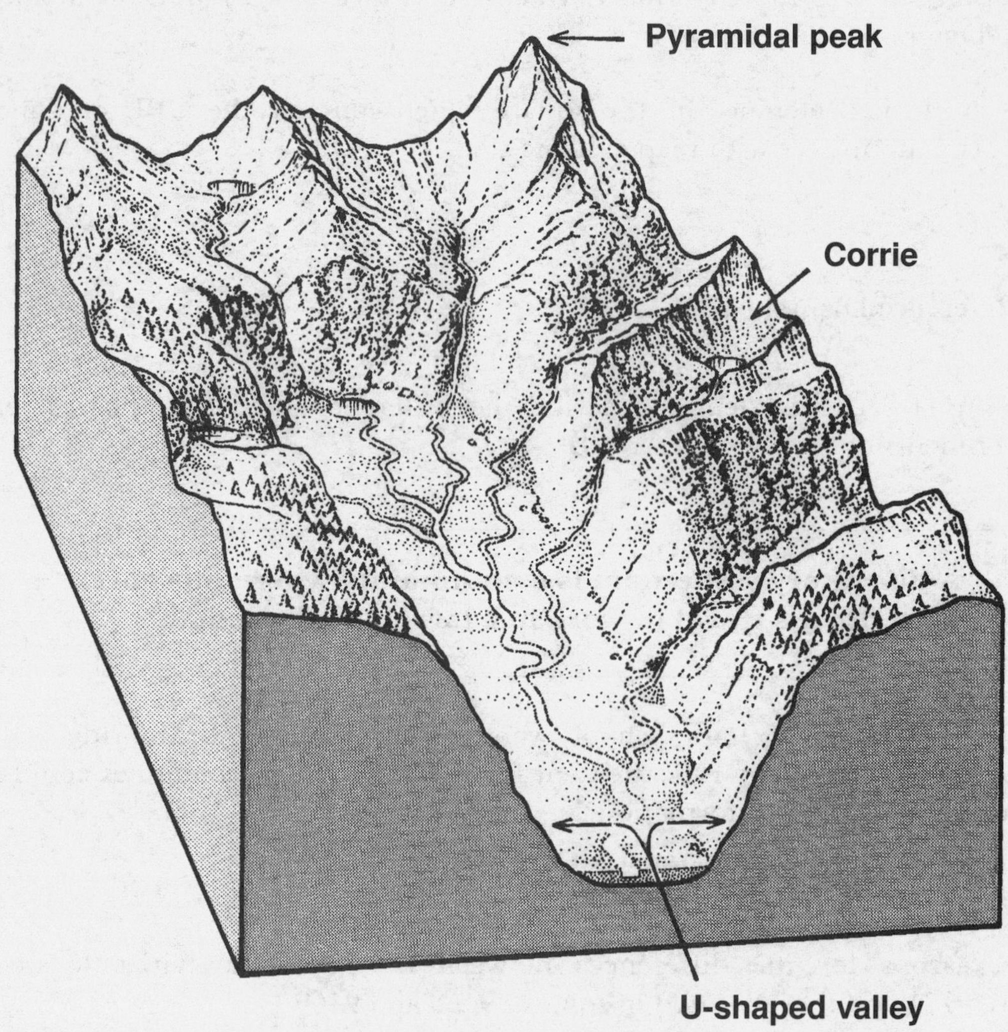

(*a*) Study Reference Diagram Q2A.

Select **one** of the labelled glaciated features shown.

Explain in detail how it was formed. You may wish to use diagrams to illustrate your answer. **4**

	Marks	
	KU	ES

2. (continued)

Reference Diagram Q2B: Some Land Uses in Glaciated Uplands

Forestry
Tourist Resorts
Skiing
Hydroelectric Power
Farming

(*b*) Select **one** land use shown in Reference Diagram Q2B.

Explain in detail why the land use is suited to a glaciated upland as shown in Reference Diagram Q2A. **4** (KU)

[Turn over

Marks
KU

3. **Reference Diagram Q3: Synoptic Chart for 25 September 2002**

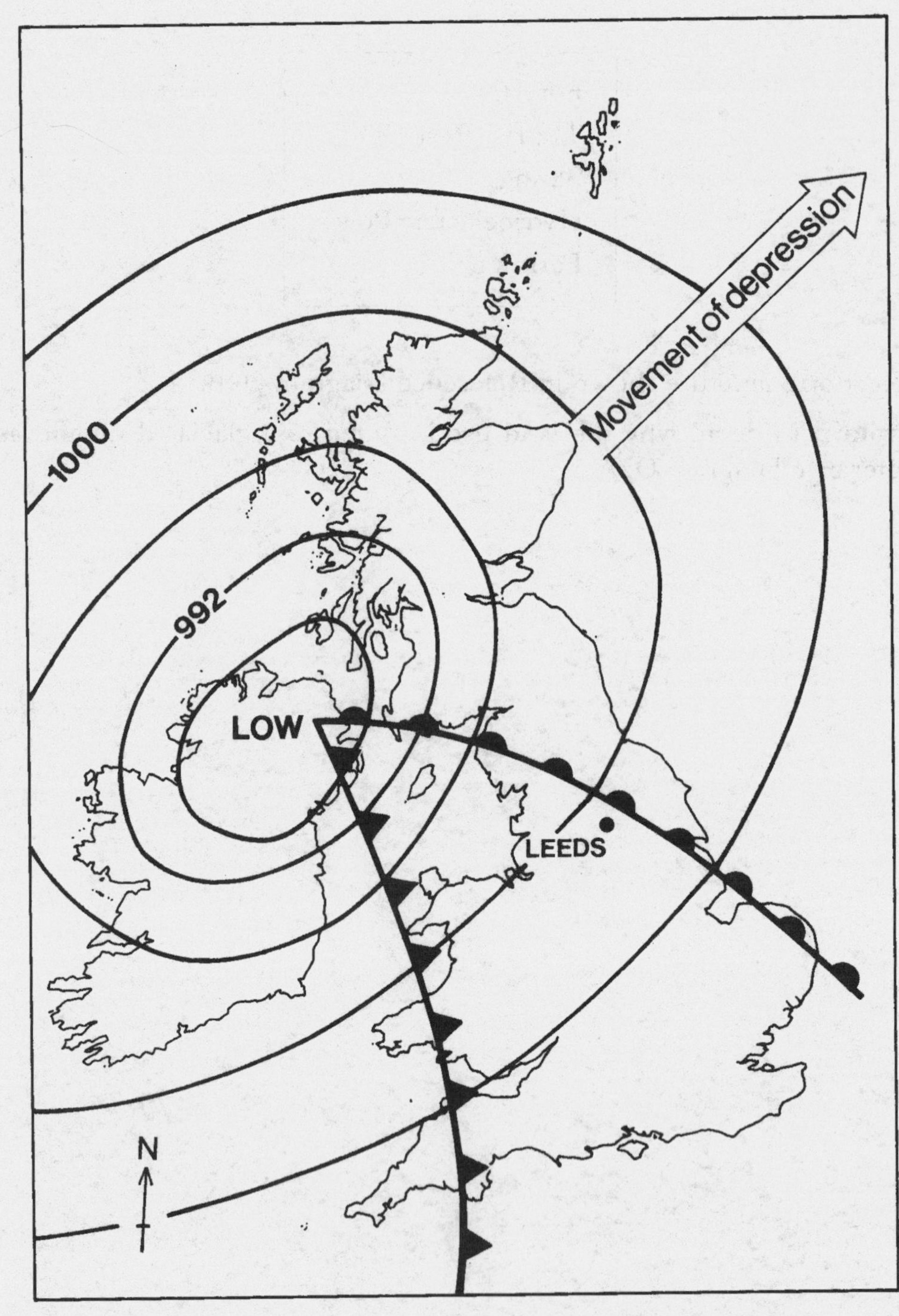

Study Reference Diagram Q3.

Explain the changes which will take place in the weather at Leeds in the next 12 hours. 5

4. Reference Diagram Q4: Threats to the Marine Environment around Scotland

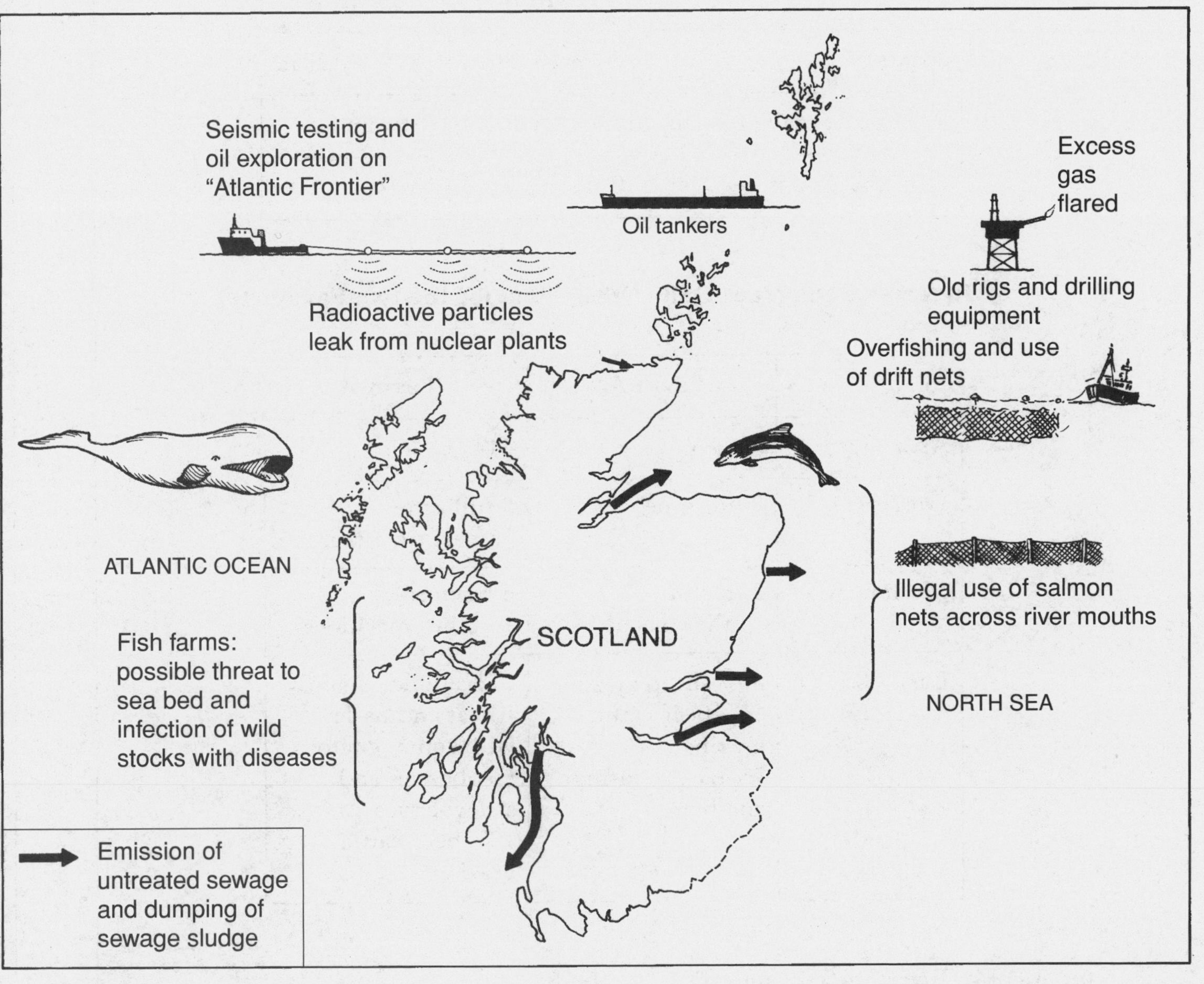

	Marks	
	KU	ES
What measures could be taken to reduce the impact of the threats to the marine environment as shown on Reference Diagram Q4?	6	

[Turn over

Marks

KU	

5. **Reference Diagram Q5A: Physical Data for two Farms in Scotland**

	Farm A	Farm B
Altitude	220 m to 450 m	75 m to 125 m
Average rainfall per year	1520 mm	630 mm
Sunshine hours per year	1000	1300

Reference Diagram Q5B: Other Data for the two Farms

	Farm A	Farm B
Area	1904 ha	444 ha
Workers	3 full time	5 full time 13 part time/seasonal
Machinery	2 tractors 8 other machines	6 tractors 14 other machines
Land use	80% sheep grazing 13% beef cattle grazing 7% barley, turnips and hay	87% arable—mainly wheat and barley with some potatoes, raspberries and strawberries 13% beef cattle grazing

(*a*) Look at Reference Diagrams Q5A and Q5B.

Give reasons for the differences between the two farms.

(*b*) Describe other techniques which could be used to present the land use data shown in Reference Diagram Q5B.

Give reasons for your choice of techniques.

Marks | KU | ES

6. Reference Diagram Q6A: Location of Toyota Car Factory at Burnaston

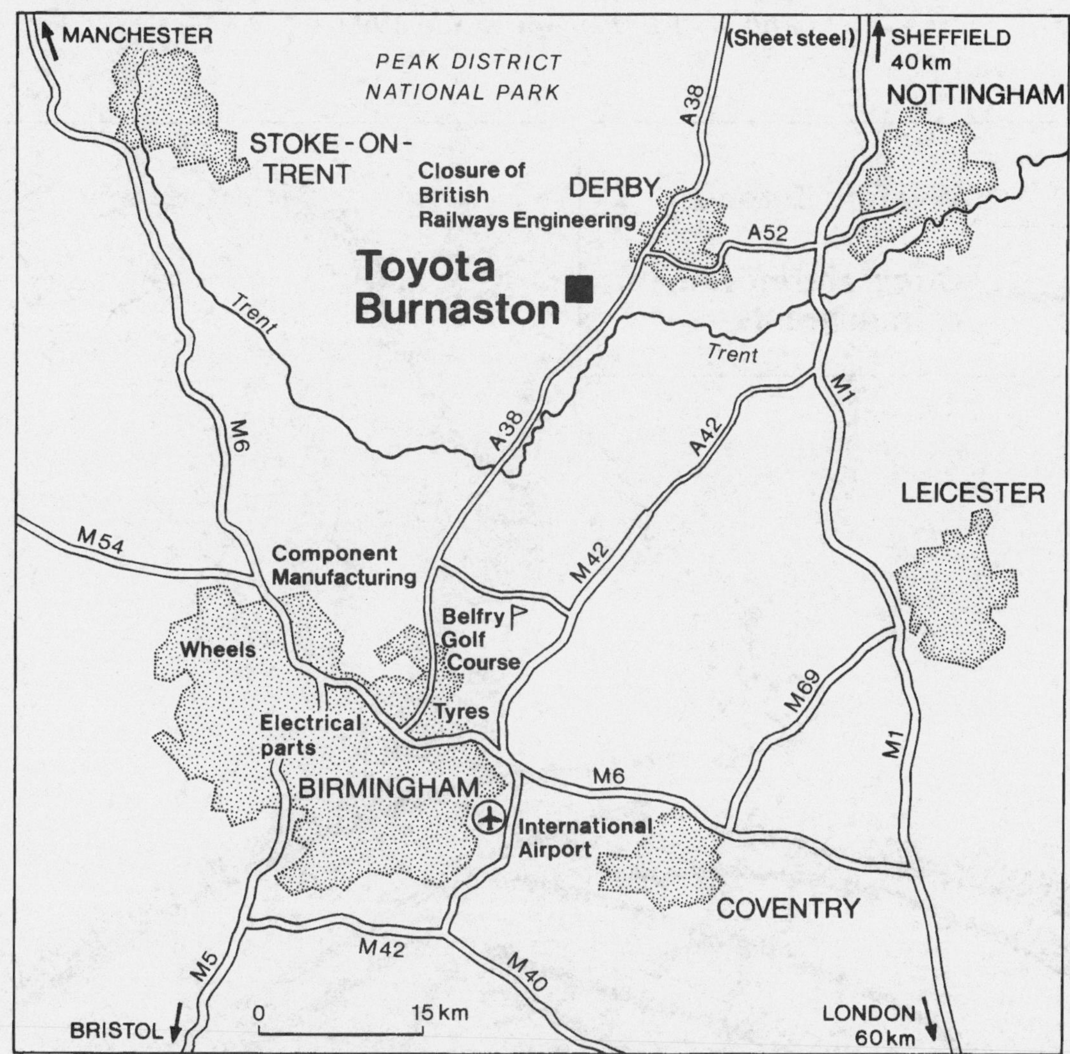

Reference Diagram Q6B: Site of Toyota's Burnaston Factory

Look at Reference Diagrams Q6A and Q6B.

What are the advantages of locating a car factory at Burnaston? **6**

Marks

KU	

7. **Reference Diagram Q7A: Destination and Origins of Migrants into and within Europe since 1990**

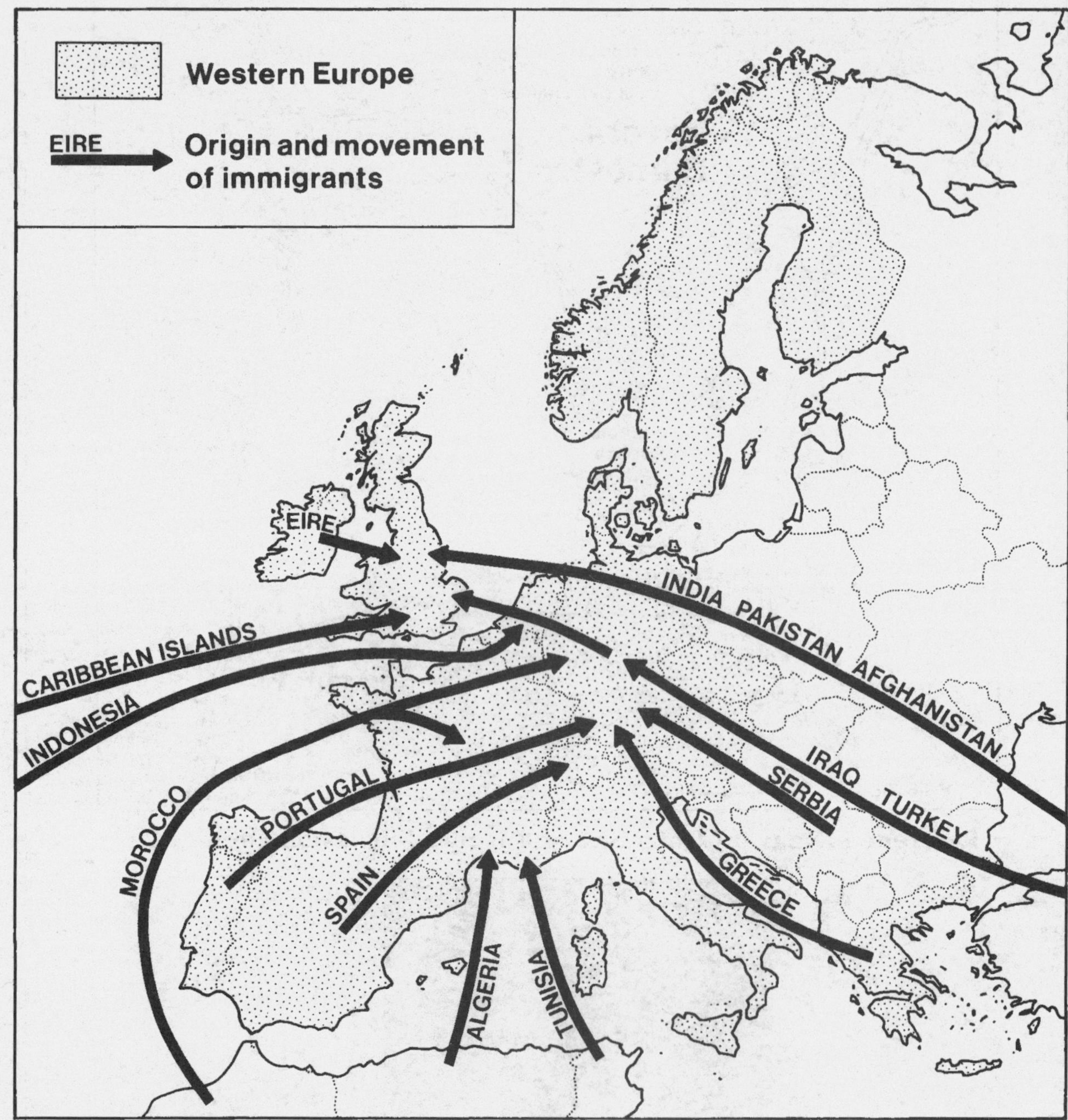

(*a*) Look at Reference Diagram Q7A above.

Describe the **pattern** of migration into and within Europe since 1990.

	Marks	
	KU	ES

7. (continued)

Reference Diagram Q7B: Extract from Newspaper Article

Families from troubled countries given asylum

About 1200 Iraqi and Afghan people were given four-year work permits to live and work in the UK. One refugee said, "I can start work tomorrow. I have useful skills which can help me to provide for my family and put something back into this country."

Some local people say that they are very unhappy about the migrants moving to the UK.

"We thought we'd be safe in this country, but my family are still being persecuted," said one young mother from Kosovo; "Not everyone welcomes us."

(*b*) Look at Reference Diagram Q7B above.

What are the advantages **and** disadvantages **to migrants** of coming to countries in the European Union, such as the United Kingdom? **4**

[Turn over

Marks KU | E

8. **Reference Diagram Q8: Location of the 10 new Members of the European Union**

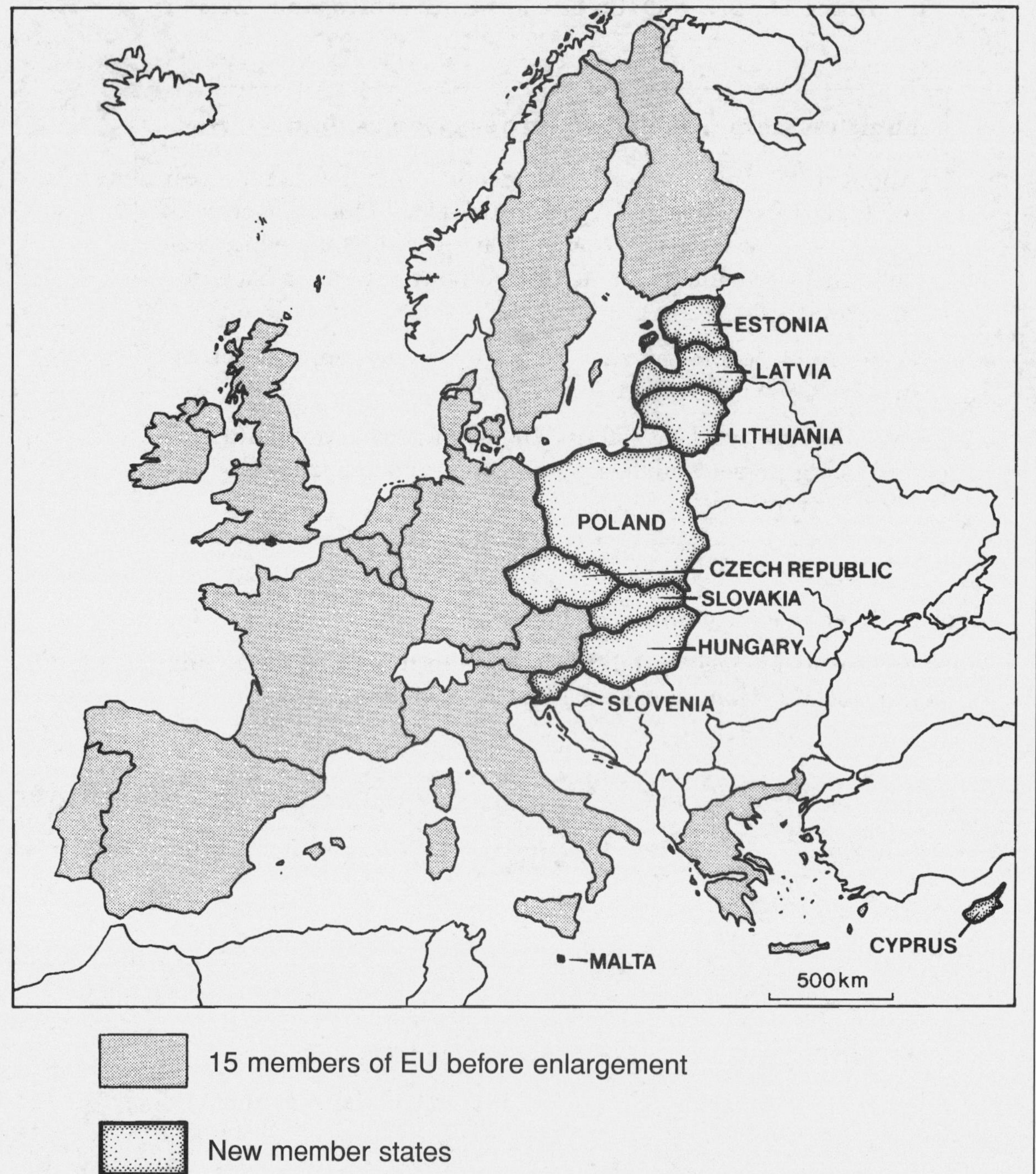

The European Union has been enlarged from its previous membership of 15 countries to a group of 25.

Explain the economic and political advantages to the 10 new countries of joining the European Union. 5

Marks KU ES

9. **Reference Diagram Q9A: Mount Nyiragongo erupts, 17 January 2002**

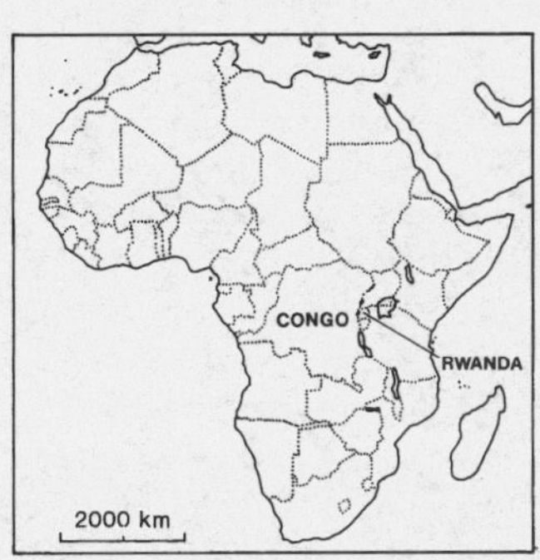

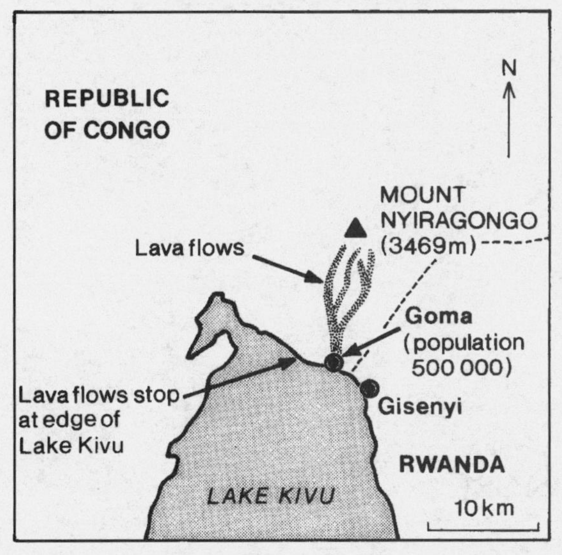

Reference Diagram Q9B

- dozens killed
- crops and farmland destroyed
- lava flows sweep through 14 villages, setting fire to fuel and power stations
- Goma Airport runway blocked by lava
- water supplies cut off
- 10 000 people made homeless
- harbour facilities on Lake Kivu destroyed

Reference Diagram Q9C

Short Term Aid	**Long Term Aid**
Tents and blankets	Road and bridge repairs
Medicines	New house building
Food supplies	Farming equipment and fertilisers

Look at Reference Diagrams Q9A, Q9B and Q9C.

Following the eruption of Mount Nyiragongo, aid was rushed to the area.

Which type of aid would be best suited to helping the people of this area following the volcanic eruption?

Give reasons for your answer. 5

[*END OF QUESTION PAPER*]

[BLANK PAGE]

2005 | General

[BLANK PAGE]

FOR OFFICIAL USE

G

KU	ES

Total Marks

1260/403

NATIONAL QUALIFICATIONS 2005

WEDNESDAY, 11 MAY
10.25 AM–11.50 AM

GEOGRAPHY STANDARD GRADE
General Level

Fill in these boxes and read what is printed below.

Full name of centre

Town

Forename(s)

Surname

Date of birth
Day Month Year

Scottish candidate number

Number of seat

1 Read the whole of each question carefully before you answer it.

2 Write in the spaces provided.

3 Where boxes like this ☐ are provided, put a tick ✓ in the box beside the answer you think is correct.

4 Try all the questions.

5 Do not give up the first time you get stuck: you may be able to answer later questions.

6 Extra paper may be obtained from the invigilator, if required.

7 Before leaving the examination room you must give this book to the invigilator. If you do not, you may lose all the marks for this paper.

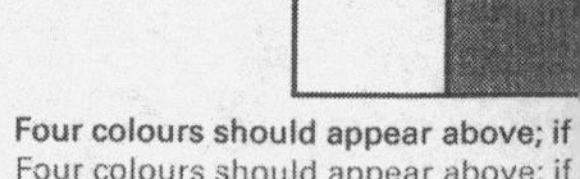

Four colours should appear above; if

Four colours should appear above; if

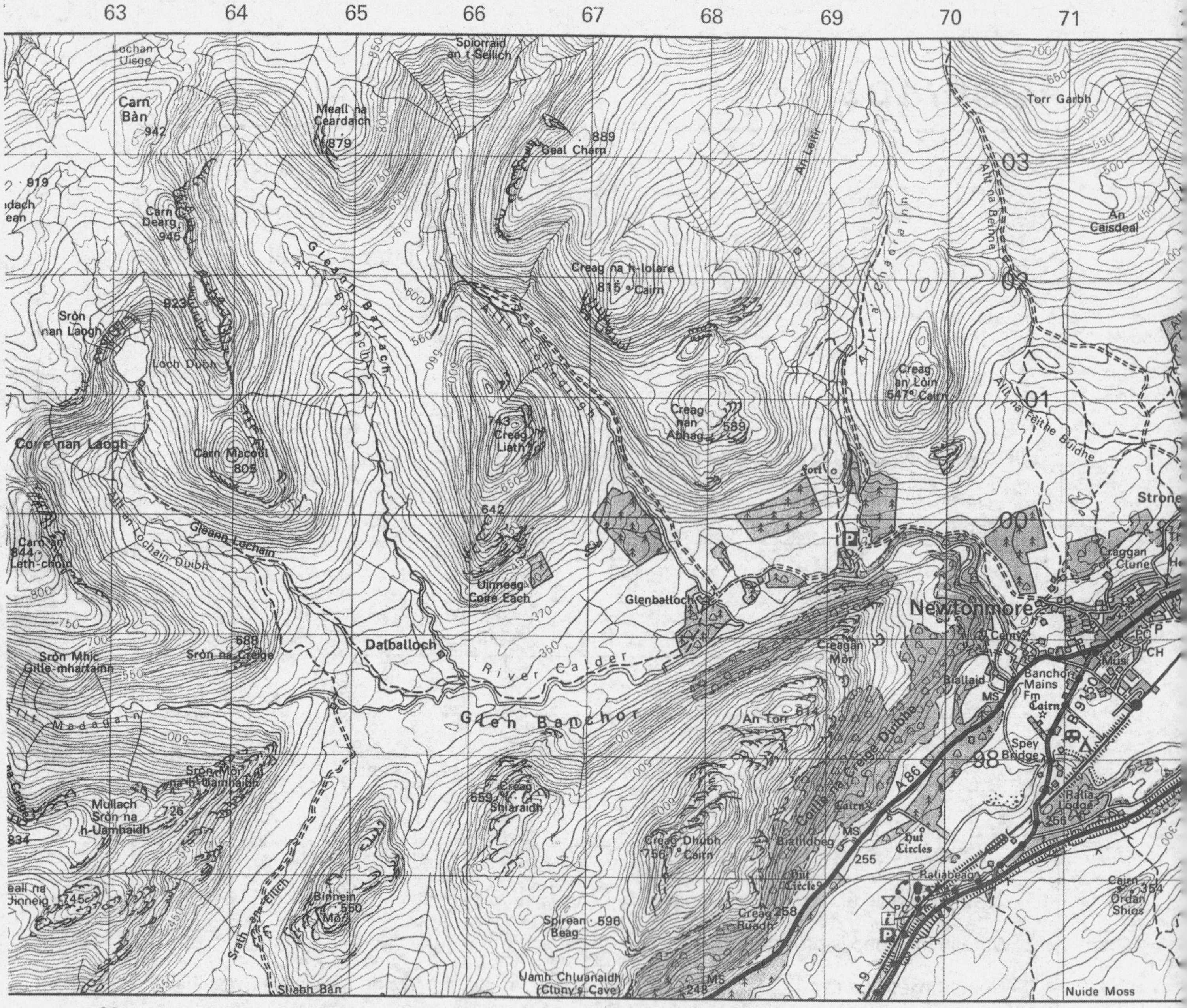

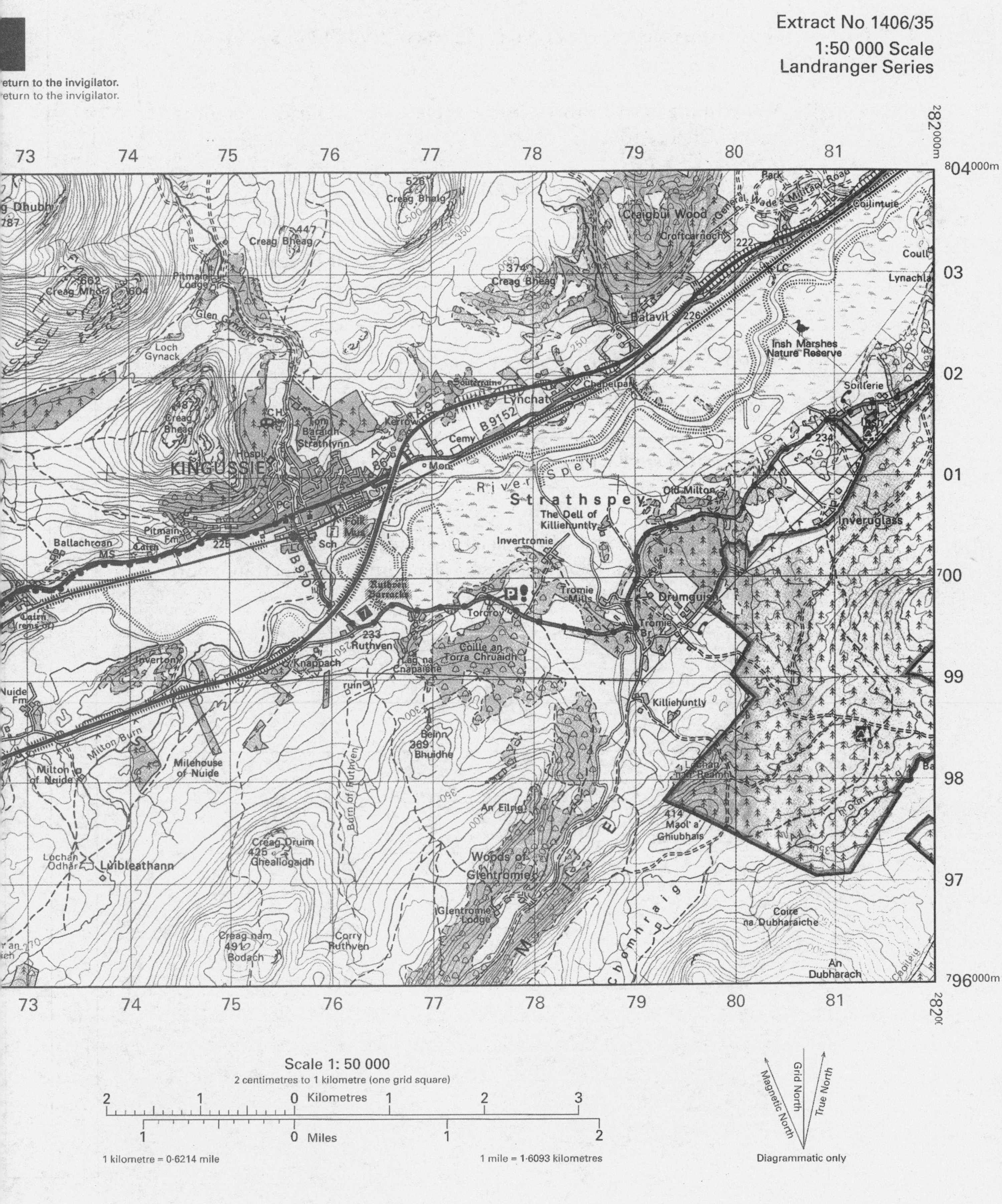

return to the invigilator.
Extract No 1406/35
1:50 000 Scale
Landranger Series
KINGUSSIE
Strathspey
River Spey
Lynchat
Chapelpark
Batavil
Craigbui Wood
Croftcarnoch
General Wade's Military Road
Insh Marshes Nature Reserve
Soillerie
Inveruglass
Old Milton
The Dell of Killiehuntly
Invertromie
Tromie Mills
Drumguish
Tromie Br
Killiehuntly
Torcroy
Ruthven Barracks
Ruthven
Knappach
Coille an Torra Chruaidh
Lag na Cnapaiche
Beinn Bhuidhe
An Eilrig
Woods of Glentromie
Glentromie Lodge
Maol a' Ghiubhais
Lochan nan Reamh
Coire na Dubharaiche
An Dubharach
Corry Ruthven
Creag nam Bodach
Creag Druim Ghealaogaidh
Lùibleathann
Lochan Odhar
Milton of Nuide
Milehouse of Nuide
Milton Burn
Nuide Fm
Invertom
Ballachroan
Pitmain Fm
Pitmain Lodge
Glen Gynack
Loch Gynack
Creag Mhor
Creag Bheag
Tom Baraidh
Strathlynn
Kerrow
Cemy
Mon
Folk Mus
Sch
Hospl
A9
A86
B9152
B970
Burn of Ruthven
Coull
Lynachlaggan
Coilintuie
Park
Scale 1: 50 000
2 centimetres to 1 kilometre (one grid square)
Kilometres
Miles
1 kilometre = 0·6214 mile
1 mile = 1·6093 kilometres
Magnetic North
Grid North
True North
Diagrammatic only

DO NOT WRITE IN THIS MARGIN

KU | ES

Marks

1. Look at the Ordnance Survey Map Extract (No 1406/35) of the Kingussie area.

(*a*) (i) Match the glacial features in the table with the grid references below. Choose from:

6399 6699 6301 7796.

Glacial Feature	Grid Reference
U-shaped valley with misfit stream	
Corrie with lochan	
Hanging valley	
Truncated spur with crags	

3

(ii) **Explain** how **one** of the glacial features named in the table above was formed. You may use a diagram(s) to illustrate your answer.

3

DO NOT WRITE IN THIS MARGIN

KU	ES

Marks

1. (continued)

(*b*) The River Spey between 720981 and 820039 has a wide flood plain. Study this section of the River Spey. Using map evidence,

(i) give **two** ways in which people have made use of the flood plain;

(ii) give **two** ways in which people have tried to overcome or avoid the problem of flooding on this section of the River Spey. 4

(*c*) Pitmain Farm is in grid square 7400. What type of farm is this likely to be?

Tick (✓) your choice.

Livestock ☐ Mixed ☐ Arable ☐

Give reasons for your answer. 3

[Turn over

DO NOT WRITE IN THIS MARGIN

KU ES

Marks

1. (continued)

(*d*) Match the site descriptions in the table with the settlements shown below:

Insh (8101) Newtonmore (7199) Kingussie (7500) Glenballoch (6799).

Description of Site	Name of Settlement
Between two tributaries to the north of the River Spey	
On land sloping gently down to the northwest, surrounded by forests	
On the floor of a U-shaped valley, next to a tributary of the River Calder	
A tributary of the River Spey runs through the middle of this settlement	

3

(*e*) Do you think the area around Newtonmore is suitable for tourism? Using map evidence, give reasons for your answer.

4

Marks | DO NOT WRITE IN THIS MARGIN | KU | ES

1. (continued)

(*f*) **Reference Diagram Q1A: Sketch Map showing part of Insh Marshes Nature Reserve**

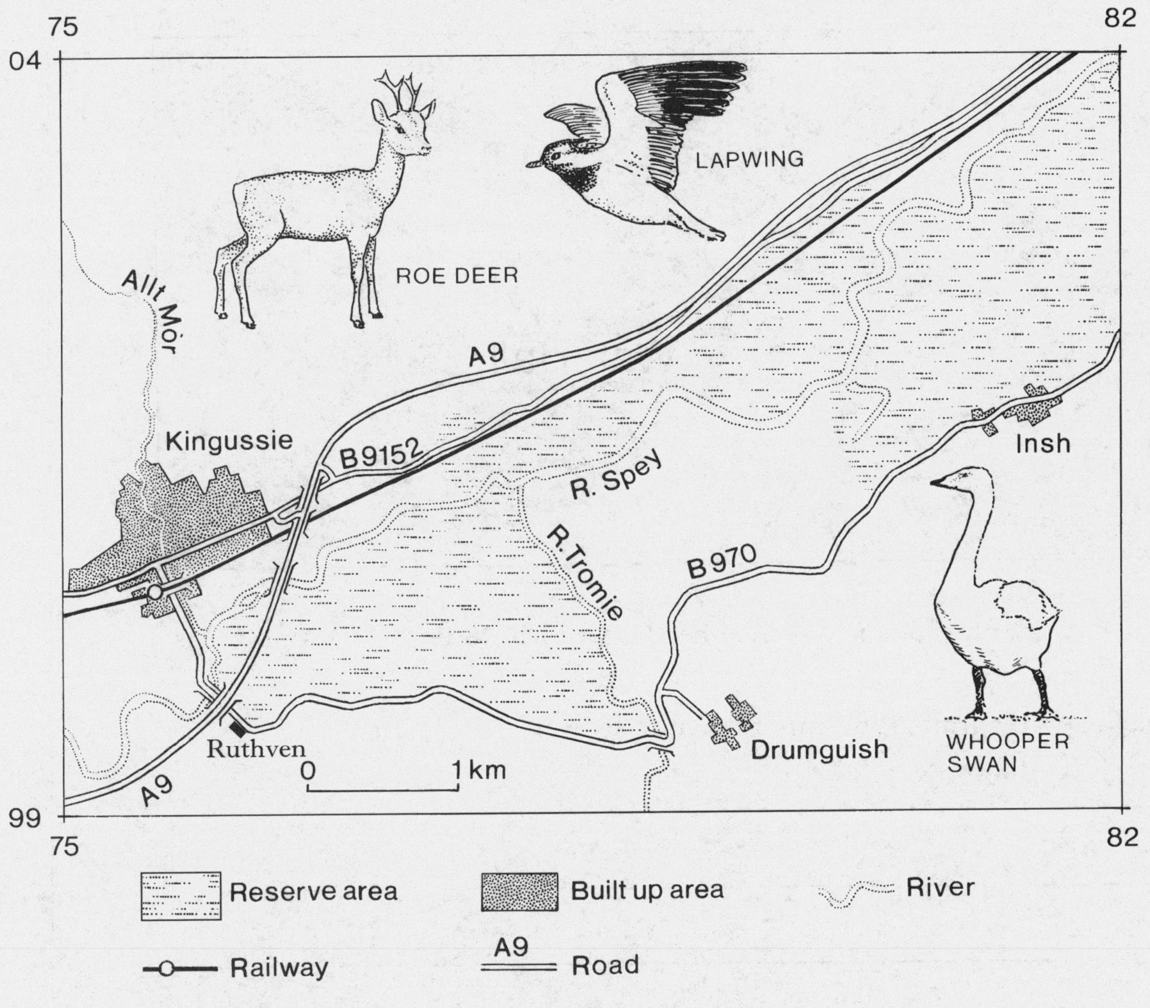

Look at the Ordnance Survey map and Reference Diagram Q1A.

The Insh Marshes Nature Reserve extends on both sides of the River Spey from grid square 7699 (Ruthven) to grid square 8103.

Using map evidence, give advantages and disadvantages of the site of this nature reserve.

Advantages ____

Disadvantages ______________________________________

4

DO NOT WRITE IN THIS MARGIN

KU	ES

Marks

2. **Reference Diagram Q2: Waterfall**

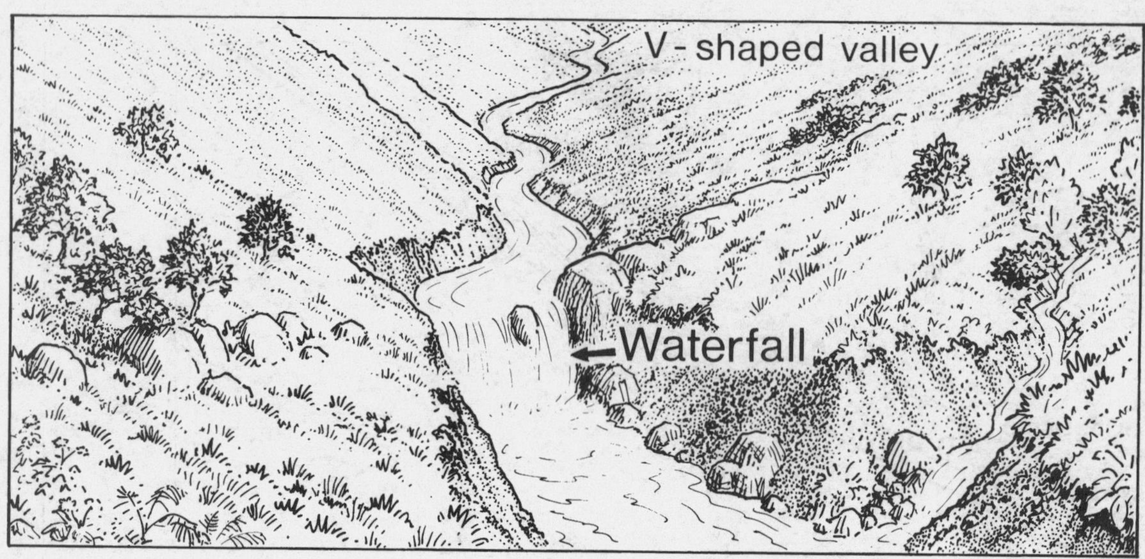

Explain how a waterfall such as the one shown in Reference Diagram Q2 is formed.

You may use a diagram(s) to illustrate your answer.

____

____

____

____

____

3

[Turn over for Question 3 on *Page eight*

DO NOT WRITE IN THIS MARGIN

KU	ES

Marks

3. Reference Diagram Q3A: Weather Station Sites

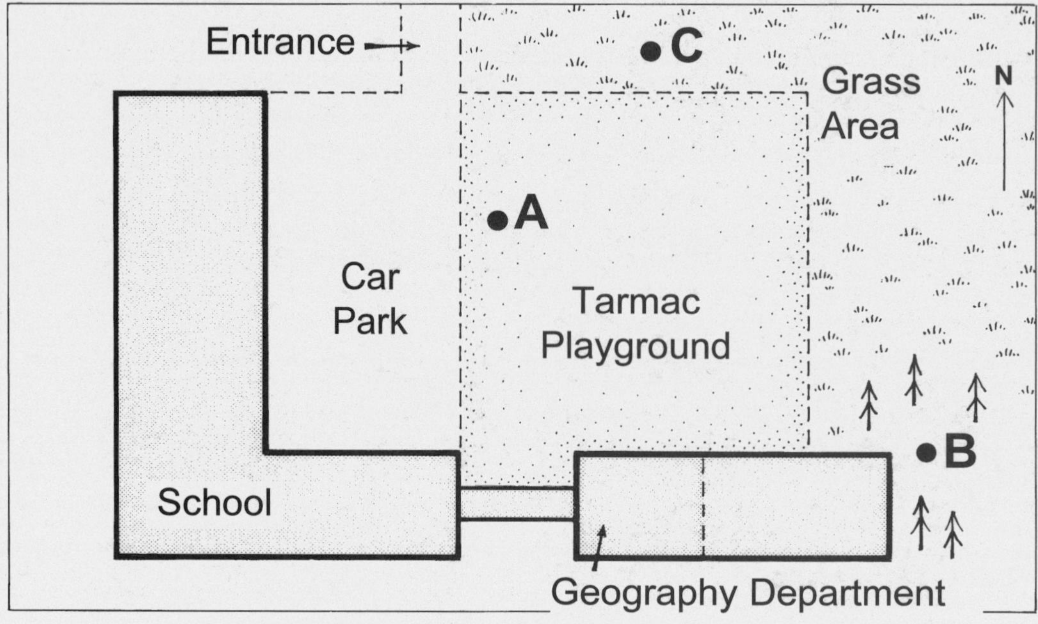

(*a*) Look at Reference Diagram Q3A.

Do you agree that site A is the best site for the school weather station?

Tick (✓) your choice.

Yes ☐ No ☐

Give reasons for your choice.

____

____

____

____

____ 3

DO NOT WRITE IN THIS MARGIN

KU	ES

Marks

3. (continued)

Reference Diagram Q3B: Air Masses affecting Britain

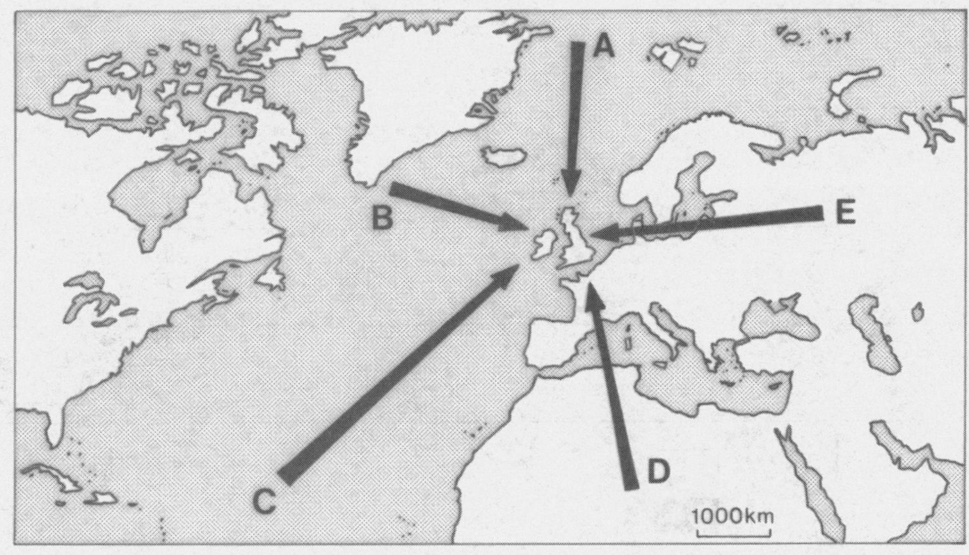

(*b*) Look at Reference Diagram Q3B.

(i) Describe the type of weather Britain might have with air mass D.

____

____

____

____ 2

(ii) **Explain** why air mass B would bring cold, wet weather.

____

____

____

____ 2

[Turn over

DO NOT WRITE IN THIS MARGIN

KU ES

Marks

4. Reference Diagram Q4A: Selected Climate Regions

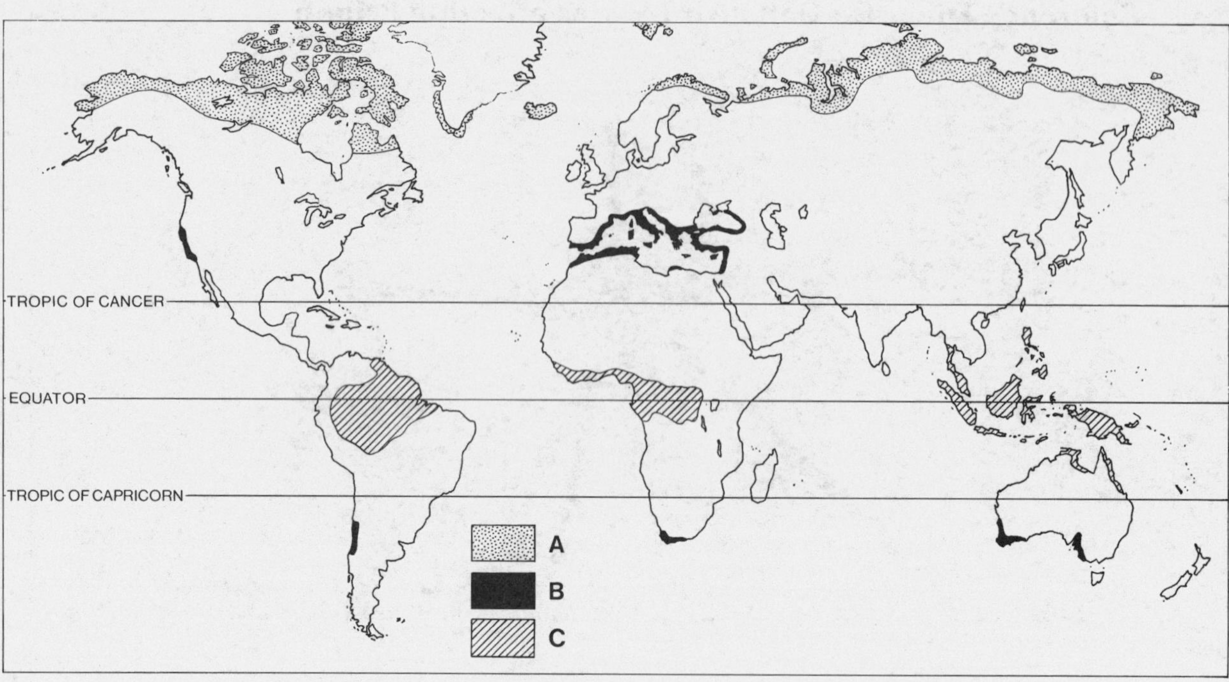

(*a*) Look at Reference Diagram Q4A above.

Complete the table below by writing in the names of the climate regions.

Area	Name of Climate Region
A	
B	
C	

3

DO NOT WRITE IN THIS MARGIN

KU	ES

Marks

4. (continued)

Reference Diagram Q4B: Desertification in Africa

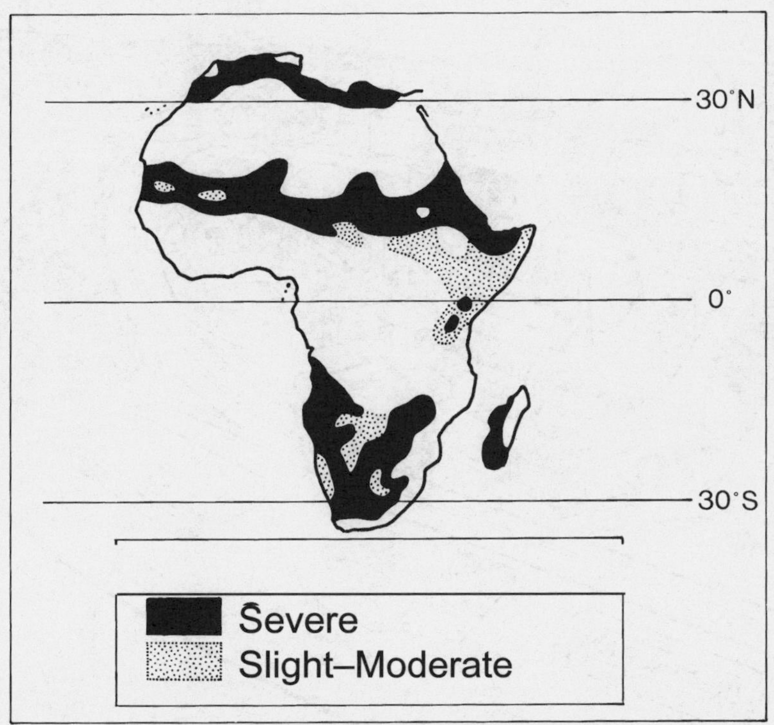

(*b*) Look at Reference Diagram Q4B.

What are the main causes of desertification?

____

____

____

____

____

____ **4**

[Turn over

5. Reference Diagram Q5: Land Uses at the Edge of a City

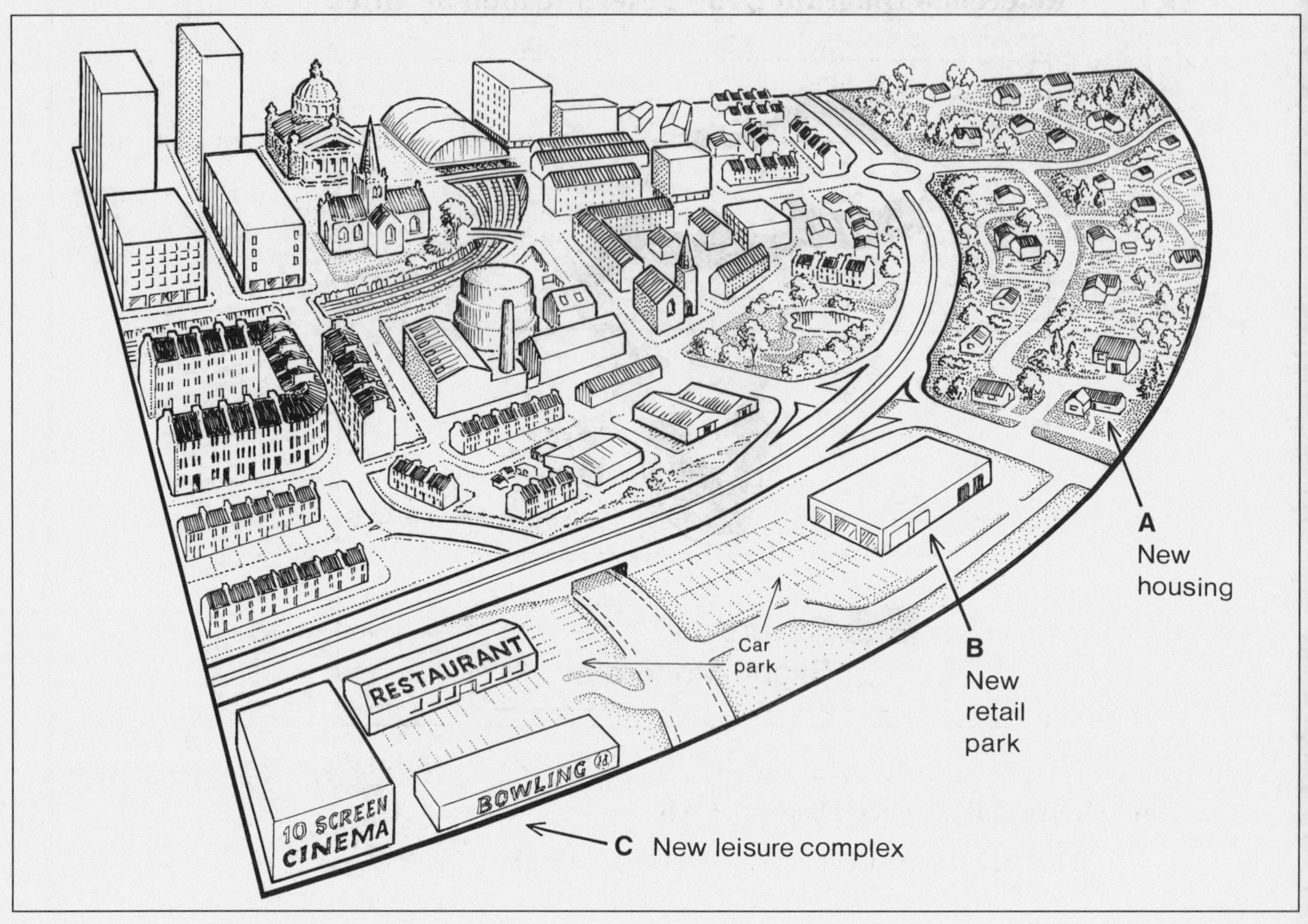

DO NOT WRITE IN THIS MARGIN

Marks	KU	ES

Look at Reference Diagram Q5.

(*a*) Choose **one** of the main land uses in the diagram—A, B or C.

Chosen land use ______________________

Explain why the edge of the city is a good location for this land use.

____

____

____

____

____ **3**

DO NOT WRITE IN THIS MARGIN

KU | ES

Marks

5. (continued)

(*b*) Identify **two** techniques which pupils could use to gather information in a study of an out-of-town shopping centre.

Give reasons for your choice.

Technique 1 ____________________

Technique 2 ____________________

Reasons for choice ____________________

____

____

____

____

____________________ 4

[Turn over

DO NOT WRITE IN THIS MARGIN

KU	ES

Marks

6. Reference Diagram Q6: Recent Trends in Farming

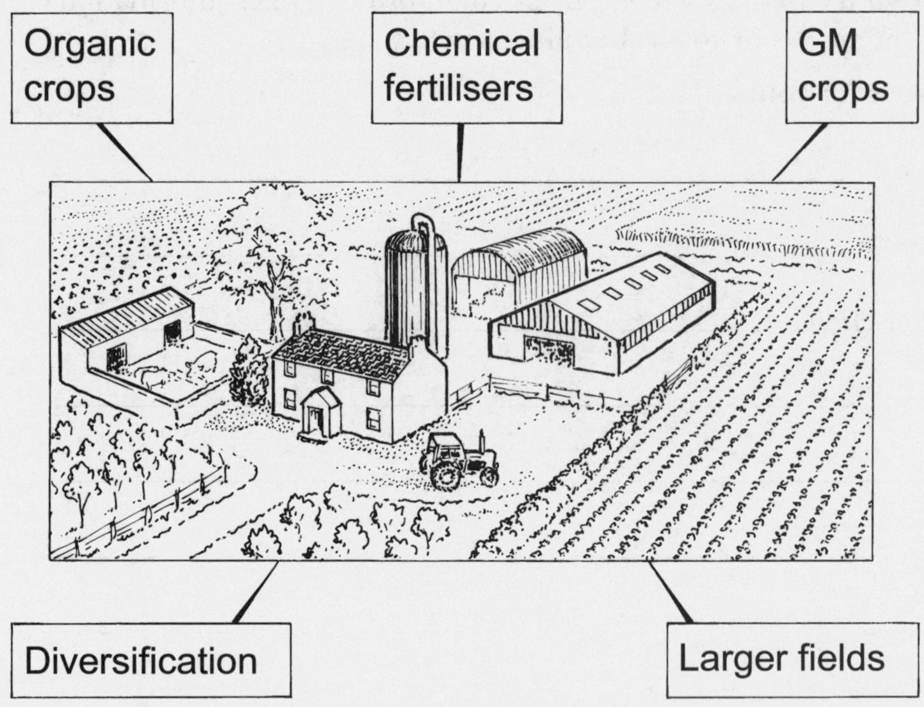

"Recent trends in farming are of great benefit to the British people."

Do you agree? Explain your answer.

____

____

____

____

____

____ **4**

7. **Reference Diagram Q7: Old Industrial Area**

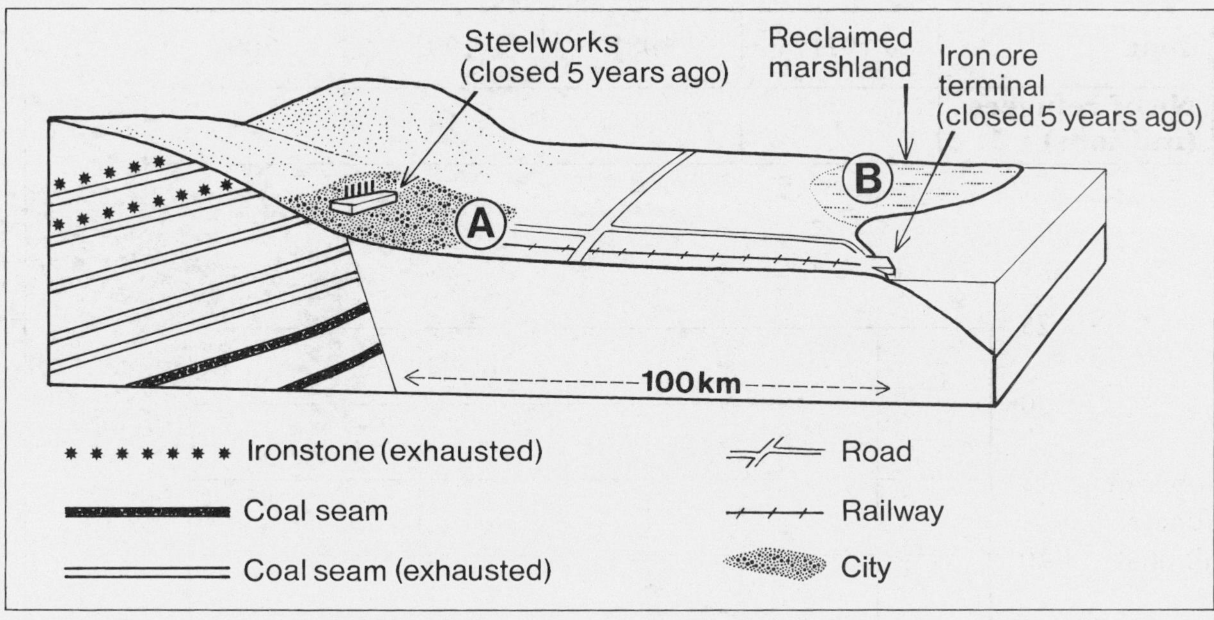

DO NOT WRITE IN THIS MARGIN

KU	ES

Marks

Look at Reference Diagram Q7.

A steel company is considering building a new integrated steelworks at either A or B.

Which site do you think they should choose?

Give reasons for your answer.

Chosen site ________________________

____

____

____

____

____

____ 4

[Turn over

DO NOT WRITE IN THIS MARGIN

KU | ES

Marks

8. Reference Diagram Q8A: World Refugees (millions) 1971–2001

Year	1971	1981	1991	2001
No of refugees (millions)	3	8	18	24

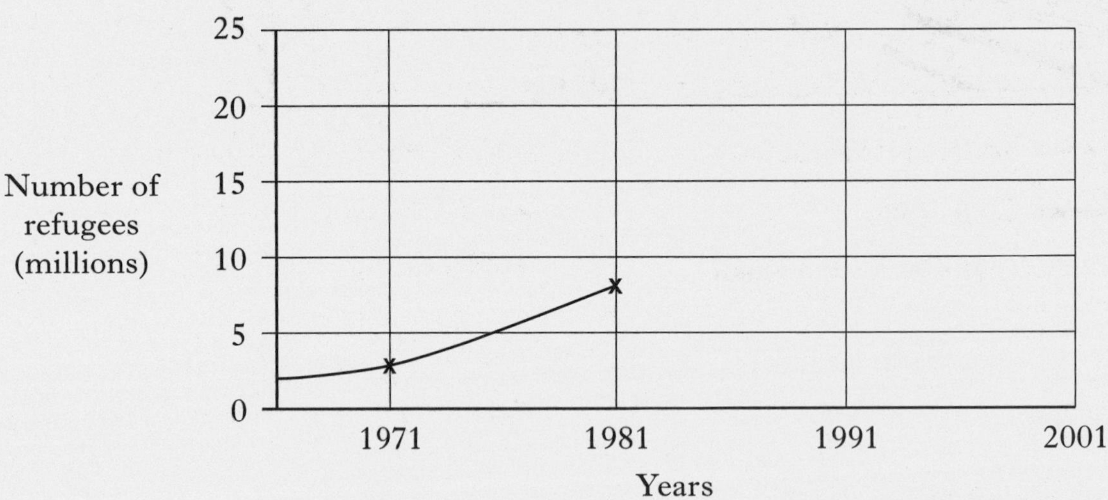

(*a*) Complete the line graph using the figures from Reference Diagram Q8A. **2**

DO NOT WRITE IN THIS MARGIN

KU	ES

Marks

8. (continued)

Reference Table Q8B: Sources of Refugees in Glasgow 2003

Country	**Percentage**
Afghanistan	6
Democratic Republic of Congo	4
Iran	9
Iraq	7
Pakistan	9
Somalia	9
Turkey	14
Others	42

(*b*) Suggest **two** other techniques which could be used to process the information in Reference Table Q8B.

Give reasons for your answers.

Technique 1 ____________________

Technique 2 ____________________

Reasons ____________________

____

____

____

____

____________________ 4

[Turn over

DO NOT WRITE IN THIS MARGIN

KU	ES

Marks

9. Reference Diagram Q9A: Quotation from Kofi Annan

> "Farmers in poor countries must be given a fair chance to compete, both in world markets and at home."

Kofi Annan (United Nations General Secretary)

Reference Diagram Q9B: Maize Trade between USA and Mexico

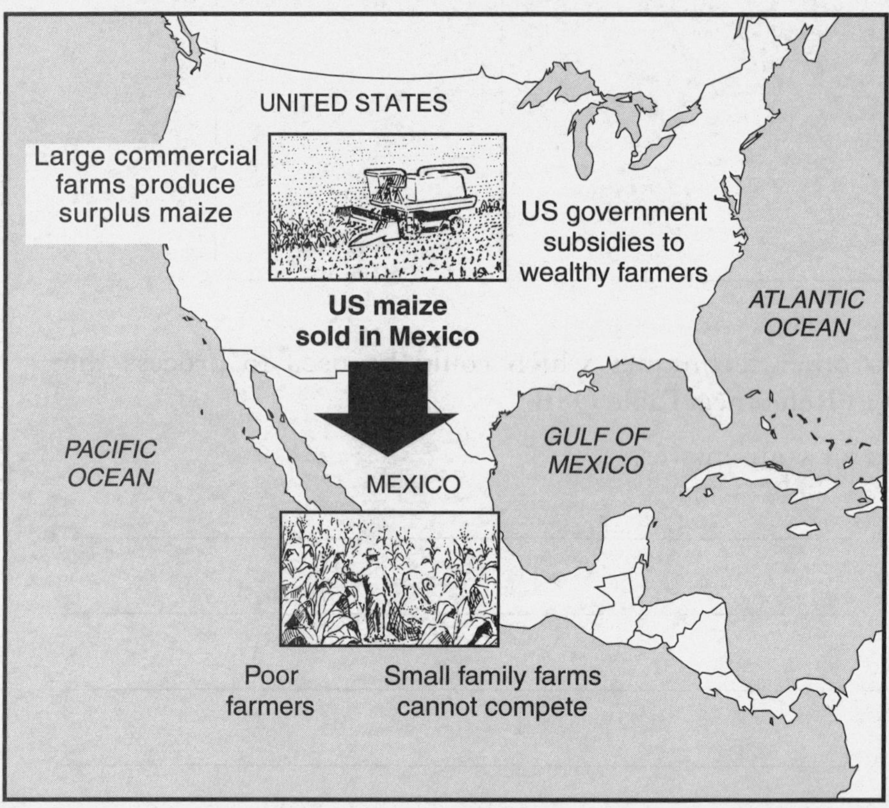

Look at Reference Diagrams Q9A and Q9B.

Explain why Mexican farmers think the maize trade between the USA and their country is unfair. 4

[Turn over for Question 10 on *Page twenty*

DO NOT WRITE IN THIS MARGIN

KU	ES

Marks

10. **Reference Diagram Q10A: Mozambique**

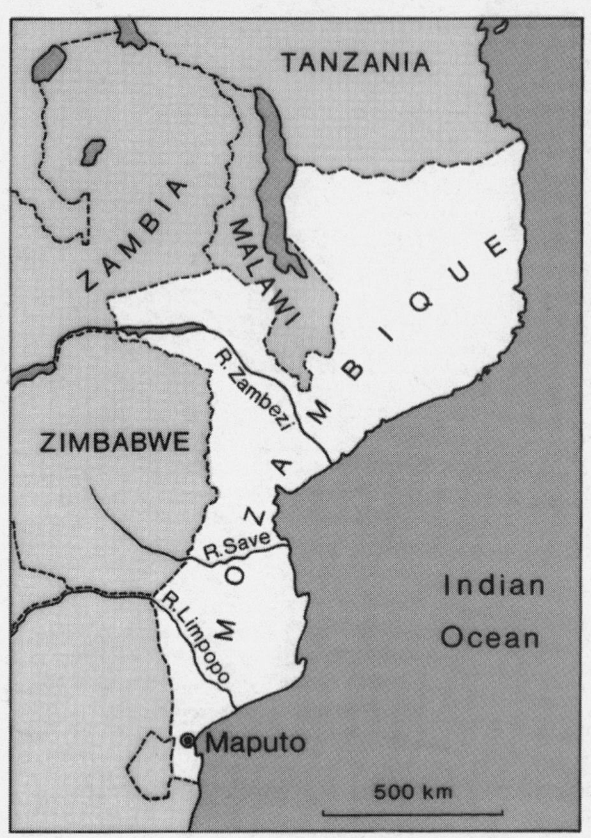

Reference Diagram Q10B: Effects of the Mozambique Floods, February/March 2000

Deaths	1000
Homeless	500 000
Farmland lost	25%
Schools destroyed	600
Estimated cost of rebuilding	\$270–\$430 million

Reference Diagram Q10C: Types of Aid

Short-term Aid	Long-term Aid
Clean water	Rebuilding homes
Food	Road building
Emergency shelter	Electricity network
Medicines	Building hospitals

DO NOT WRITE IN THIS MARGIN

	KU	ES

Marks

10. (continued)

Look at Reference Diagrams Q10A, Q10B and Q10C.

In 2000, two cyclones hit Mozambique causing the Rivers Save, Zambezi and Limpopo to burst their banks. Almost half of Mozambique's land was flooded.

Which type of aid, short-term or long-term, would have been most useful to Mozambique?

Explain your answer in detail. **4**

[*END OF QUESTION PAPER*]

[BLANK PAGE]

[BLANK PAGE]

C

1260/405

NATIONAL
QUALIFICATIONS
2005

WEDNESDAY, 11 MAY
1.00 PM – 3.00 PM

GEOGRAPHY
STANDARD GRADE
Credit Level

All questions should be attempted.

Candidates should read the questions carefully. Answers should be clearly expressed and relevant.

Credit will always be given for appropriate sketch-maps and diagrams.

Write legibly and neatly, and leave a space of about one cm between the lines.

Marks may be deducted for bad spelling and bad punctuation, and for writing that is difficult to read.

All maps and diagrams in this paper have been printed in black only: no other colours have been used.

THB 1260/405 6/19370

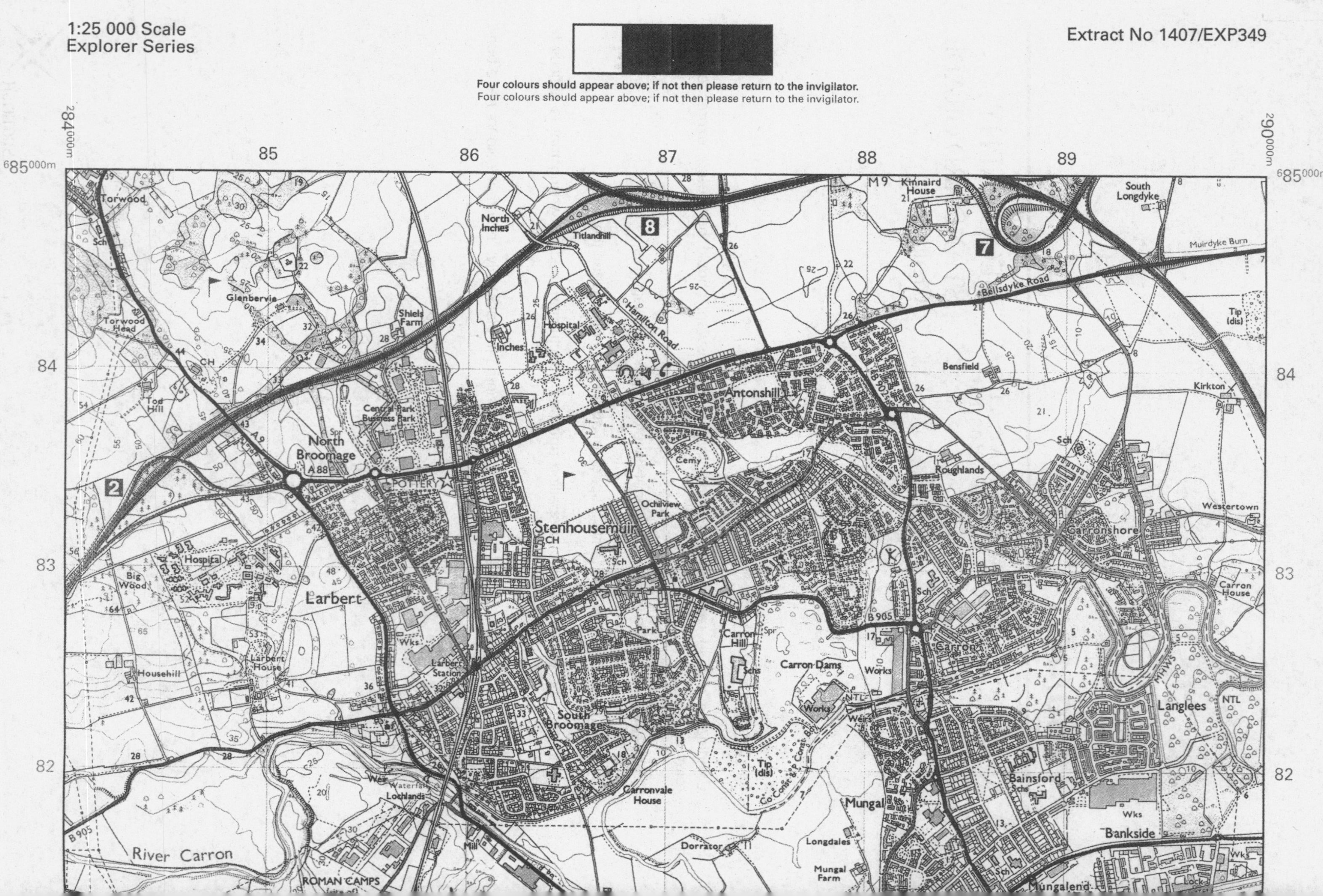
1:25 000 Scale
Explorer Series
Extract No 1407/EXP349
Four colours should appear above; if not then please return to the invigilator.
Four colours should appear above; if not then please return to the invigilator.
River Carron
Stenhousemuir
Larbert
Antonshill
North Broomage
South Broomage
Carron
Carronshore
Langlees
Bainsford
Bankside
Mungal
Mungalend
Carron Dams
Carron Hill
Carronvale House
Hamilton Road
Bellsdyke Road
Glenbervie
Torwood
Kinnaird House
South Longdyke
Kirkton
Westertown
Roughlands
Bensfield
Ochilview Park
Dorrator
Longdales
Mungal Farm
ROMAN CAMPS
Lochlands
Househill
Big Wood
Tod Hill
Shiels Farm
North Inches
Titlandhill
Muirdyke Burn
Central Park Business Park

Scale 1: 25 000
4 centimetres to 1 kilometre (one grid square)
Kilometres
Miles
1 kilometre = 0·6214 mile
1 Mile = 1·6093 kilometres
True North
Grid North
Magnetic North
Diagrammatic only
Falkirk Wheel
Due to open 2001
Forth & Clyde Canal
Union Canal
Glen Village
Hallglen
Woodlands
Bantaskin
Summerford
Tamfourhill
Greenbank
Grahamston
Merchiston
Camelon
Carmuirs
Wester Carmuirs
Middlefield
Lock Sixteen
Callendar Park
Parkfoot
Princes Park
Glenrig
Seafield
Craigieburn
Craigburn Wood
Canada Wood
Greenrig Strip
Tamfourhill Wood
Howierig
Howierig Wood
Greenrig
Bonnyhill Farm
Auchengean Wood
Auchengean
Westerglen Farm
Westerglen Transmitting Sta
Wester Strip
Easter Strip
Mavisbank
Mavisbank Wood
Wester Pirleyhill
Pirleyhill Bridge
Glen Farm
Cleuch Plantation
Kilbean Wood
Fox Covert
ROMAN CAMP (site of)
ANTONINE WALL
MILITARY WAY
ROMAN FORT
Rough Castle
Opencast Workings
Cairn
Monument
Car Park
Industrial Estate
Bantaskine Estate
Greenbank Farm
Old House
Shafts (dis)
Falkirk Grahamston Station
Camelon Sta
A803
B8080

1. **Reference Diagram Q1**

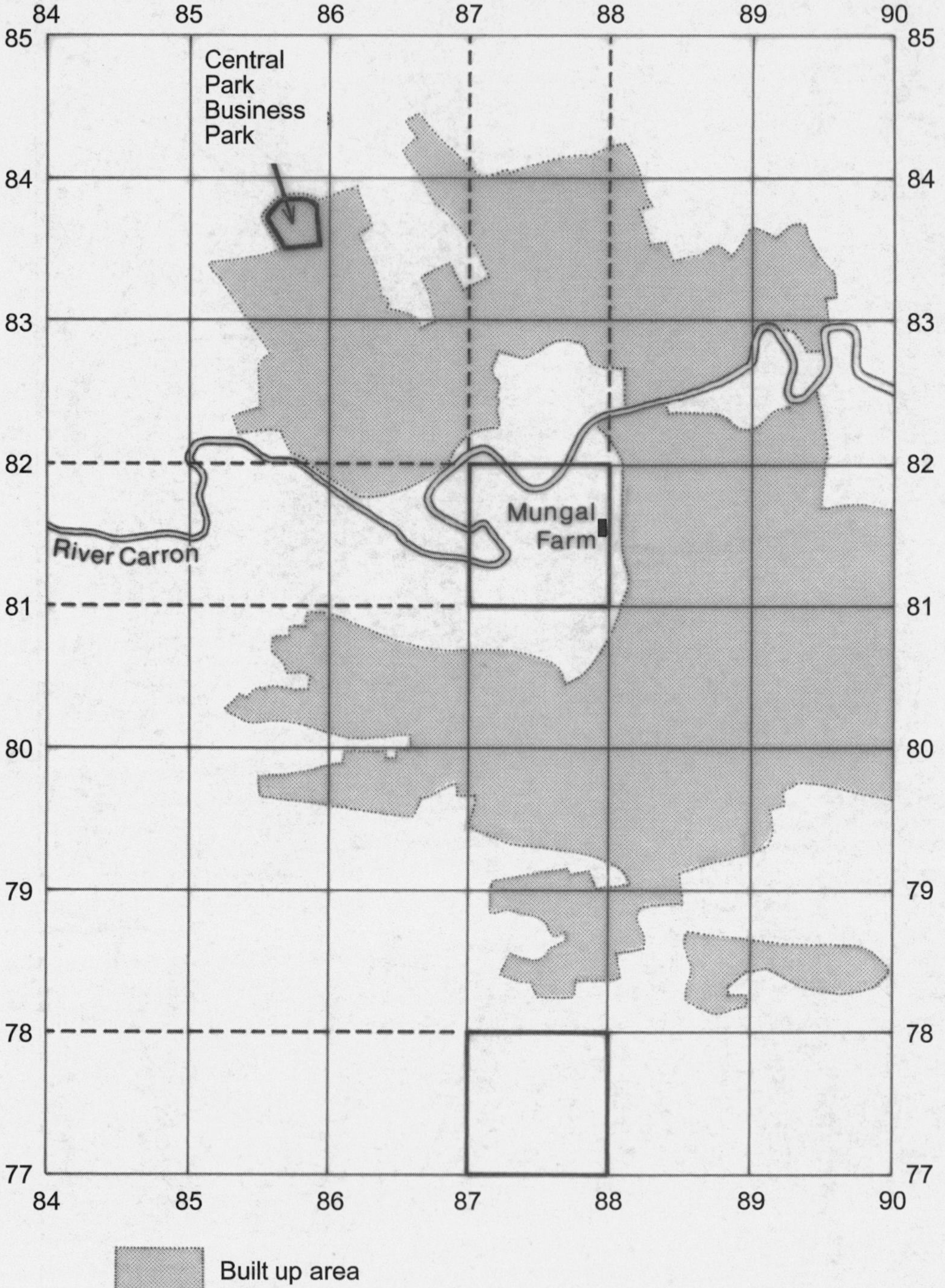

	Marks KU	ES

1. (continued)

This question refers to the OS Map Extract (No 1407/EXP349) of the Falkirk Area and the Reference Diagram Q1 on *Page two*.

(*a*) Describe the **physical** features of the River Carron **and** its valley from Lochlands (859818) to Carron House (897829). 4

(*b*) What is the main present day function of Falkirk?

Choose from:

industrial service centre tourism and recreation.

Use map evidence to support your answer. 5

(*c*) Mungal Farm is found at 880815.

Using map evidence, give the advantages **and** disadvantages of the location of this farm. 4

(*d*) Look at grid squares 8781 and 8777.

Give reasons for the low population density in **each** grid square. 4

(*e*) Use map evidence to **explain** the location of the Central Park Business Park in grid square 8583. 5

(*f*) Do you agree that grid square 8880 contains the CBD of Falkirk?

Explain your answer. 4

[Turn over

Marks | KU | E

2. **Reference Diagram Q2: U-shaped Valley**

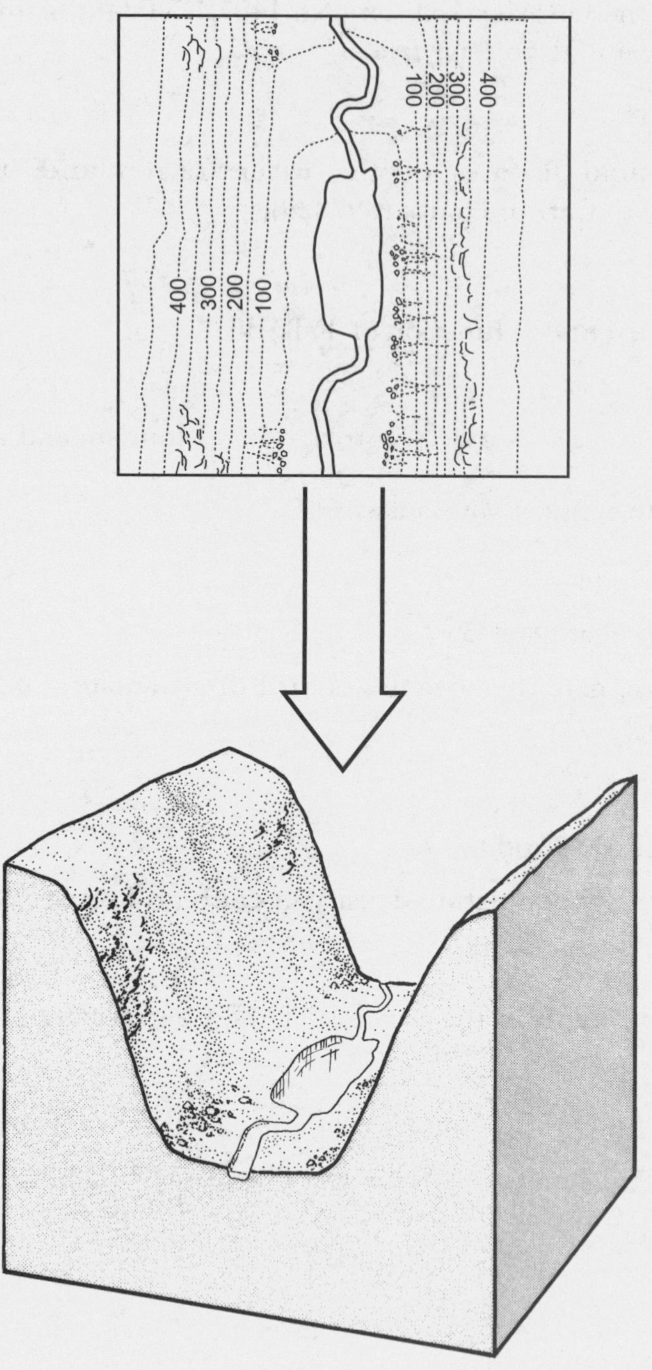

Study Reference Diagram Q2 above.

Explain the formation of a U-shaped valley.

You may use diagrams to illustrate your answer. 4

Marks KU ES

3. **Reference Diagram Q3: Land Use Conflict in Loch Lomond and Trossachs National Park**

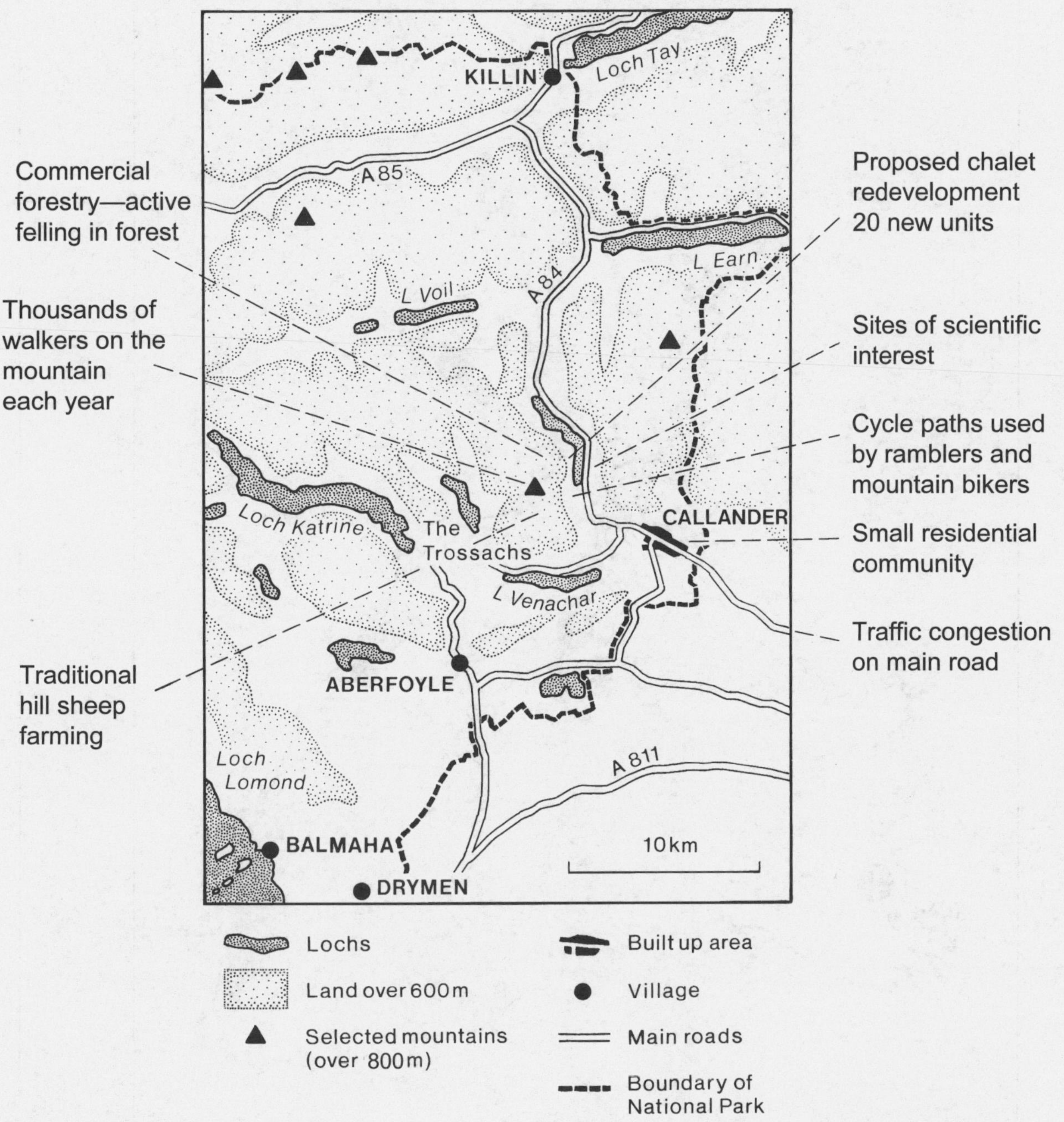

Study Reference Diagram Q3 above.

(*a*) Select **two** different land uses.

Explain in detail why they may be in conflict with each other. 5

(*b*) A group of pupils wants to investigate land use conflicts in the National Park. Describe **two** gathering techniques they could use to collect appropriate data.

Give reasons for your choice. 6

[Turn over

Marks

KU

4. Reference Diagram Q4A: Weather Conditions in the British Isles

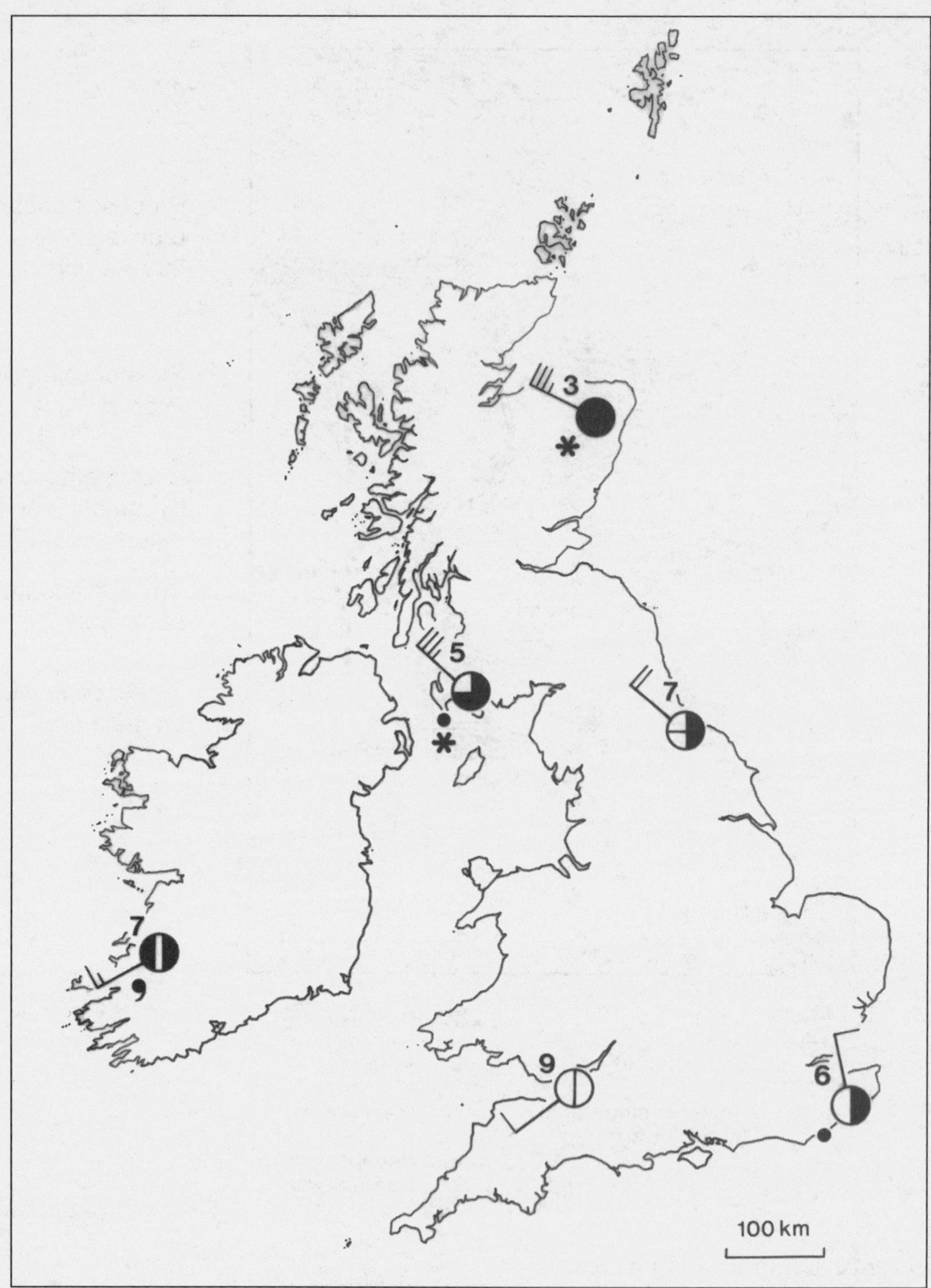

(*a*) Look at Reference Diagram Q4A.

Compare, in detail, weather conditions in North East Scotland with those in South East England.

	Marks	
	KU	ES

4. (continued)

Reference Diagram Q4B: Synoptic Chart for 1200 hrs, 14 November 2004

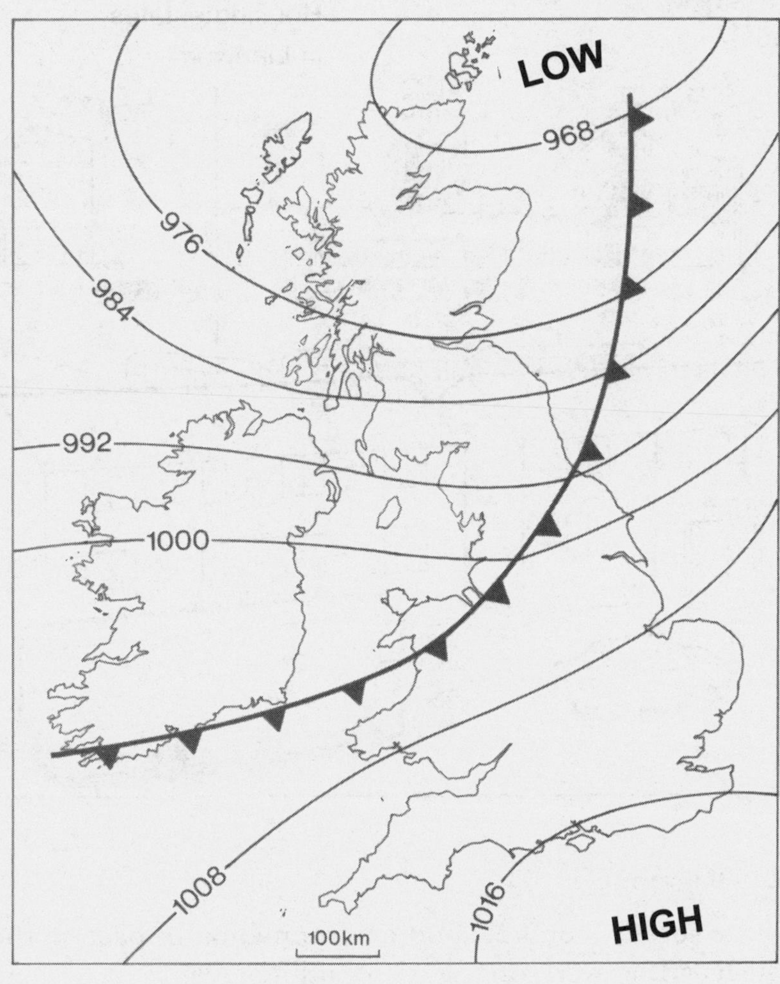

(*b*) Look at Reference Diagrams Q4A and Q4B.

Do you agree that the weather conditions shown in Reference Diagram Q4A match the synoptic chart in Reference Diagram Q4B?

Explain your answer in detail. 5

[Turn over

Marks | KU |

5. **Reference Diagram Q5: Llanwern Steelworks, South Wales**

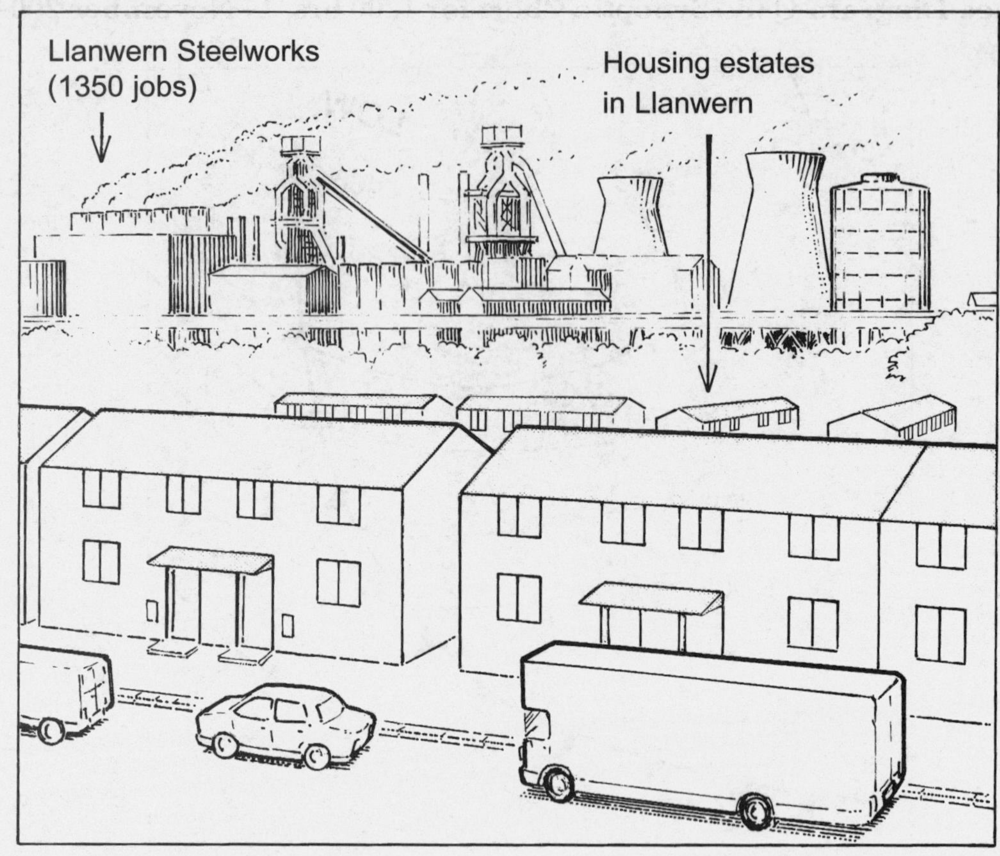

Look at Reference Diagram Q5.

Explain in detail the social, economic and environmental impact of the closure of a large steelworks such as Llanwern on the surrounding area. **5**

Marks | KU | ES

6. **Reference Diagram Q6A: Changing Farmscape in UK**

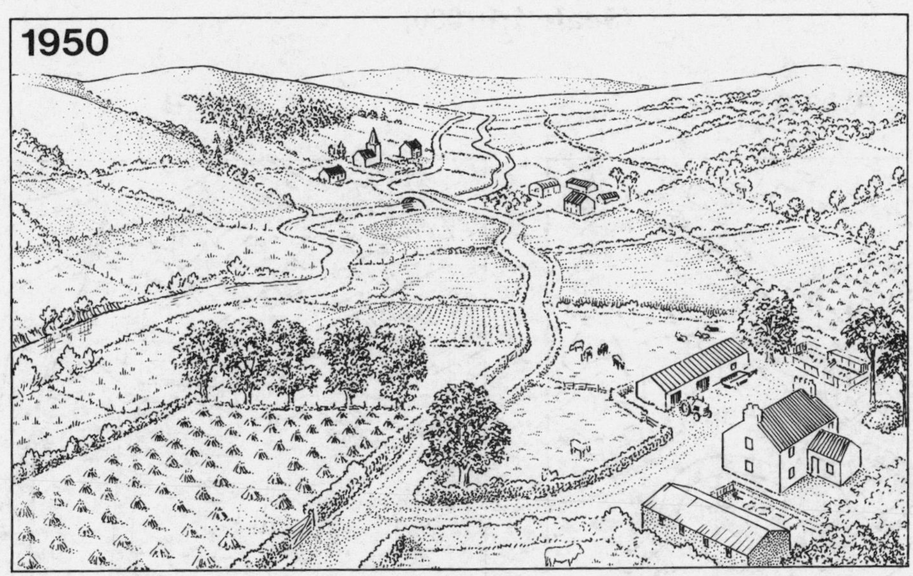

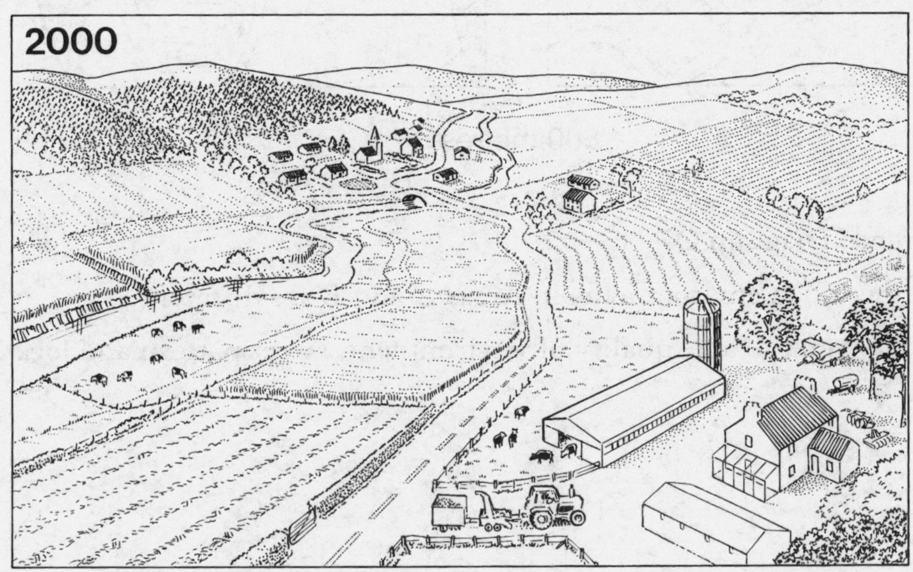

Reference Diagram Q6B: Changes in Farm Size

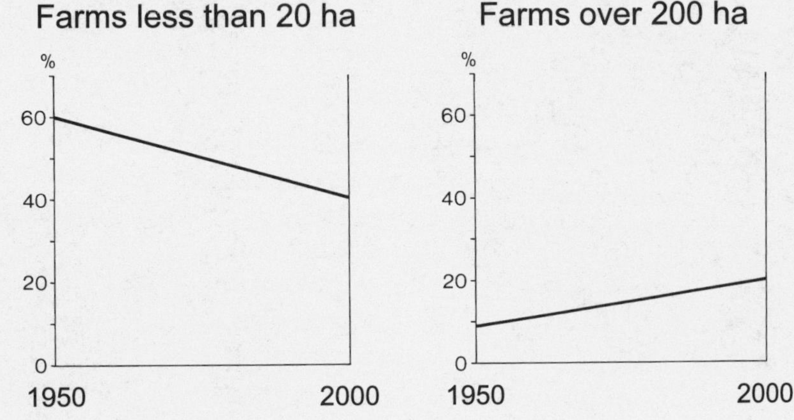

Look at Reference Diagrams Q6A and Q6B.

Explain the advantages **and** disadvantages of the changes shown. 6

Marks | KU

7. **Reference Diagram Q7: Street Maps of two Areas in Greater Glasgow (Scale 1:10 000)**

Area A

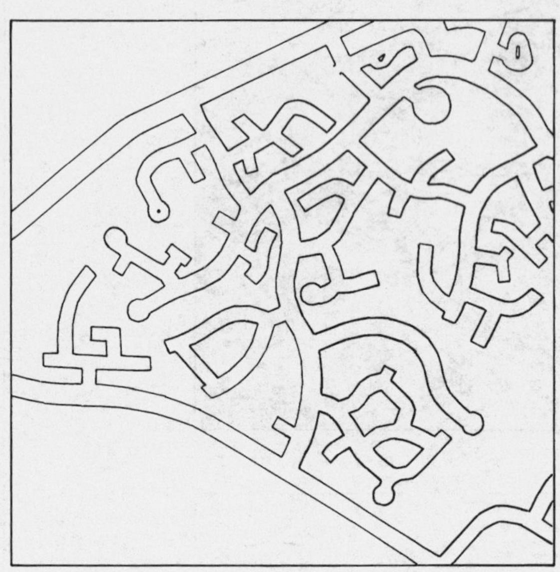

Area B

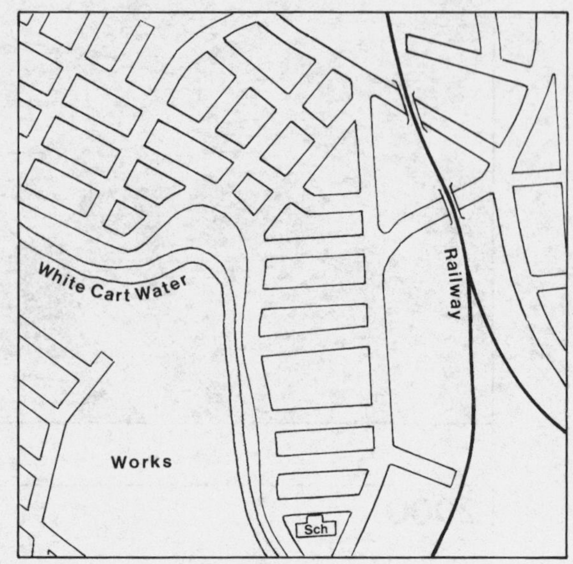

500 metres

Look at Reference Diagram Q7.

Explain why the urban environments in Areas A and B are different.

Your answer may refer to age, quality of environment, street pattern and location. 6

8. **Reference Diagram Q8: Exports of selected Economically Less Developed Countries (Developing Countries)**

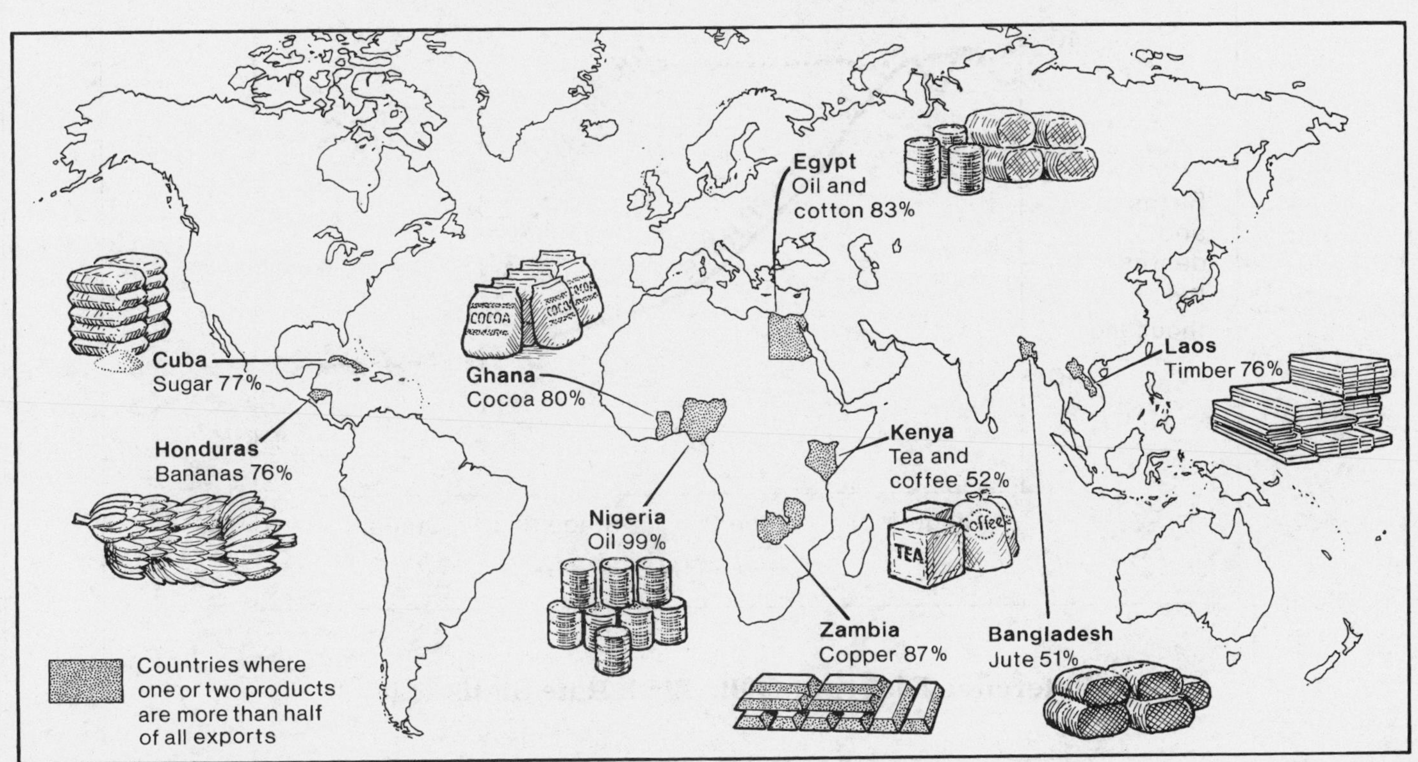

	Marks	
	KU	ES
(*a*) Look at Reference Diagram Q8. **Explain** why some Economically Less Developed Countries (Developing Countries) are especially at risk from changing world prices for the goods which they export.	4	
(*b*) Which other processing techniques could be used to display the export percentage figures shown on Reference Diagram Q8? Give reasons for your choice of techniques.		6

[Turn over for Question 9 on *Page twelve*

Marks KU

9. **Reference Diagram Q9A: Demographic Transition Model**

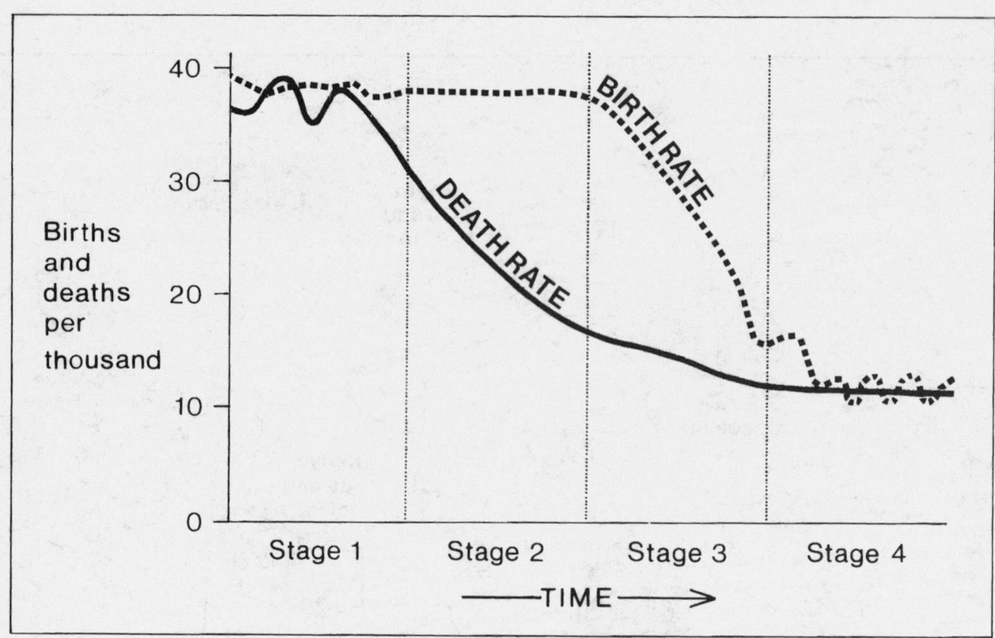

Reference Diagram Q9B: Birth Rate Statistics

Country	Birth Rate/1000
United Kingdom	13
Ethiopia	38

Study Reference Diagrams Q9A and Q9B above.

Many ELDCs* are at Stage 2 in the demographic transition model while EMDCs* are more likely to be at Stage 4.

Give reasons for the differences in birth rates between ELDCs such as Ethiopia and EMDCs such as the UK. **4**

* ELDCs = Economically Less Developed Countries
* EMDCs = Economically More Developed Countries

[*END OF QUESTION PAPER*]

2006 | General

[BLANK PAGE]

FOR OFFICIAL USE

G

KU	ES

Total Marks

1260/403

NATIONAL QUALIFICATIONS 2006

WEDNESDAY, 10 MAY
10.25 AM–11.50 AM

GEOGRAPHY
STANDARD GRADE
General Level

Fill in these boxes and read what is printed below.

Full name of centre

Town

Forename(s)

Surname

Date of birth
Day Month Year

Scottish candidate number

Number of seat

1 Read the whole of each question carefully before you answer it.

2 Write in the spaces provided.

3 Where boxes like this ☐ are provided, put a tick ✓ in the box beside the answer you think is correct.

4 Try all the questions.

5 Do not give up the first time you get stuck: you may be able to answer later questions.

6 Extra paper may be obtained from the invigilator, if required.

7 Before leaving the examination room you must give this book to the invigilator. If you do not, you may lose all the marks for this paper.

PB 1260/403 6/3/24870

1:50 000 Scale
Landranger Series

Extract No 1488/178

Four colours should appear above; if not then please return to the invigilator.

Four colours should appear above; if not then please return to the invigilator.

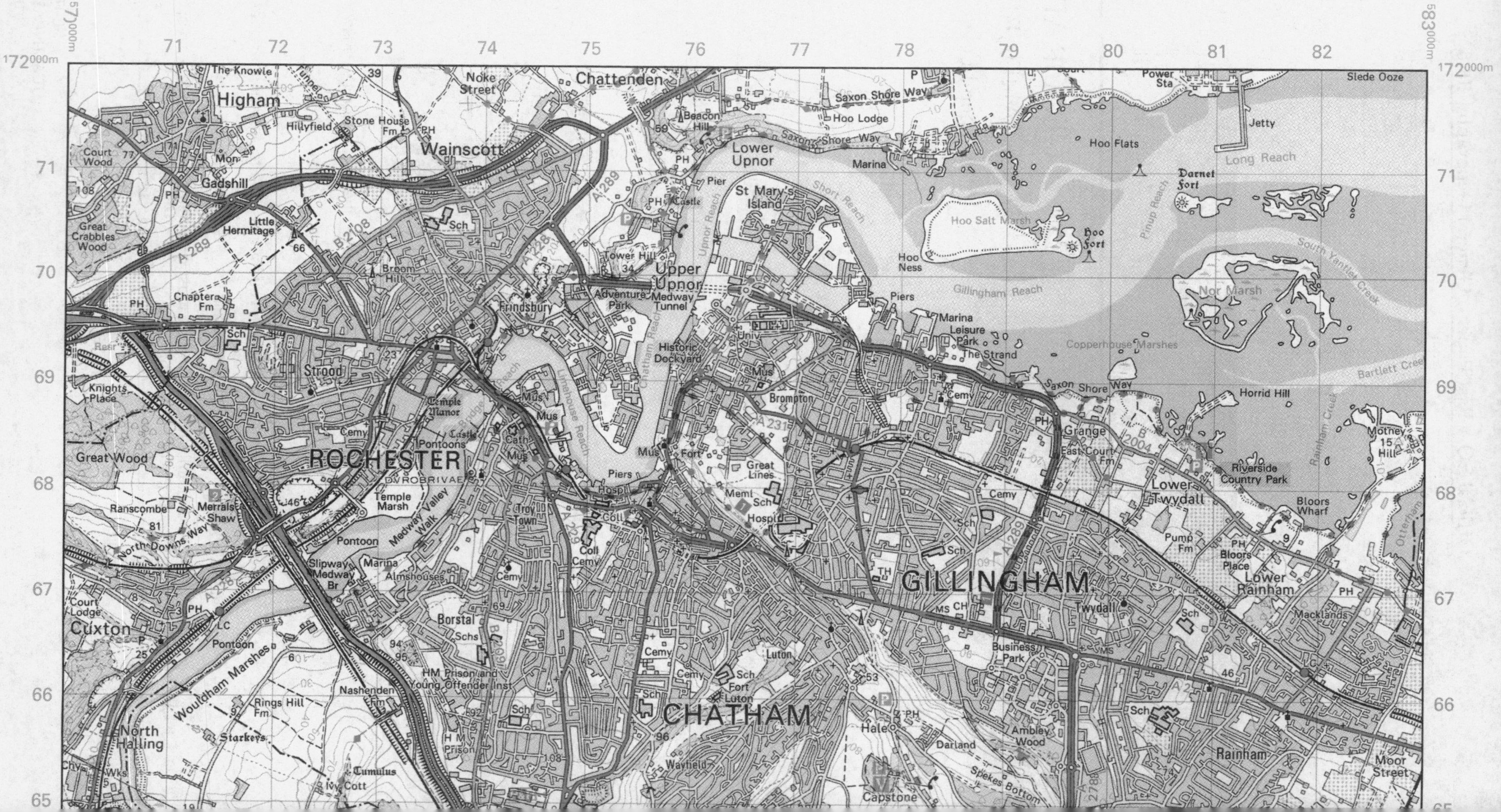

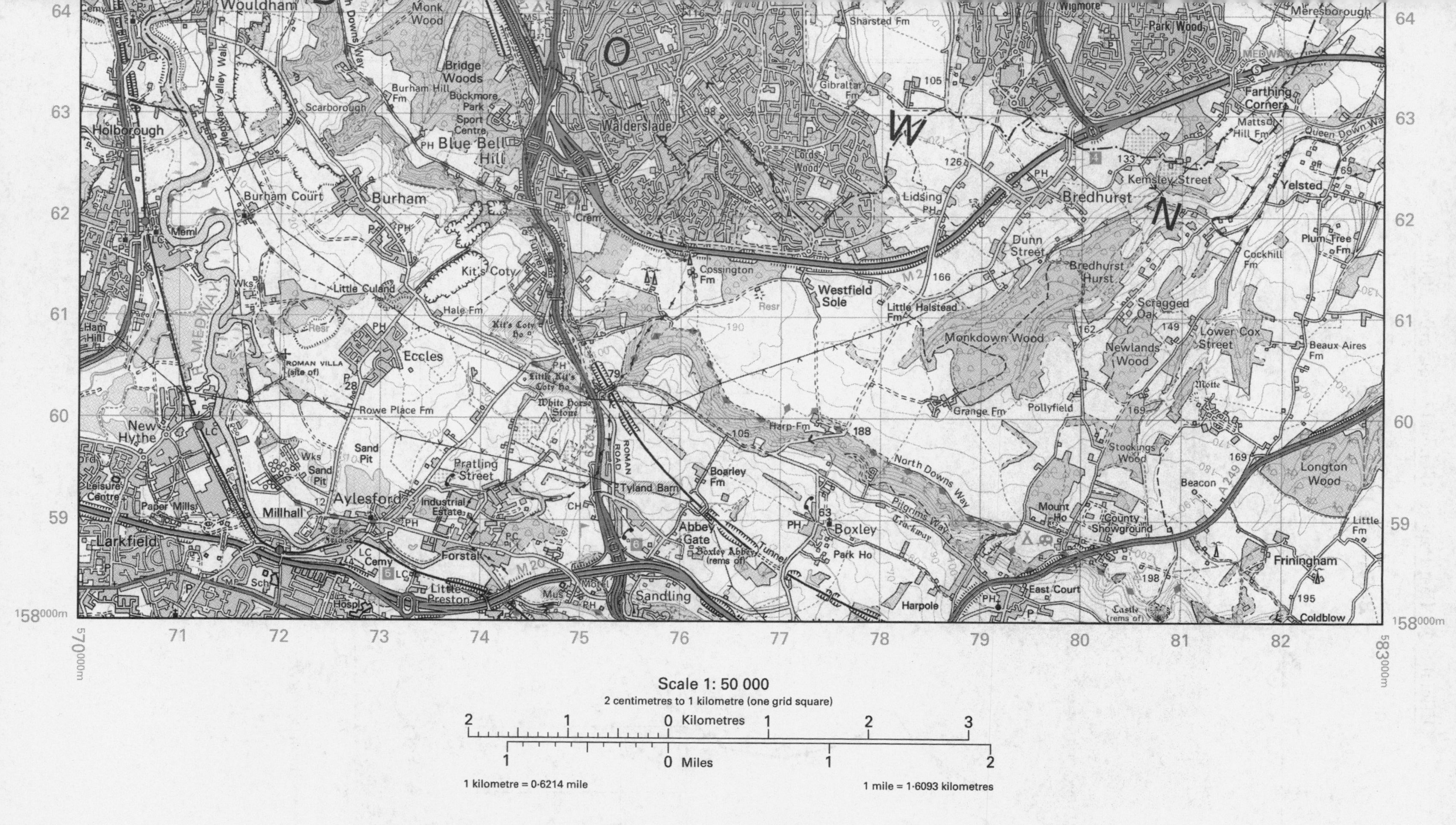

Scale 1: 50 000

2 centimetres to 1 kilometre (one grid square)

2 1 0 Kilometres 1 2 3

1 0 Miles 1 2

1 kilometre = 0·6214 mile

1 mile = 1·6093 kilometres

1. **Reference Diagram Q1**

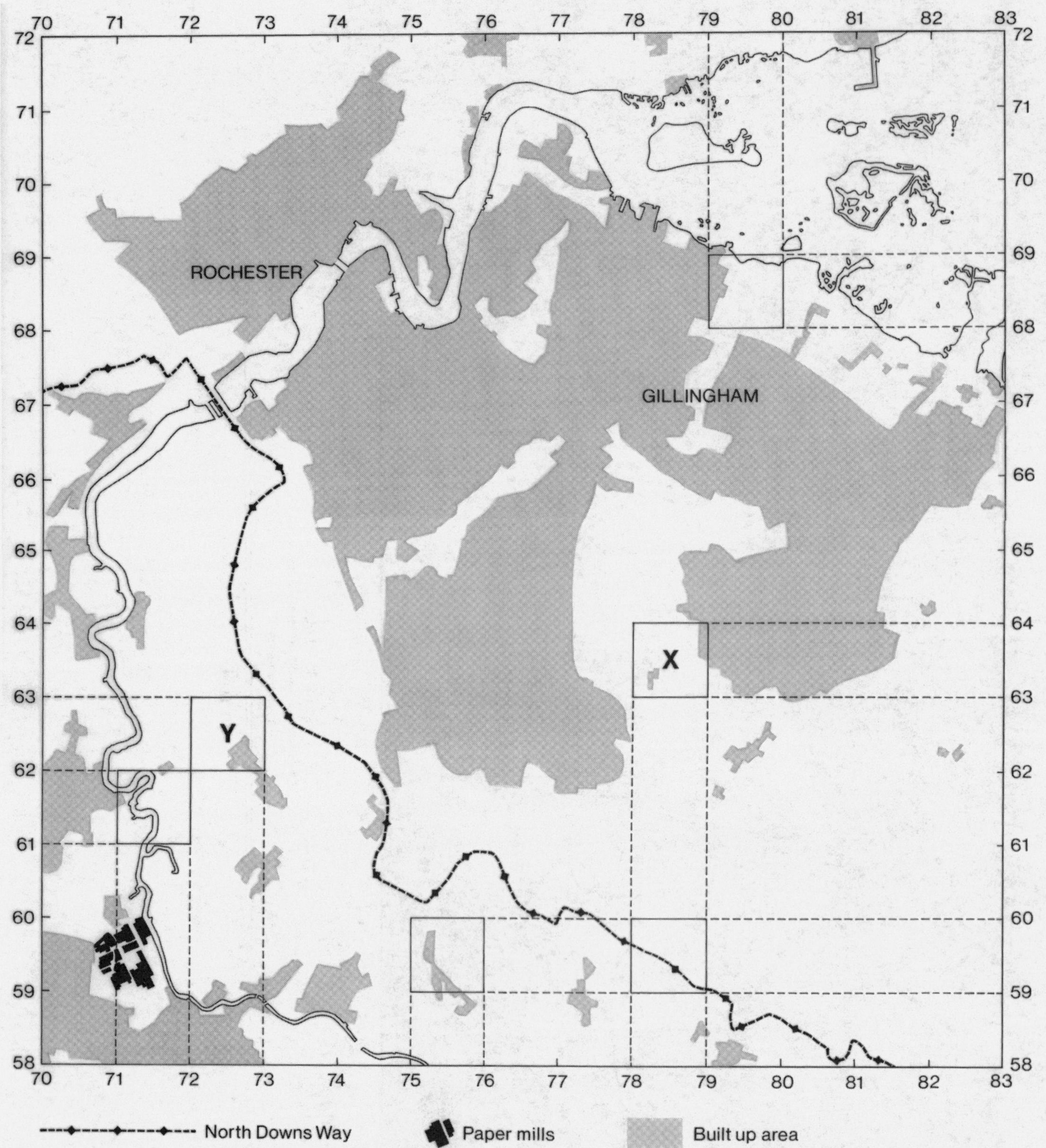

DO NOT WRITE IN THIS MARGIN

KU	ES

Marks

1. (continued)

Look at the Ordnance Survey Map Extract (No 1488/178) of the Thames Estuary area and Reference Diagram Q1 on Page two.

(*a*) **Explain** why an oxbow lake is likely to develop in grid square 7161.

You may use diagrams to illustrate your answer.

4

(*b*) Find the North Downs Way on Reference Diagram Q1 and on the Ordnance Survey Map.

The North Downs Way is a footpath for recreational walkers.

Using map evidence, give the advantages **and** disadvantages of this route.

4

[Turn over

DO NOT WRITE IN THIS MARGIN

KU | ES

Marks

1. (continued)

(*c*) Give different reasons why there are trees in the following grid squares.

7559 ______________________________

____

7859 ______________________________

____

7968 ______________________________

______________________________ **3**

(*d*) It is proposed to develop either Area X (7863) or Area Y (7262) for new housing.

Which area, X or Y, do you think is more suitable?

Explain your answer **in detail**.

____

____

____

____

____

______________________________ **4**

DO NOT WRITE IN THIS MARGIN

KU | ES

Marks

1. (continued)

(*e*) There is a large paper mill in grid square 7159.

Explain why this site is a suitable location for the paper mill.

You **must** use map evidence.

4

(*f*) Rochester and Gillingham are built either side of the River Medway.

In what ways has the River Medway **both** benefited **and** created problems for these settlements?

4

[Turn over

DO NOT WRITE IN THIS MARGIN

KU	ES

Marks

2. Reference Diagram Q2: A Landscape of Glacial Deposition

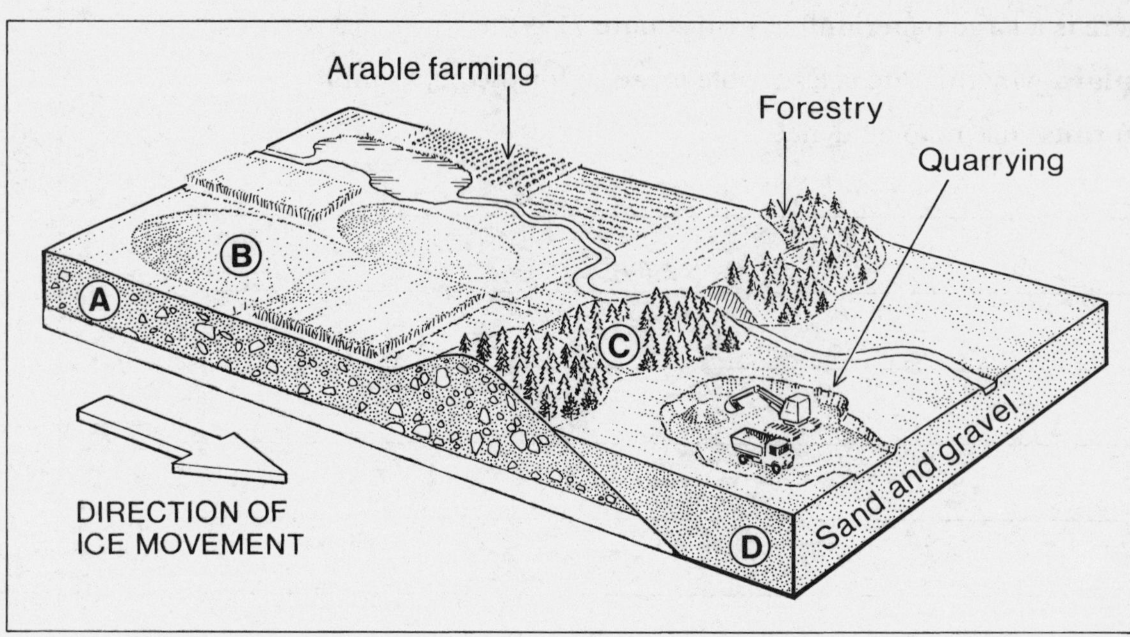

(*a*) Match each of the features of glacial deposition in the table to the correct letter (A, B, C, D) on the Reference Diagram.

Feature	Letter
Drumlin	
Terminal moraine	
Outwash plain	
Boulder clay	

3

DO NOT WRITE IN THIS MARGIN

KU | ES

Marks

2. (continued)

(*b*) **Explain** why **two** of the land uses shown on Reference Diagram Q2 are suitable for the areas in which they are located.

Land Use 1 ______________________

____

____

____

____

Land Use 2 ______________________

____

____

____

____ **4**

[Turn over

DO NOT WRITE IN THIS MARGIN

KU ES

Marks

3. Reference Diagram Q3A: Janice's Radio Phone-in

DO NOT WRITE IN THIS MARGIN

KU | ES

Marks

3. (continued)

Reference Diagram Q3B: Synoptic Chart, 10 August 2004

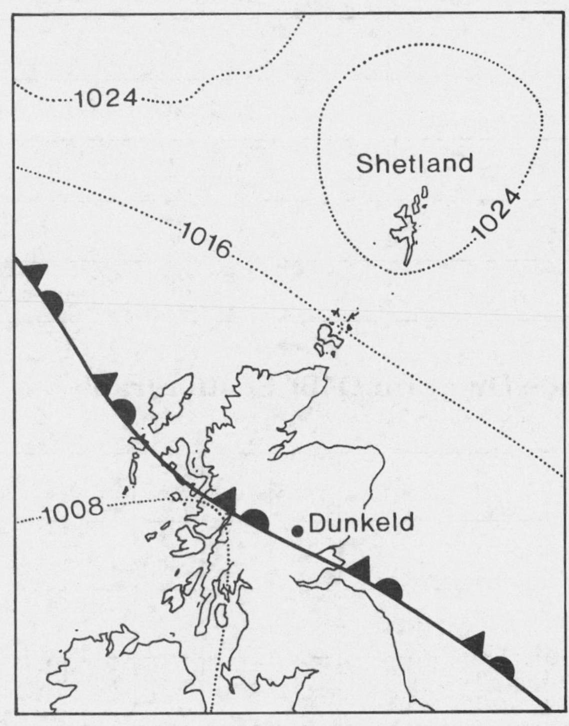

Look at Reference Diagrams Q3A and Q3B.

Explain the different weather experiences which Janice's two callers had on 10 August 2004.

____

____

____

____

_______________ 4

[Turn over

DO NOT WRITE IN THIS MARGIN

Marks | KU | ES

4. Reference Diagram Q4A: Data for six Weather Stations in Canadian Tundra on 3 May 2004

Station	Hours of Sunshine	Mean Temperature °C
A	2	1
B	6	4
C	8	6
D	3	2
E	5	3
F	2	4

Reference Diagram Q4B: Scattergraph

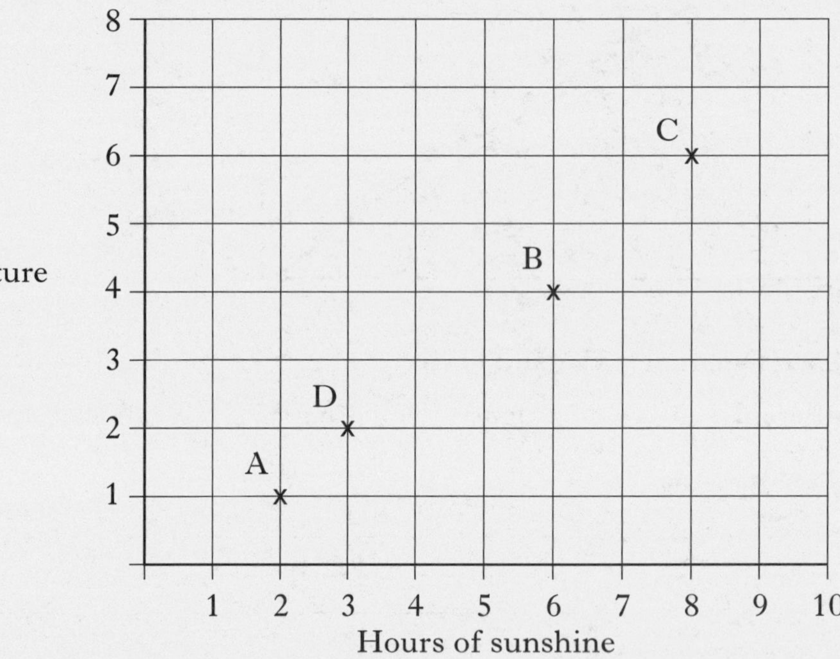

(*a*) Use the information in Reference Diagram Q4A to complete the scattergraph in Reference Diagram Q4B above. 2

(*b*) "The scattergraph shows that temperature in the Tundra is directly linked to the hours of sunshine."

Do you agree with this statement?

Give reasons for your answer.

____

____

____

______________________________________ 2

DO NOT WRITE IN THIS MARGIN

KU	ES

Marks

5. Reference Diagram Q5: Developments in the North Sea

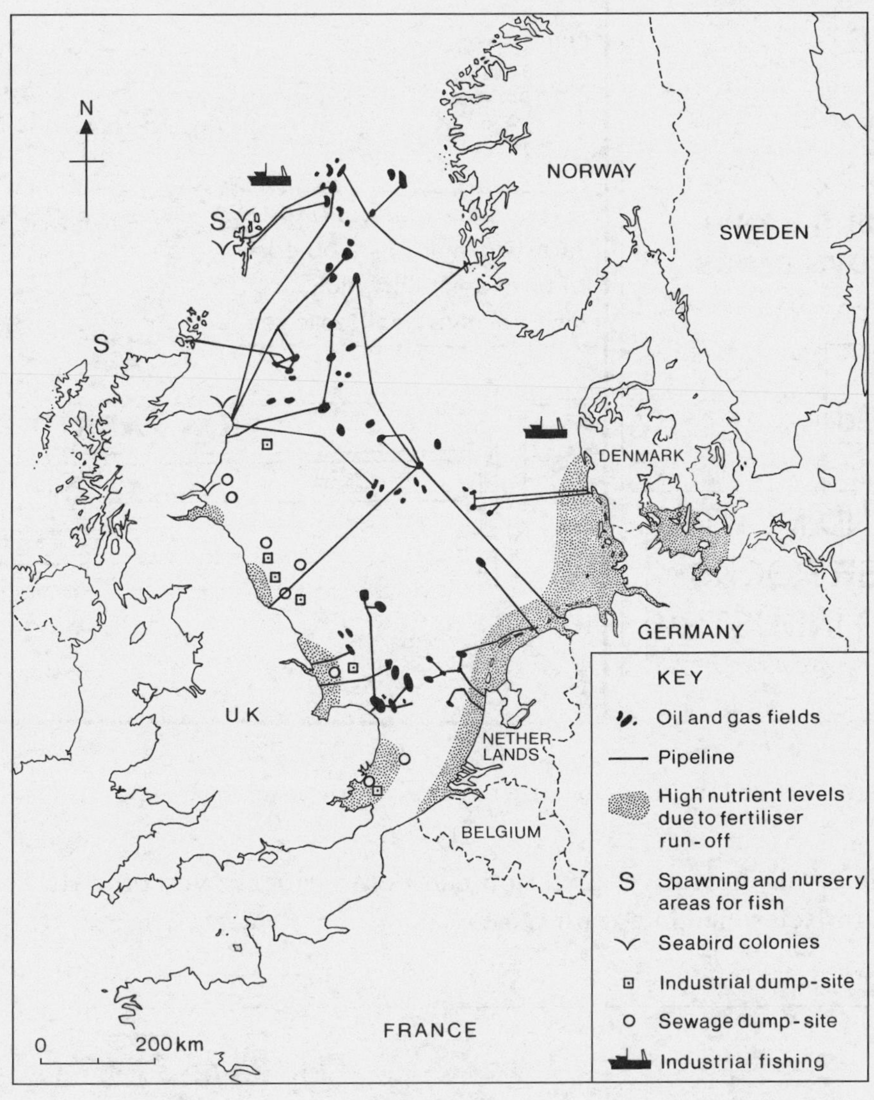

"We must stop exploiting the North Sea. We are destroying its environment."
EU Politician

Do you agree with the statement above?

Give reasons for your answer.

4

6. **Reference Diagram Q6A: Newspaper Headlines** **Reference Diagram Q6B: Examples of Diversification* on a Farm**

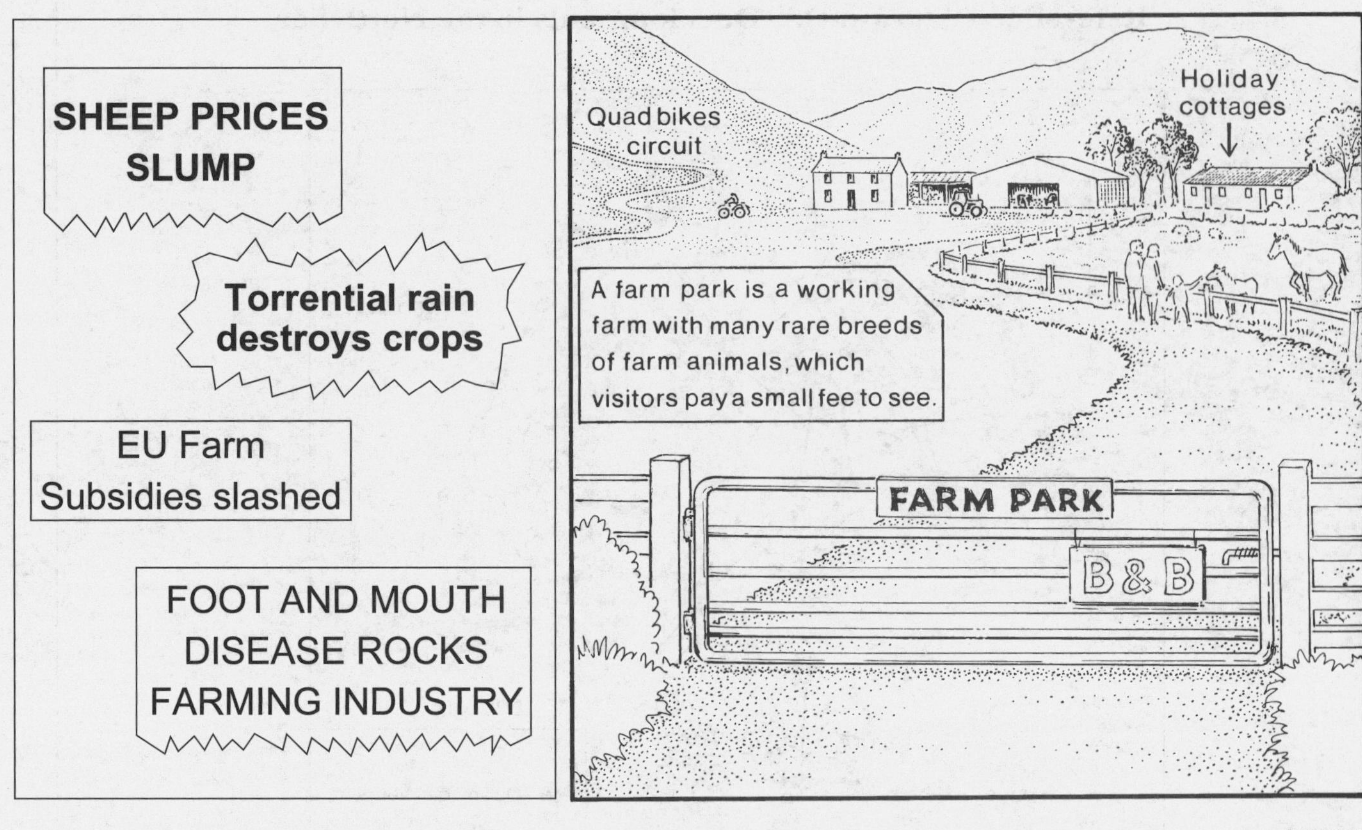

*Diversification = using other land uses to improve farm income

DO NOT WRITE IN THIS MARGIN

	KU	ES

Explain, in some detail, how diversification can help farmers overcome the problems shown in Reference Diagram Q6A.

Marks

4

DO NOT WRITE IN THIS MARGIN

KU	ES

Marks

7. Reference Diagram Q7: Factors affecting Location of Industry

(*a*) Look at Reference Diagram Q7.

Is Government Aid the most important factor in attracting industry to an area?

Give reasons for your answer.

4

(*b*) Which techniques could pupils use to gather information about the industrial estate?

Give reasons for your choices.

4

DO NOT WRITE IN THIS MARGIN

KU	ES

Marks

8. Reference Diagram Q8: Population Data for two Countries

Population Data A **Population Data B**

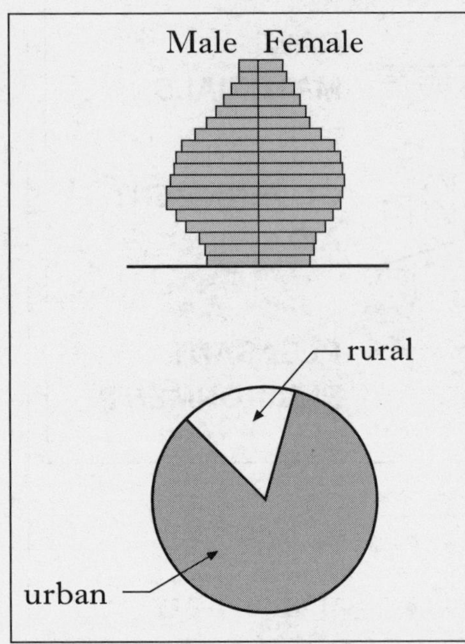

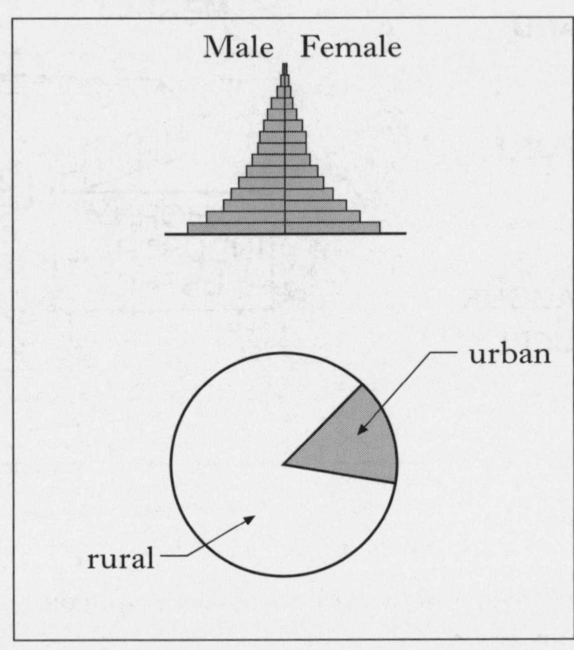

Which set of population data, A or B, is more typical of an Economically Less Developed Country (ELDC)?

Give reasons for your choice.

____

____

____

____

____

____ **4**

9. **Reference Diagram Q9: Japan's Trade Pattern**

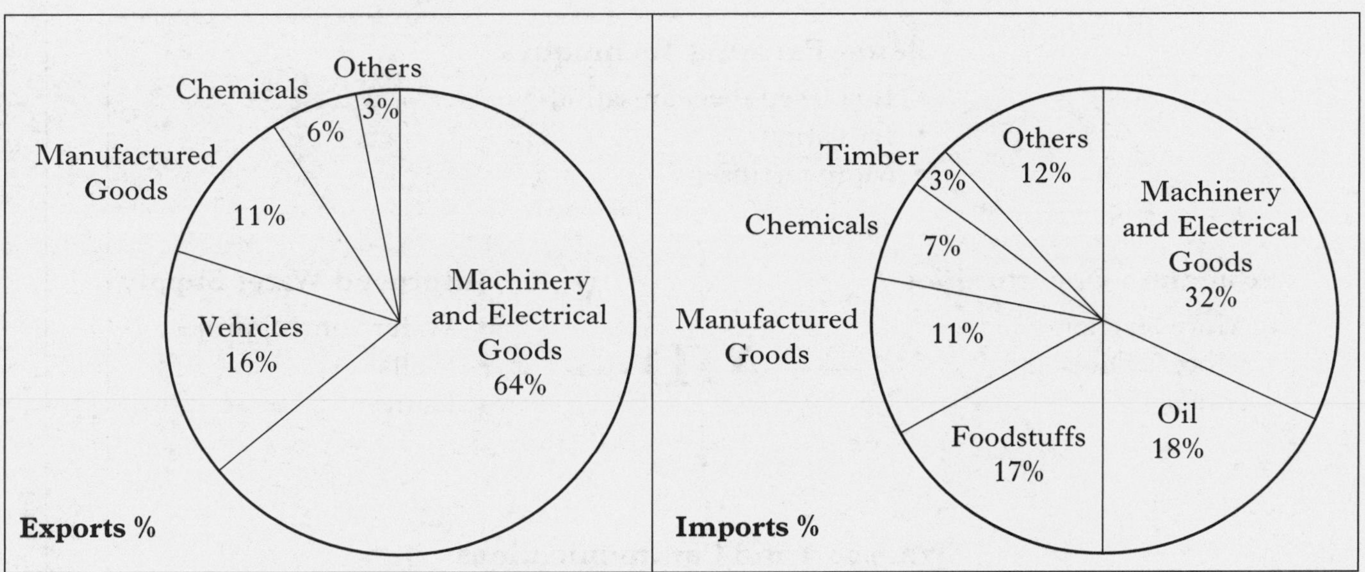

DO NOT WRITE IN THIS MARGIN

KU	ES

Marks

(*a*) Look at Reference Diagram Q9 above.

Do you think this trade pattern is typical of an Economically More Developed Country (EMDC)?

Give reasons for your answer. **4**

(*b*) Suggest other processing techniques which could be used to show the information in the pie charts.

Give reasons for your answer. **4**

 [Turn over for Question 10 on *Page sixteen*

DO NOT WRITE IN THIS MARGIN

KU | ES

Marks

10. **Reference Diagram Q10: Uses of Aid**

Better Farming Techniques
- Increased mechanisation
- Irrigation
- More fertiliser

Education Opportunities
- More teachers
- More schools and colleges

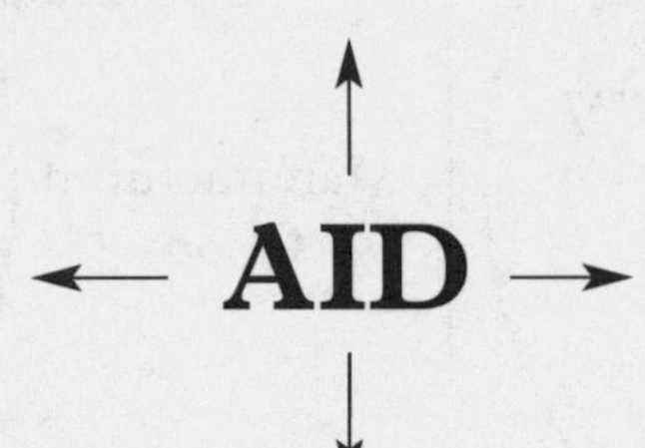

Improved Water Supply
- Water control project
- Wells
- Dams

Transport and Communications improved
- Better roads
- Better telecommunications

Which **two** of the above uses of aid do you think would be of **most** benefit to Economically Less Developed Countries (ELDCs)?

Give reasons for your choices.

Choice 1 ______________________________

____

____

____

____

Choice 2 ______________________________

____

____

____

____ 4

[*END OF QUESTION PAPER*]

2006 | Credit

[BLANK PAGE]

C

1260/405

NATIONAL QUALIFICATIONS 2006

WEDNESDAY, 10 MAY
1.00 PM – 3.00 PM

GEOGRAPHY
STANDARD GRADE
Credit Level

All questions should be attempted.

Candidates should read the questions carefully. Answers should be clearly expressed and relevant.

Credit will always be given for appropriate sketch-maps and diagrams.

Write legibly and neatly, and leave a space of about one cm between the lines.

All maps and diagrams in this paper have been printed in black only: no other colours have been used.

PB 1260/405 6/3/17070

1:50 000 Scale
Landranger Series

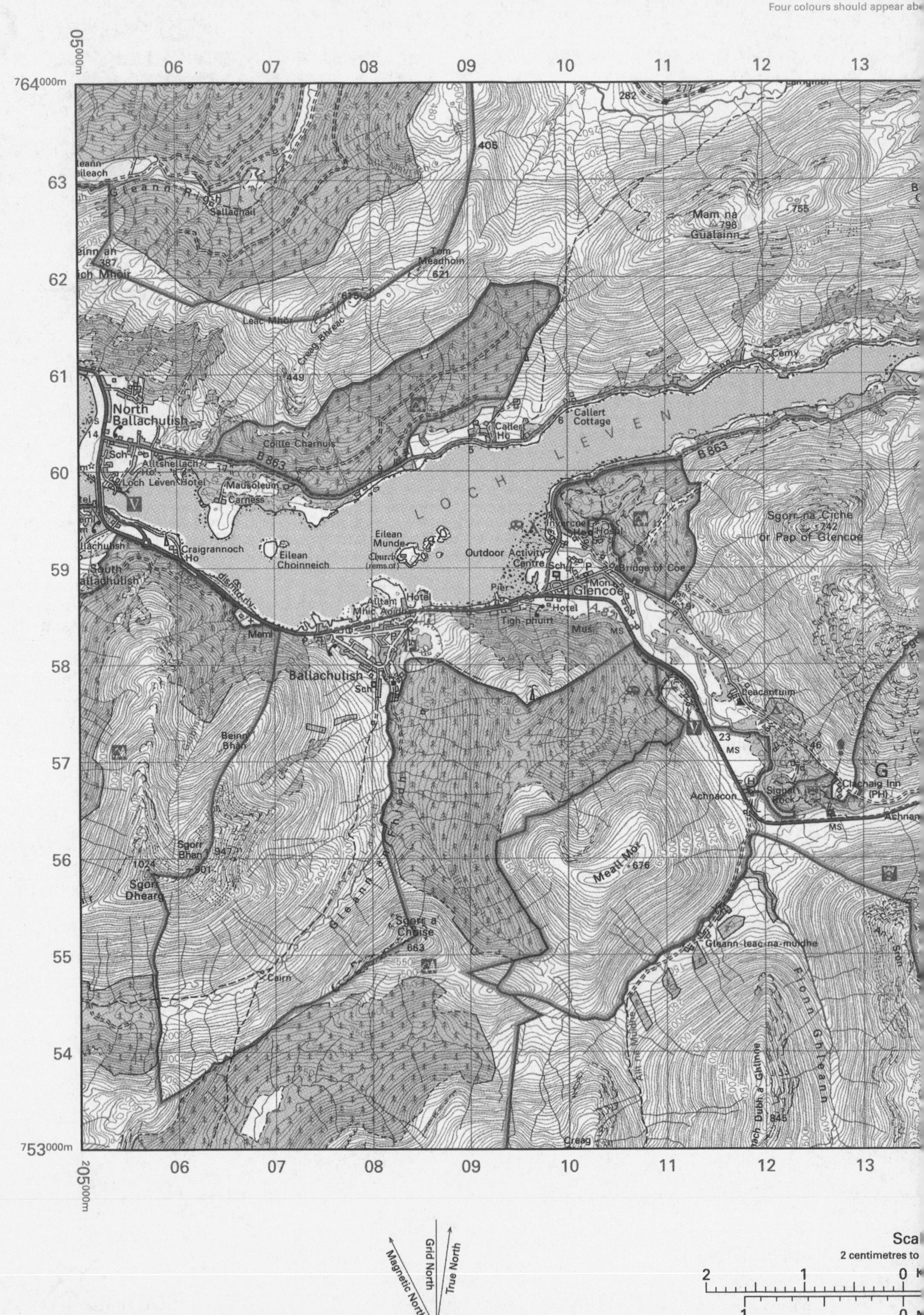

Diagrammatic only

1 kilometre = 0·6214 mile

Extract No 1489/41

lease return to the invigilator.

lease return to the invigilator.

15 16 17 18 19 20 21 22 2^{3000m}

$^{7}64^{000m}$ 63 62 61 60 59 58 57 56 55 54 $^{7}53^{000m}$

Fhuarain
Allt Nathrach
Mamore Lodge (Hotel)
Meall an Doire Dharaich
Kinlochmore
Waterfall
B 863
Meall na Duibhe 573
Kinlochleven
Laitir Bo Fionn
Waterfall
734
Garbh Bheinn 867
River Leven
508
Meall Ruigh a' Bhricleathaid
Allt a' Choire Odhair-mhoir
Old Military Road
Allt a' Choire Odhair-bhig
Meall Garbh
886
Stob Coire Leith
Meall Dearg 953
Aonach Eagach
873
Sron Gharbh
943
The Chancellor
Am Bodach
903
Sron a' Choire Odhair-bhig
Beinn Bheag 616
Stob Mhic Mhartuin 707
A' Chailleach
Devil's Staircase
A82
Achtriochtan
River Coe
PASS OF GLENCOE
Allt-na-reigh
The Study
Cairn
Waterfall
Meeting of Three Waters
Loch Achtriochtan
Ossian's Cave
The Three Sisters
Lochan na Fola
Altnafeadh
Lagangarbh
892
Aonach Dubh
Coire nan Lochan
Gearr Aonach
692
811
Stob nan Cabar
River Coupall
Stob Coire nan Lochan 1115
Beinn Fhada
Stob Coire Raineach 925
Coire na Tulaich
Lairig Eilde
Buachaille Etive Beag
902
Buachaille Etive Mor
1022 Stob Dearg
1150
931
902
Lairig Gartain
Coire Cloiche Finne
1072 Stob Coire Sgreamhach
958 Stob Dubh
ROYAL FOREST
941
Stob na Doire 1011

15 16 17 18 19 20 21 22 2^{23000m}

grid square)

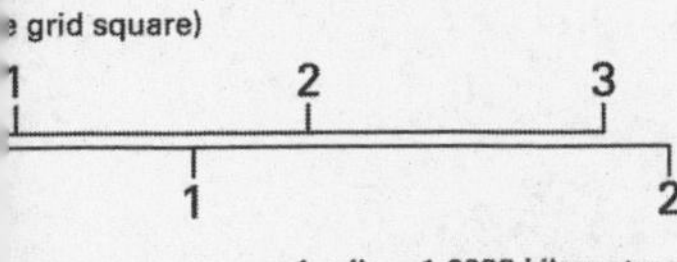

Extract produced by Ordnance Survey 2005

1. **Reference Diagram Q1A**

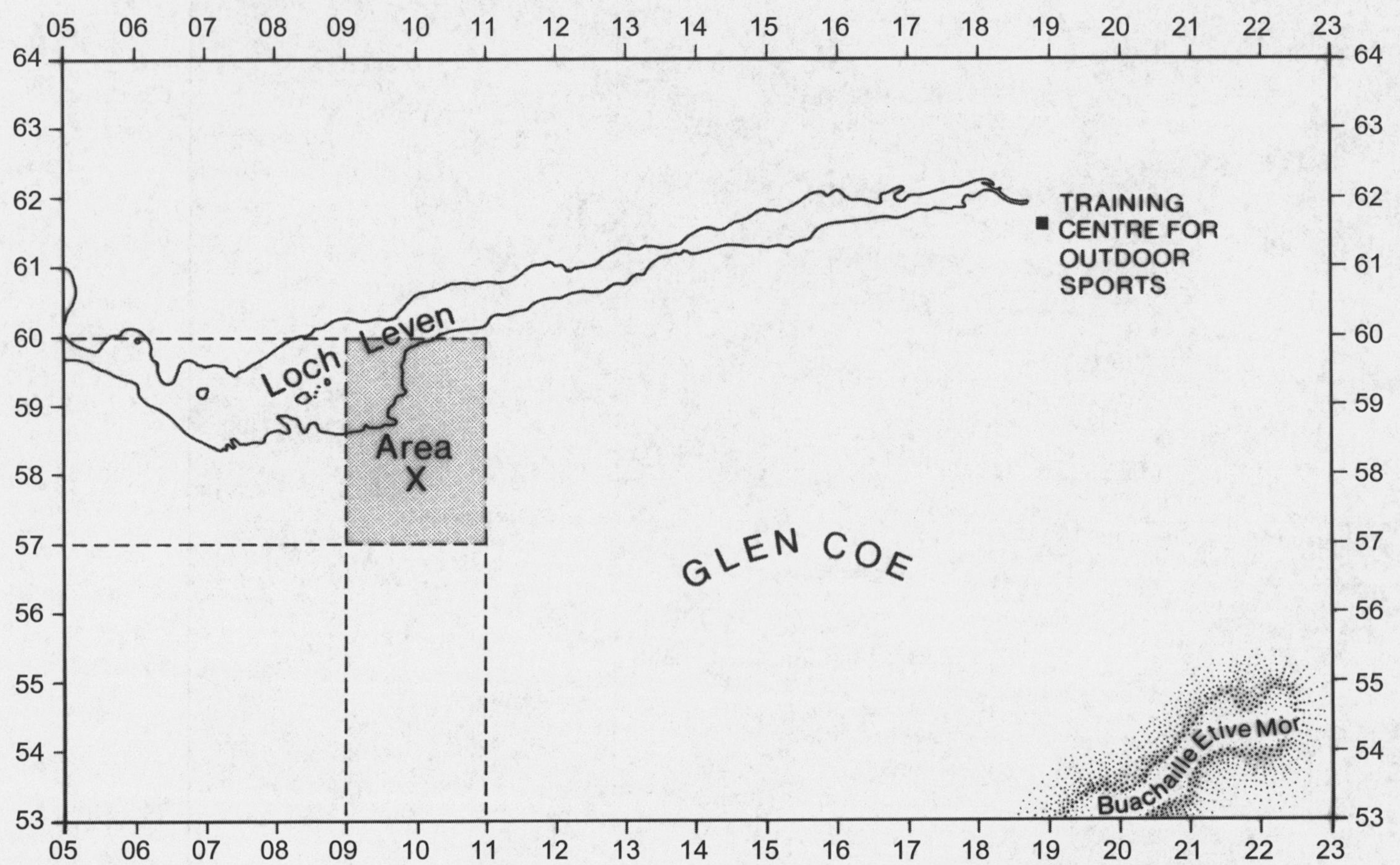

	Marks KU	Marks ES

1. (continued)

This question refers to the OS Map Extract (No 1489/41) of the Glen Coe area and Reference Diagram Q1A on *Page two*.

Reference Diagram Q1B: View looking West from 197618

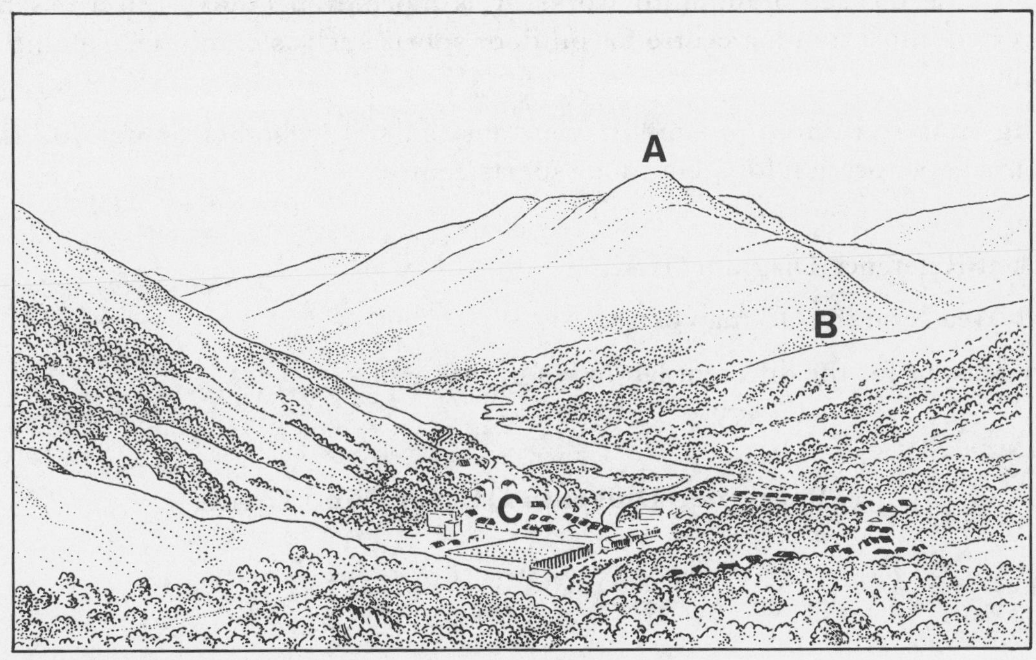

(*a*) Look at Reference Diagram Q1B and the map extract.

Reference Diagram Q1B is a view looking west from 197618.

Identify the **three** features marked A, B and C.

Choose from:

Allt Nathrach; Kinlochleven; Mam na Gualainn; Kinlochmore; Beinn na Caillich. 3

(*b*) (i) Match each of the features named below with the correct grid reference.

Features: **arete; hanging valley; truncated spur; corrie.**

Choose from grid references: 165553, 057563, 197584, 201556. 3

(ii) **Explain** how **one** of the features listed in (*b*)(i) was formed.

You may use diagrams to illustrate your answer. 4

[Turn over

	Marks	
	KU	ES

1. (continued)

(*c*) "Glen Coe and the surrounding area is one of Scotland's most popular tourist areas."

Spokesperson for the Scottish Tourist Industry

Part of the disused aluminium works at Kinlochleven (1861, 1862) has been converted into a training centre for outdoor sports such as climbing, walking and ice climbing.

Using map evidence to support your answer, state whether or not you think this is a good location for an outdoor sports centre.

(*d*) Look at Reference Diagram Q1A.

Find Area X on the OS map extract.

Give reasons for the different land uses in this area. 5

Reference Diagram Q1C: A Wind Farm

(*e*) A developer is proposing to build a wind farm of up to thirty wind turbines on Buachaille Etive Mòr (see Reference Diagrams Q1A and Q1C).

Do you think this proposal should go ahead?

You **must** use map evidence to support your answer.

Marks KU ES

2. Reference Diagram Q2: Synoptic Chart for 15 January 1995

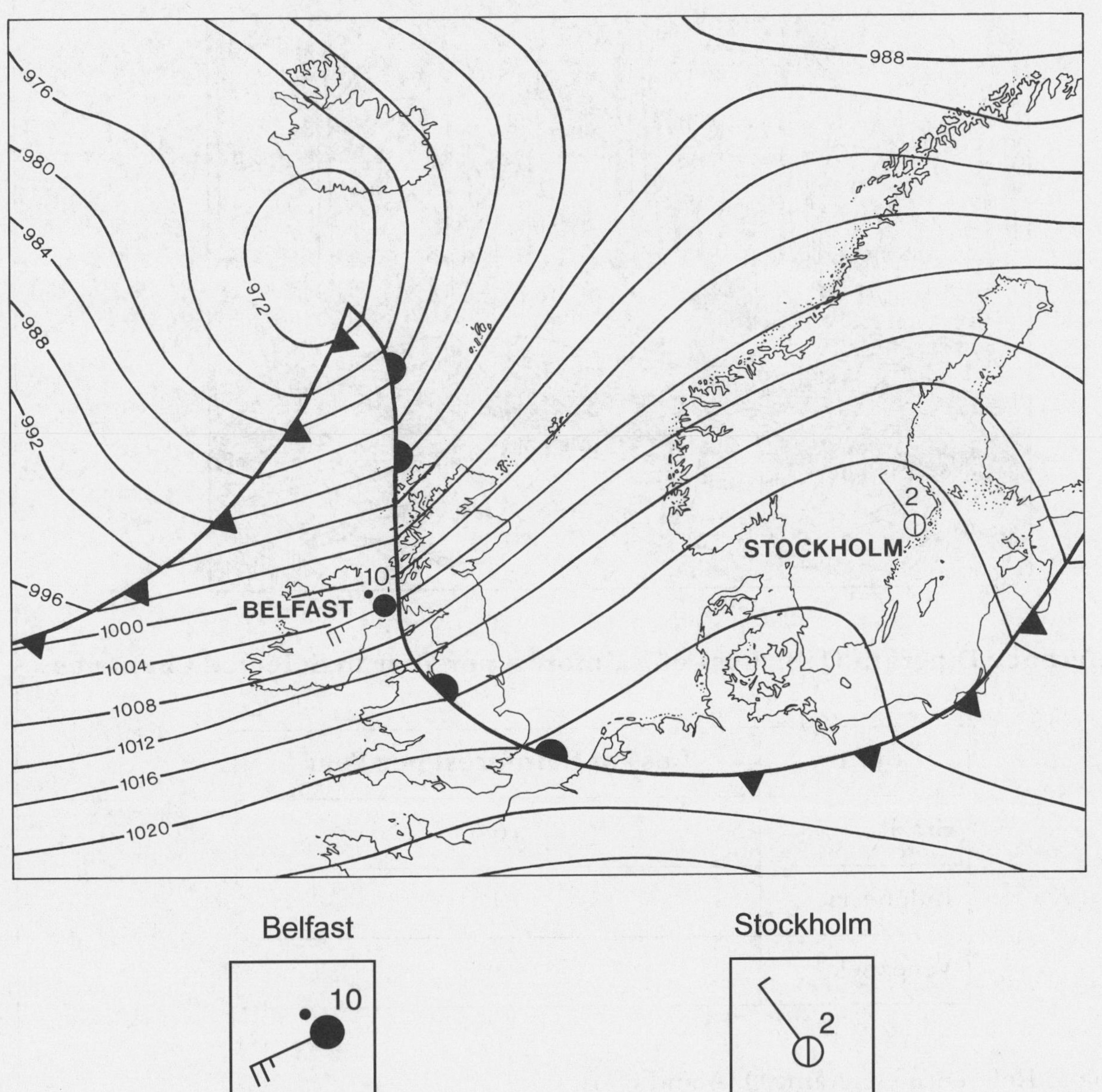

Look at Reference Diagram Q2.

Explain the **differences** in the weather conditions between Belfast and Stockholm. 6

[Turn over

	Marks	
	KU	

3. **Reference Diagram Q3A: Destruction of Rainforest**

Reference Diagram Q3B: Loss of Rainforest per Year in Selected Countries

Country	Loss of Rainforest per Year
Brazil	6%
Indonesia	10%
Venezuela	12%

Look at Reference Diagrams Q3A and Q3B.

Explain why the world's rainforests continue to be destroyed. 5

Marks

KU	ES

4. **Reference Diagram Q4A: Recent Changes in Farming**

- Farmers paid to "set aside" land
- Farmers converting to produce organic food
- Removal of hedges to make fields larger
- Increased mechanisation

(*a*) Study Reference Diagram Q4A.

Do you think these changes **benefit** the countryside?

Give reasons for your answer. 6

Reference Diagram Q4B: Land Use Data for Crow Farm East Anglia

Land Use	**Area (hectares)**
Barley	13·5
Wheat	12·5
Farm yard and buildings	1·2
Sugar beet	12·0
Vegetables	5·5
Set aside	8·5

(*b*) Study Reference Diagram Q4B.

Give **two** other techniques which would be appropriate to process this data.

Explain your choices. 5

[Turn over

Marks KU

5. **Reference Diagram Q5A: Land Values in a City**

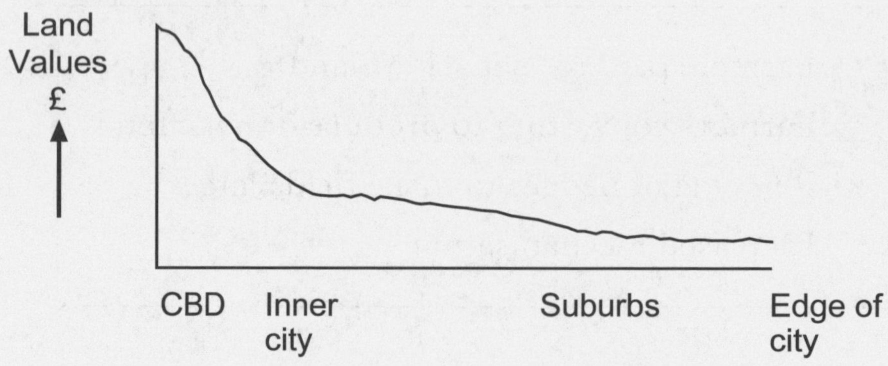

Reference Diagram Q5B: Features of Housing Areas

Inner City	Suburbs
Nearer CBD	**Nearer edge of city**
In grid-iron pattern with long, straight streets	Varied street pattern with many short streets in a cul-de-sac arrangement
Houses close to industry	Housing separate from industry
Tenements and/or terraces	Variety of house types, with many detached and semi-detached
Little open space/greenery	More spacious with many gardens
Environmental problems	Pleasant environment

	Marks KU	Marks ES
5. (continued)		
Look at Reference Diagrams Q5A and Q5B.		
(*a*) **Explain** the features of **either** the Inner City **or** the Suburbs shown in Reference Diagram Q5B.	6	
(*b*) Describe techniques which could be used to gather information about differences between the environments of two urban areas. Give reasons for your choice of techniques.		5

[Turn over

6. Reference Diagram Q6: Population Growth in Tokyo and Jakarta

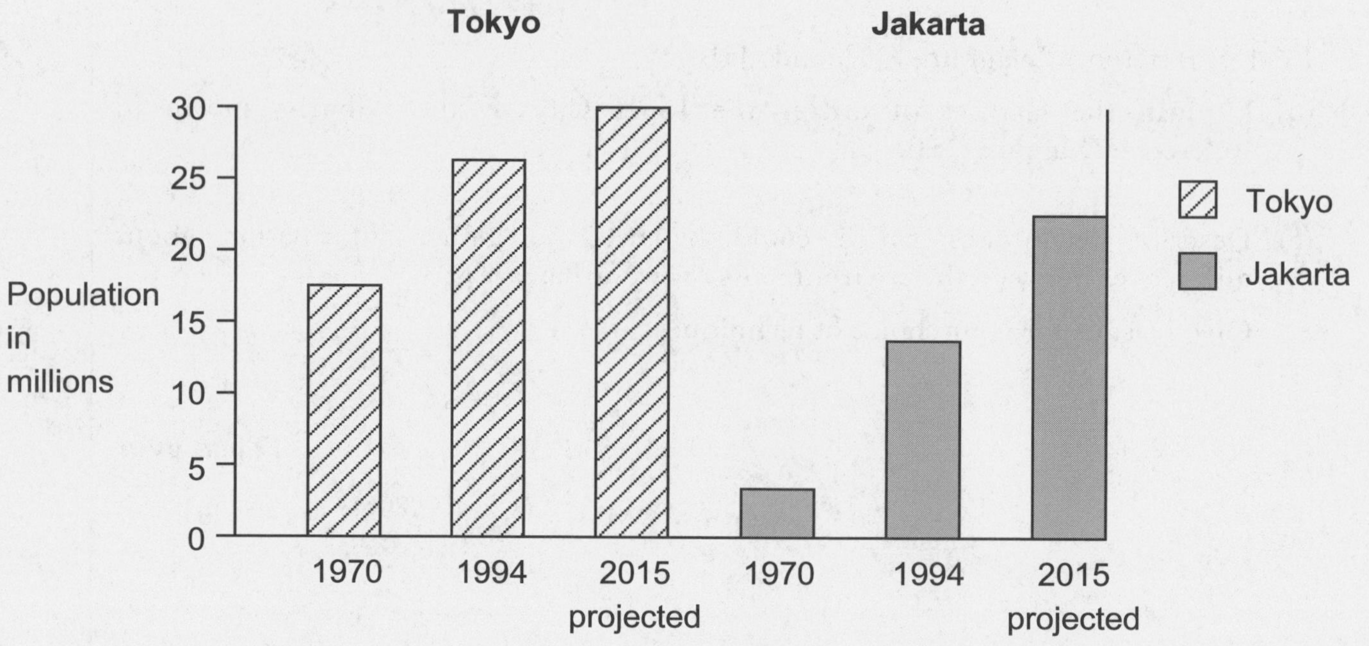

Marks KU

(*a*) Compare **in detail** the population growth in the two cities.

Tokyo is the capital of Japan, an Economically More Developed Country (EMDC). Jakarta is the capital of Indonesia, an Economically Less Developed Country (ELDC).

(*b*) This population growth will cause more problems for Tokyo than for Jakarta.

Do you agree?

Give reasons for your answer.

Marks

KU	ES

7. Reference Diagram Q7: Factors affecting Population Distribution

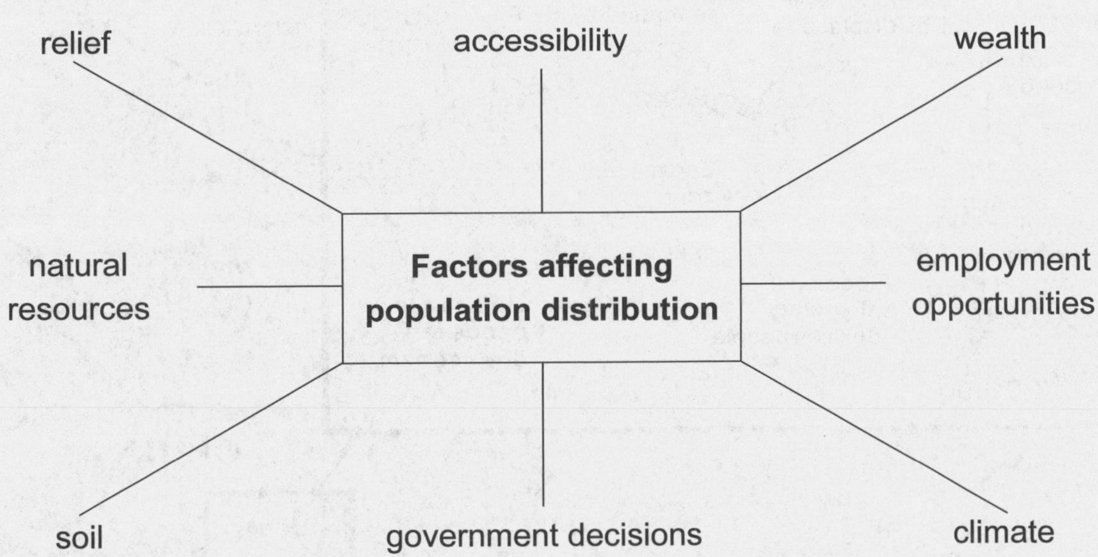

Which factors, physical **or** human, have the greater influence on population distribution?

Give reasons for your choice. 6

[Turn over for Question 8 on *Page twelve*

8. **Reference Diagram Q8: Location of the Three Gorges Dam**

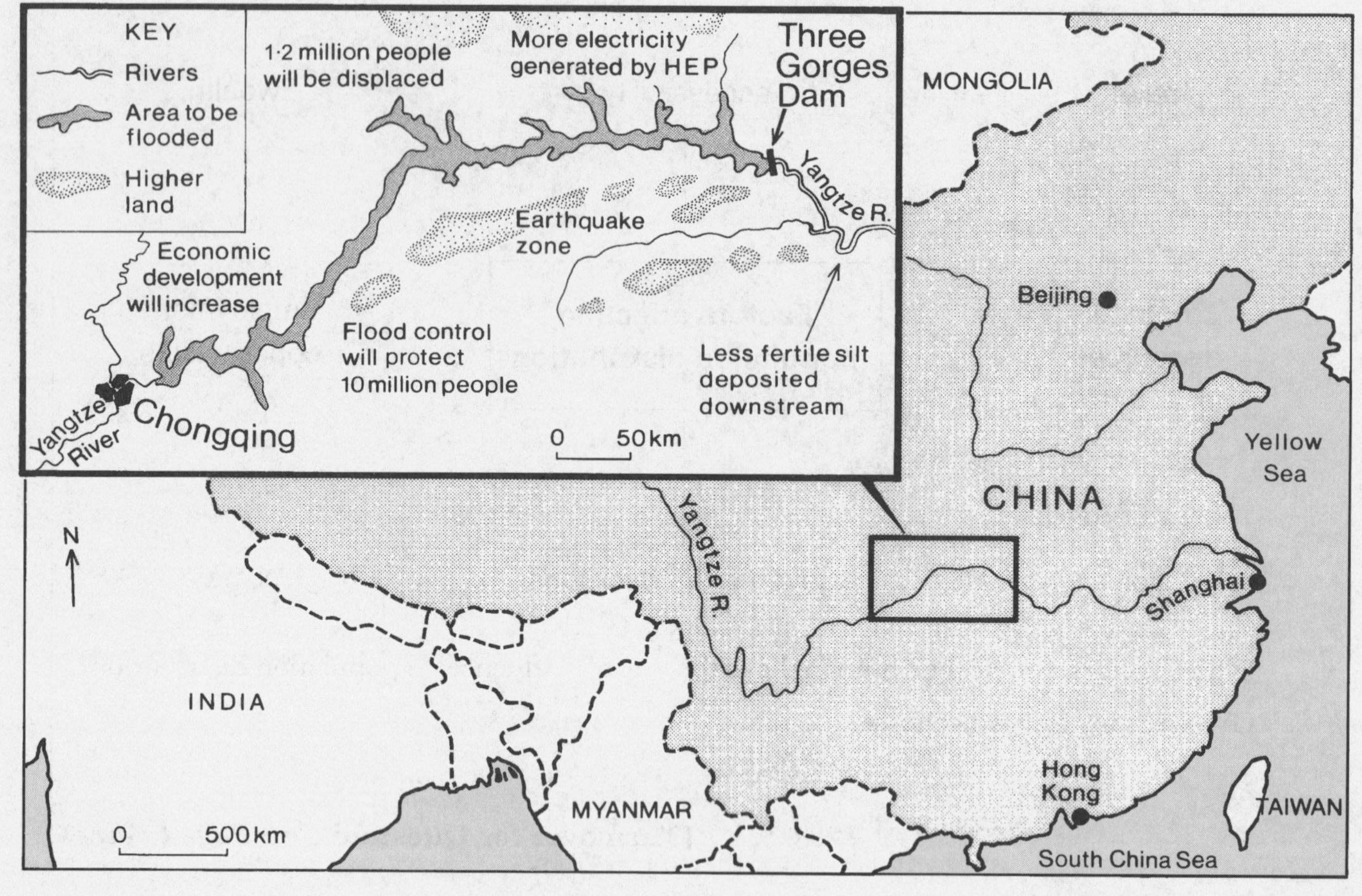

Marks	
KU	

The Three Gorges Dam project was built with money from China and investments from Japan, Canada, Germany and Switzerland. These investments were made in order to develop trade links with China.

What are the advantages **and** disadvantages for China and its trading partners of using these investments to build the Three Gorges Dam?

[*END OF QUESTION PAPER*]

[BLANK PAGE]

FOR OFFICIAL USE

G

KU	ES

Total Marks

1260/403

NATIONAL QUALIFICATIONS 2007

TUESDAY, 8 MAY
10.25 AM–11.50 AM

GEOGRAPHY
STANDARD GRADE
General Level

Fill in these boxes and read what is printed below.

Full name of centre

Town

Forename(s)

Surname

Date of birth
Day Month Year

Scottish candidate number

Number of seat

1 Read the whole of each question carefully before you answer it.

2 Write in the spaces provided.

3 Where boxes like this ☐ are provided, put a tick ✓ in the box beside the answer you think is correct.

4 Try all the questions.

5 Do not give up the first time you get stuck: you may be able to answer later questions.

6 Extra paper may be obtained from the invigilator, if required.

7 Before leaving the examination room you must give this book to the invigilator. If you do not, you may lose all the marks for this paper.

PB 1260/403 6/28870

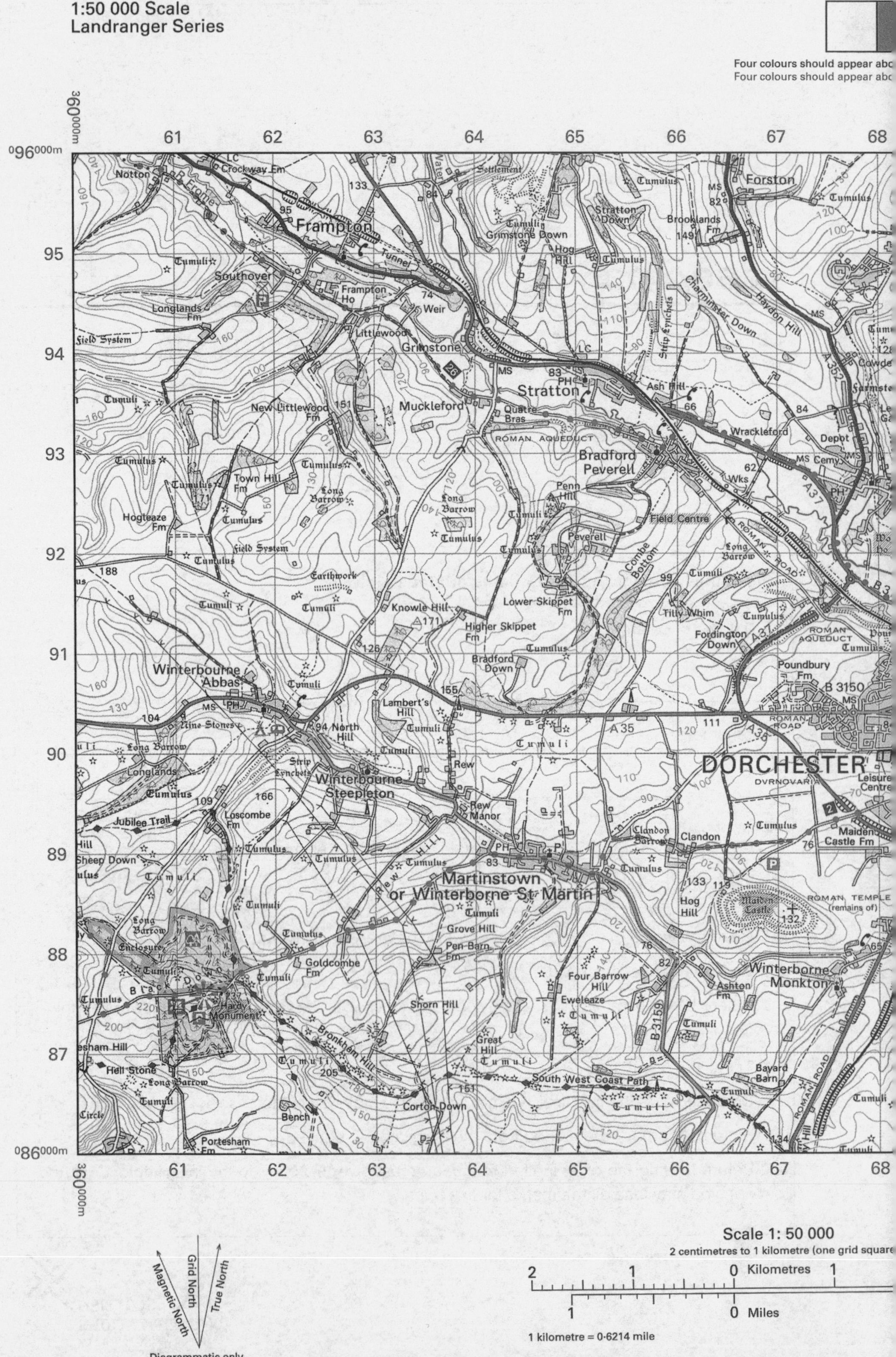
1:50 000 Scale
Landranger Series
Four colours should appear abo
Four colours should appear abo
Frampton
Southover
Grimstone
Stratton
Mucklefield
Bradford Peverell
Forston
Charminster Down
Wrackleford
Winterbourne Abbas
Winterbourne Steepleton
Martinstown or Winterborne St Martin
DORCHESTER
DVRNOVARIA
Maiden Castle
Winterborne Monkton
Hardy Monument
South West Coast Path
Poundbury Fm
Clandon
Scale 1: 50 000
2 centimetres to 1 kilometre (one grid square
Kilometres
Miles
1 kilometre = 0·6214 mile
Grid North
True North
Magnetic North
Diagrammatic only

Extract No 1557/194

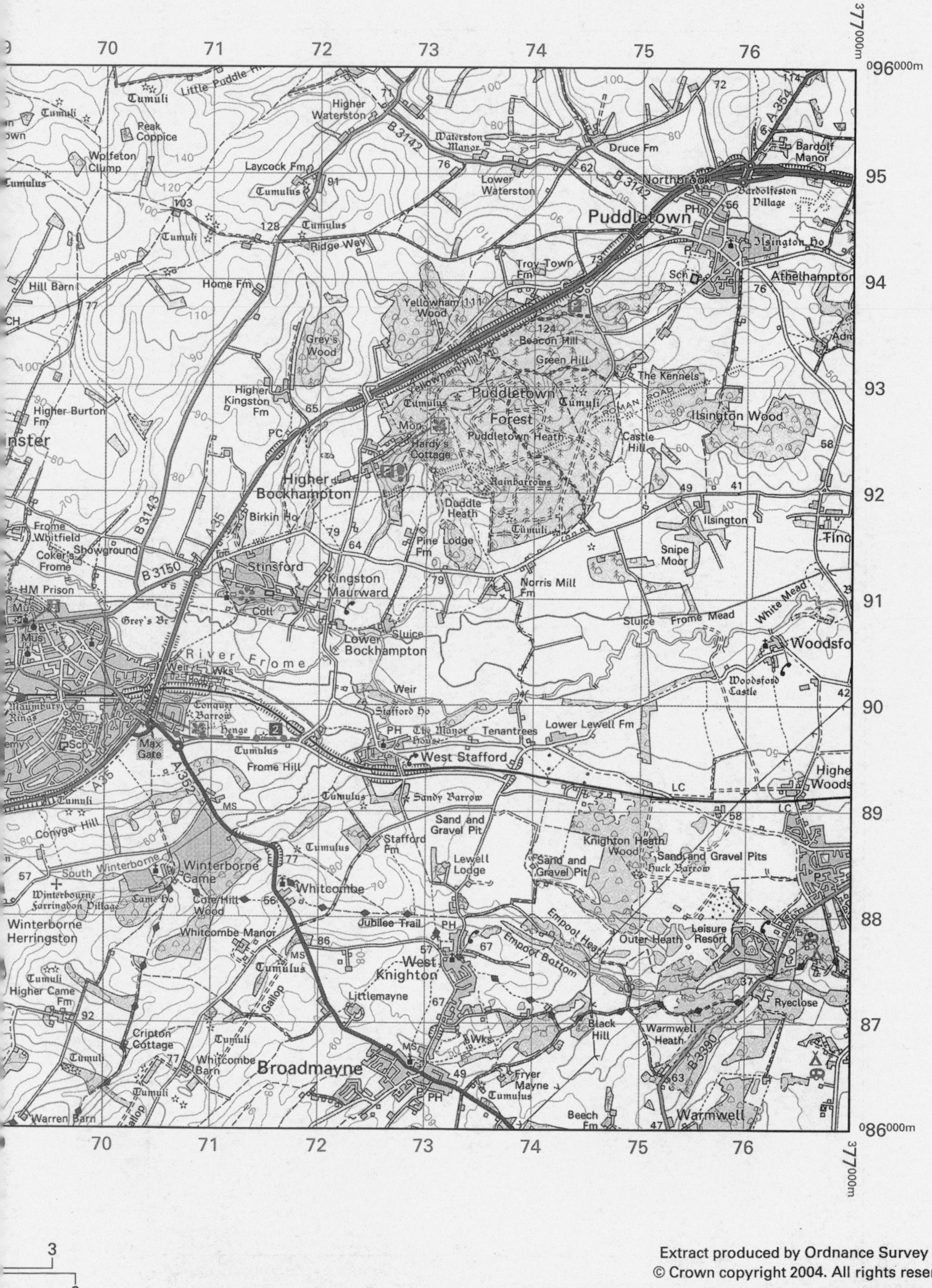

ase return to the invigilator.
ase return to the invigilator.

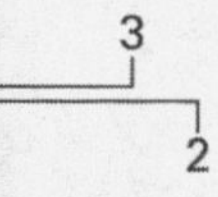

1. **Reference Diagram Q1: The Dorchester Area**

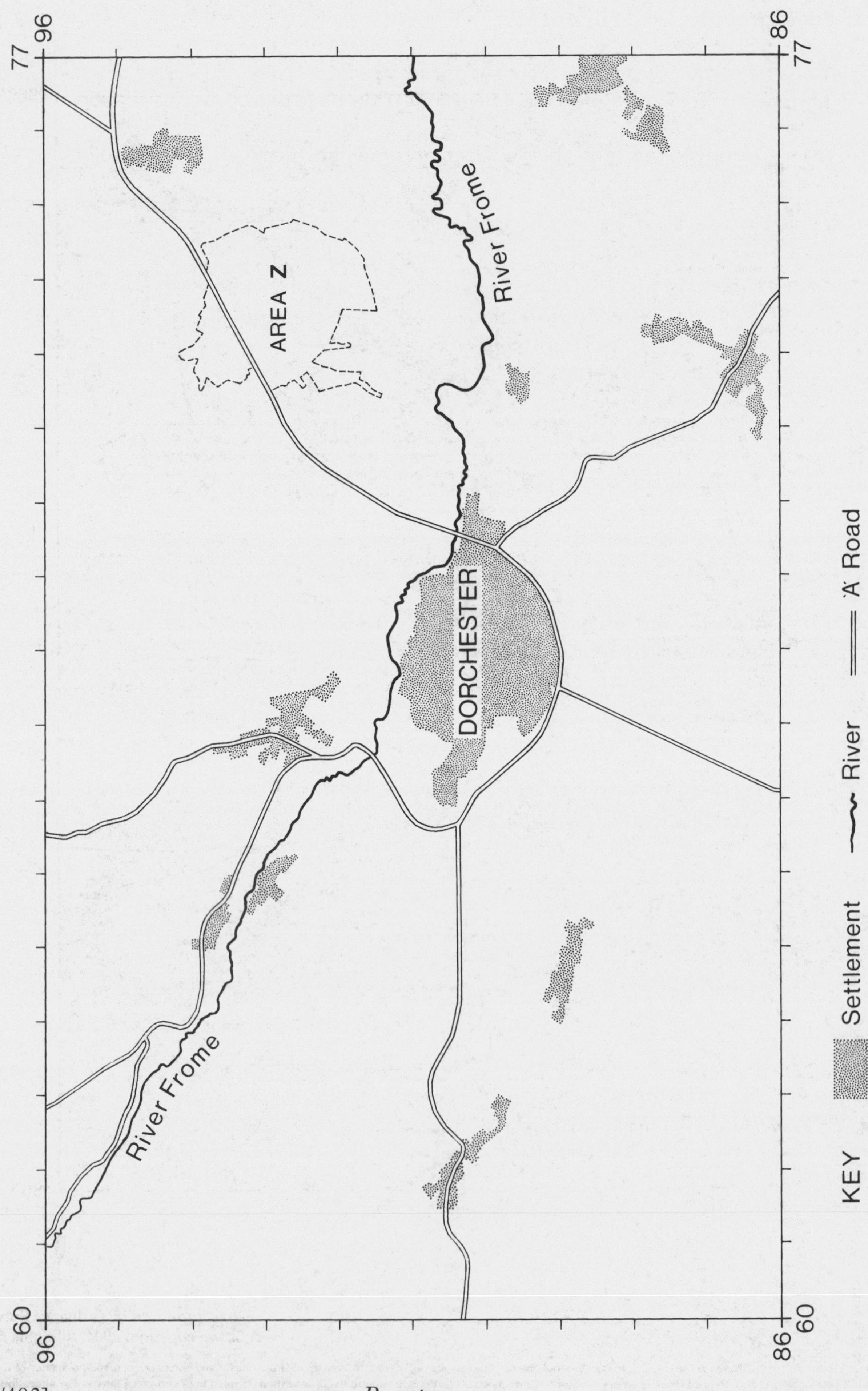

DO NOT WRITE IN THIS MARGIN

KU ES

Marks

1. (continued)

Look at the Ordnance Survey Map Extract (No 1557/194) of the Dorchester area and Reference Diagram Q1 on Page two.

(*a*) Complete the table below by matching the physical features to the correct grid references.

Choose from: 6586 7490 6193 6286

Physical Feature	Grid Square
Steep southwest facing slopes	
Flat land	
Broad ridge running East–West	
V-shaped valley	

3

(*b*) Describe the **physical** features of the River Frome **and** its valley between grid references 610959 and 700909.

____

____

____

____

____

______________________________ **4**

[Turn over

DO NOT WRITE IN THIS MARGIN

KU	ES

Marks

1. (continued)

(*c*) Give **two** techniques which could be used to gather information about the physical characteristics of the River Frome.

Give reasons for your choice of techniques.

Technique 1: ____________________

Reason: ____________________

____

Technique 2: ____________________

Reason: ____________________

____________________ 4

(*d*) It is proposed to develop Area Z into a country park (see Reference Diagram Q1).

Using map evidence, give arguments for **and** against this proposal.

For: ____________________

____

____

____

Against: ____________________

____

____

____________________ 4

DO NOT WRITE IN THIS MARGIN

KU ES

Marks

1. (continued)

(*e*) **Explain** why Dorchester has expanded west into grid square 6790 and not north into grid square 6991.

Refer to both grid squares in your answer. **3**

(*f*) Which is the more likely function of Dorchester?

Tick (✓) your choice.

Tourist resort ☐ Market town ☐

Give map evidence to support your choice. **3**

(*g*) What are the **disadvantages** of the location of Maiden Castle Farm (grid square 6789)? **3**

DO NOT WRITE IN THIS MARGIN

KU	ES

Marks

2. **Reference Diagram Q2: A Glaciated Lowland**

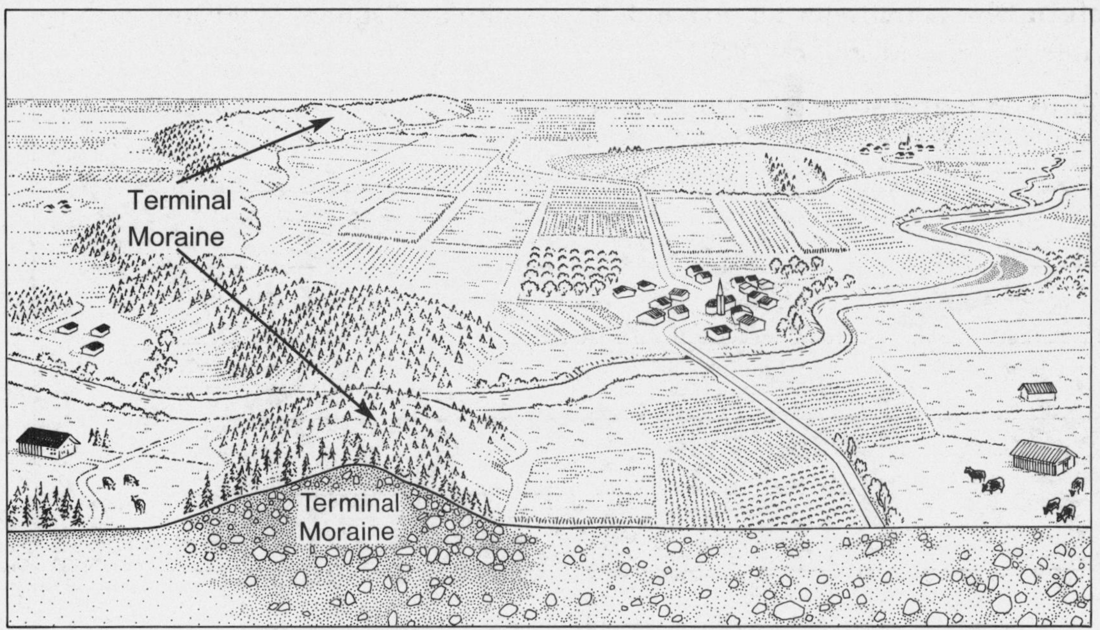

Look at Reference Diagram Q2.

Explain how a terminal moraine is formed.

You may wish to use diagram(s) to illustrate your answer.

(*Space for diagrams*)

3

DO NOT WRITE IN THIS MARGIN

KU	ES

Marks

3. Reference Diagram Q3: Air Masses affecting the British Isles

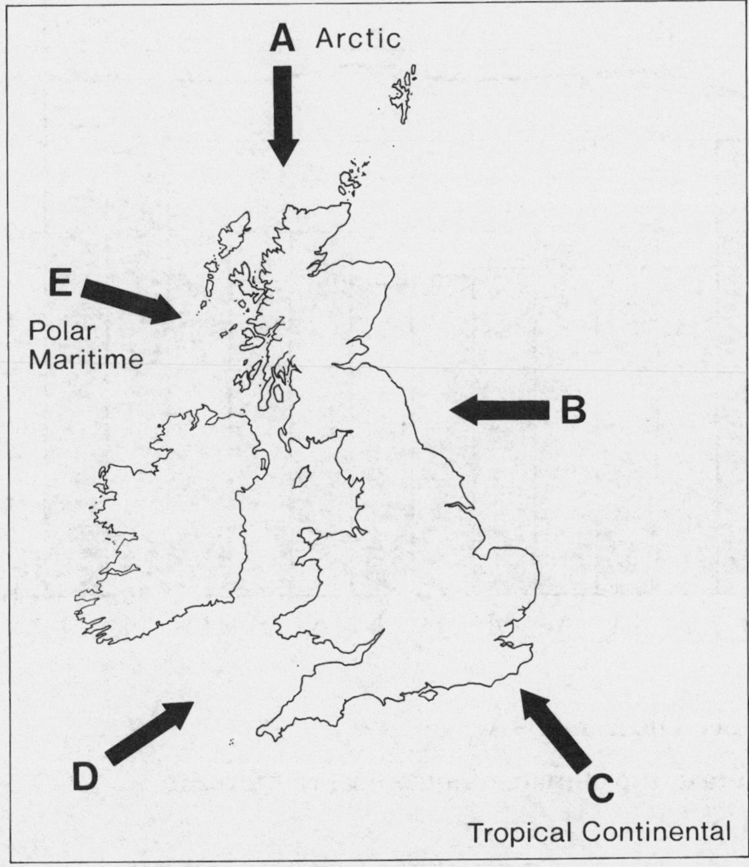

Look at Reference Diagram Q3.

(*a*) Name air masses B and D.

B ______________________

D ______________________ 2

(*b*) **Describe** the benefits **and** problems of a long spell of weather caused by air mass C in summer.

____

____

____

____

______________________ 4

[Turn over

DO NOT WRITE IN THIS MARGIN

Marks | KU | ES

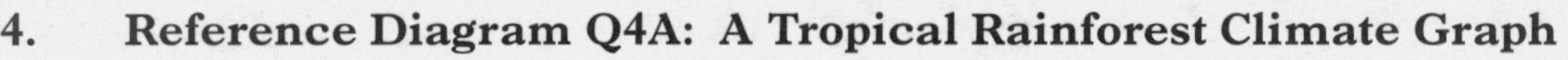

4. Reference Diagram Q4A: A Tropical Rainforest Climate Graph

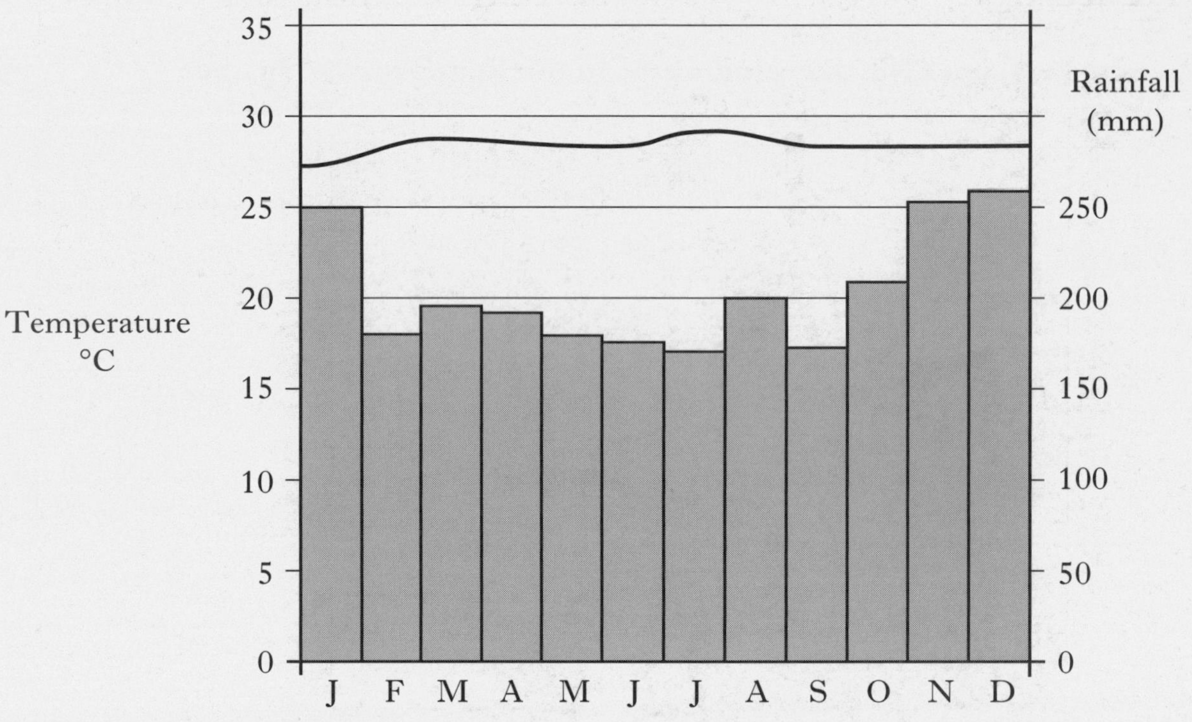

(*a*) Look at Reference Diagram Q4A.

Describe, **in detail**, the climate of a tropical rainforest.

3

DO NOT WRITE IN THIS MARGIN

KU | ES

Marks

4. (continued)

Reference Diagram Q4B: Developments in the Rainforests of Brazil

(*b*) Look at Reference Diagram Q4B.

"Developments in rainforests have brought many benefits to local people."

Do you agree with the above statement?

Explain your answer.

____

____

____

____

____

____ **4**

[Turn over

5. **Reference Diagram Q5A: Brockan Farm in 1977**

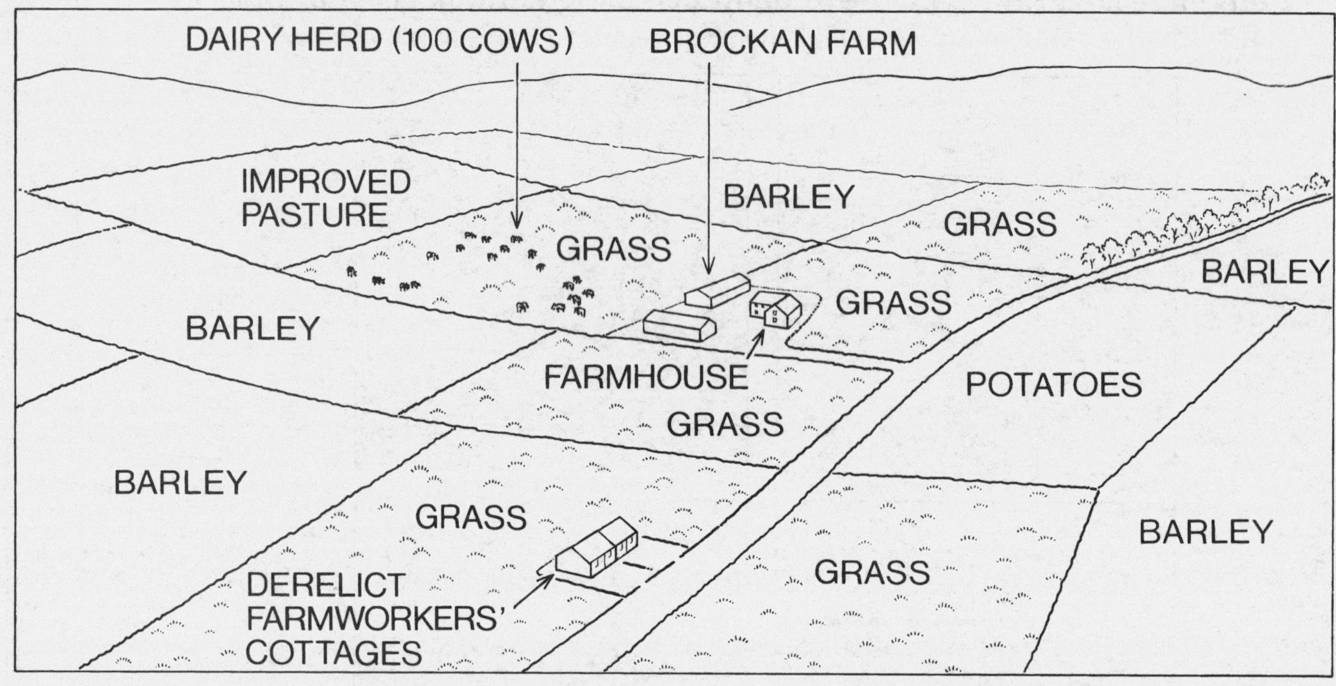

Reference Diagram Q5B: Brockan Farm in 2007

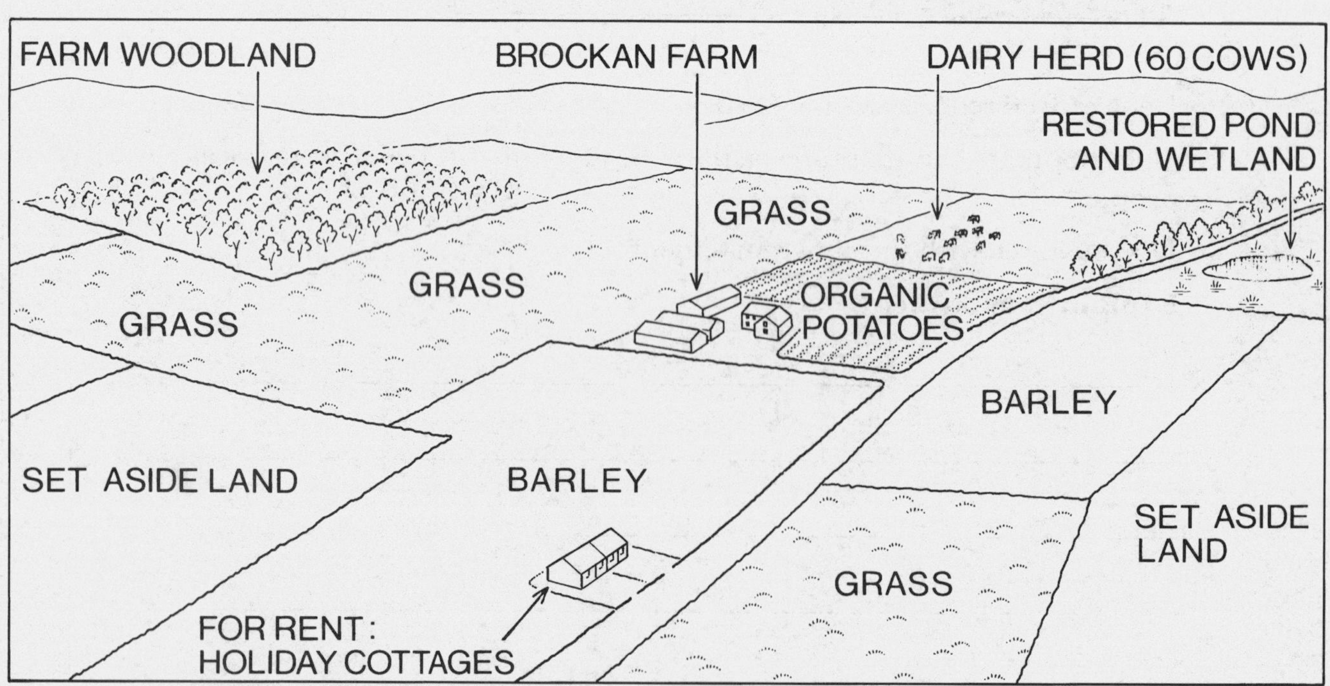

DO NOT WRITE IN THIS MARGIN

KU | ES

Marks

5. (continued)

(*a*) Study Reference Diagrams Q5A and Q5B. Suggest reasons for the changes shown on Brockan Farm between 1977 and 2007.

4

Reference Diagram Q5C: Land Use on Brockan Farm, 2007

Land Use	% of Total Land
Grass	45%
Barley	25%
Woodland	10%
Set aside	10%
Organic potatoes	5%
Restored wetland	5%

(*b*) Study Reference Diagram Q5C.

Complete the divided bar graph below.

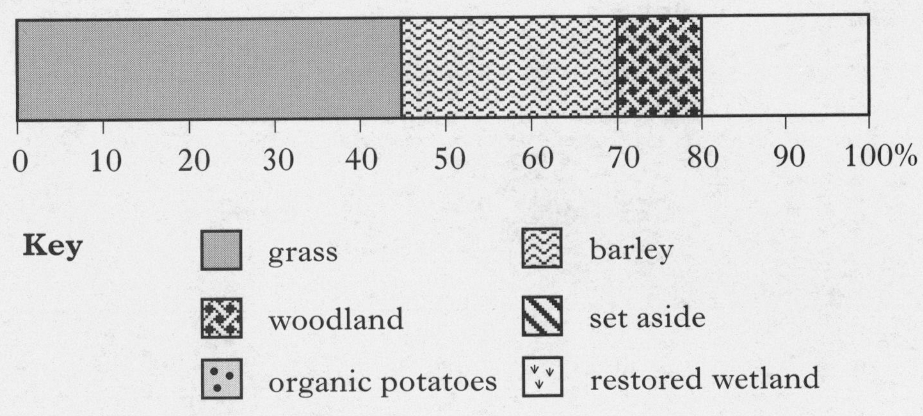

3

[Turn over

6. Reference Diagram Q6: Location of a Cement Works

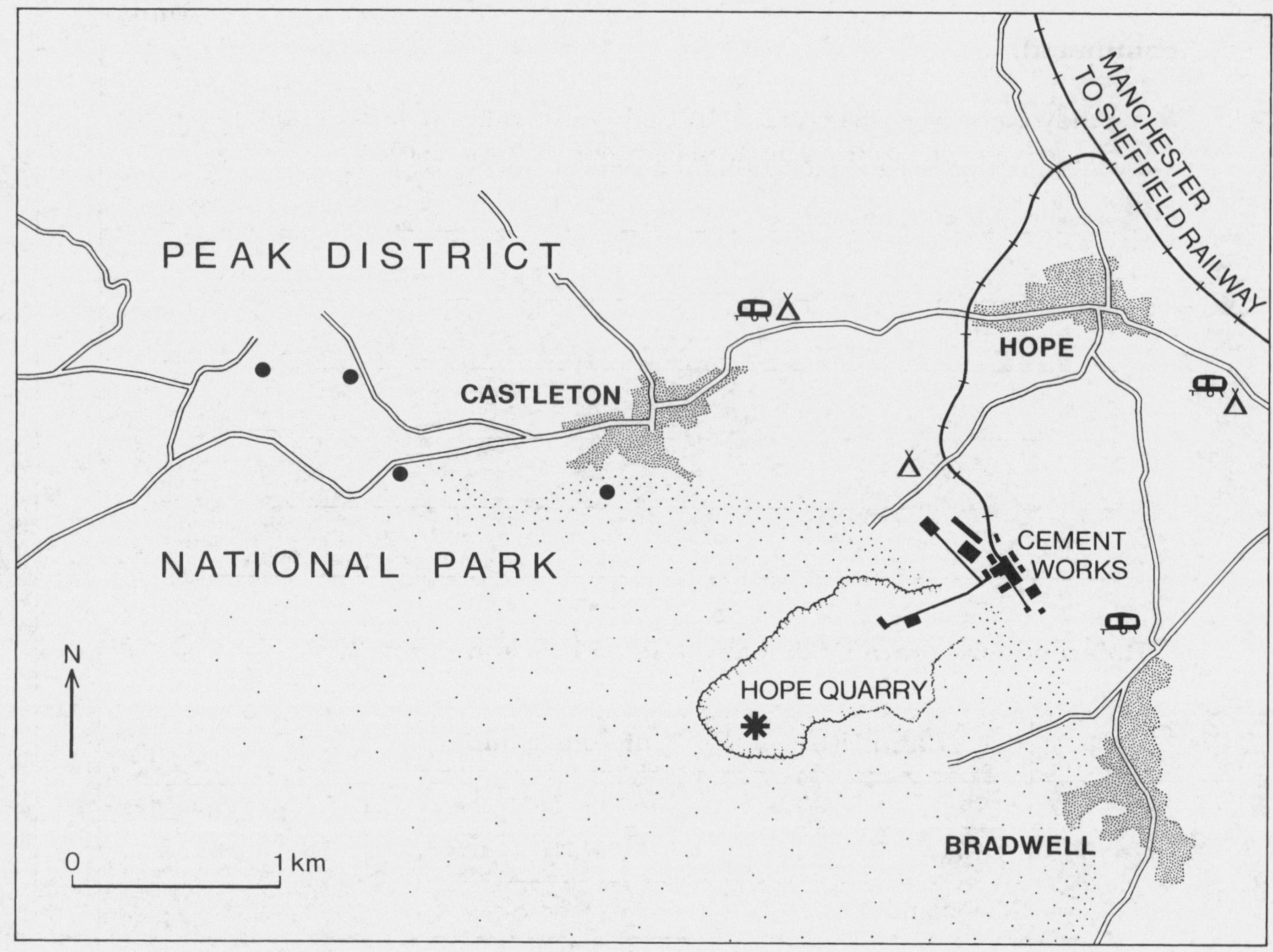

✱ LIMESTONE, THE MAIN RAW MATERIAL IN THE MANUFACTURE OF CEMENT

KEY

- ● LIMESTONE CAVES (OPEN TO PUBLIC)
- CARAVAN SITE
- CAMPSITE
- BUILT UP AREA
- RAILWAY
- ROAD
- LIMESTONE HILLS

DO NOT WRITE IN THIS MARGIN

KU	ES

Marks

6. (continued)

Study Reference Diagram Q6.

Do you think this is a good location for a cement works?

Give reasons for your answer.

4

[Turn over

DO NOT WRITE IN THIS MARGIN

KU	ES

Marks

7. **Reference Diagram Q7: Population Data—India**

Year	Population in Millions
1945	336
1955	395
1965	482
1975	600
1985	749
1995	934
2005	1095

Look at Reference Diagram Q7.

(*a*) "In an Economically Less Developed Country such as India, the population figures taken from census records are likely to be unreliable."

UN spokesperson

Do you agree with the above statement?

Give reasons for your answer.

3

DO NOT WRITE IN THIS MARGIN

KU ES

Marks

7. (continued)

(*b*) What other techniques could be used to show the information in Reference Diagram Q7?

Explain your choice(s).

4

[Turn over

DO NOT WRITE IN THIS MARGIN

KU	ES

Marks

8. Reference Diagram Q8: Migration from Haiti to USA, 1990–95

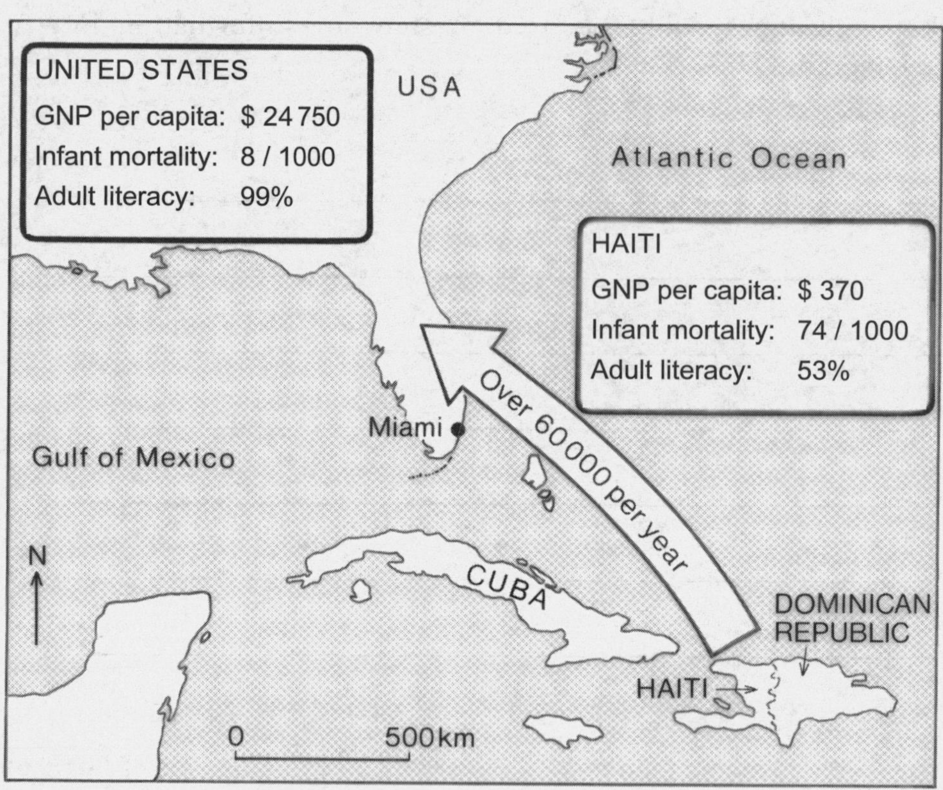

Look at Reference Diagram Q8.

Referring to the data shown, **explain** why so many people migrated from Haiti to USA between 1990 and 1995.

____

____

____

____

____

____

____ 4

9. Reference Diagram Q9: Selected World Oil Consumption, 2005

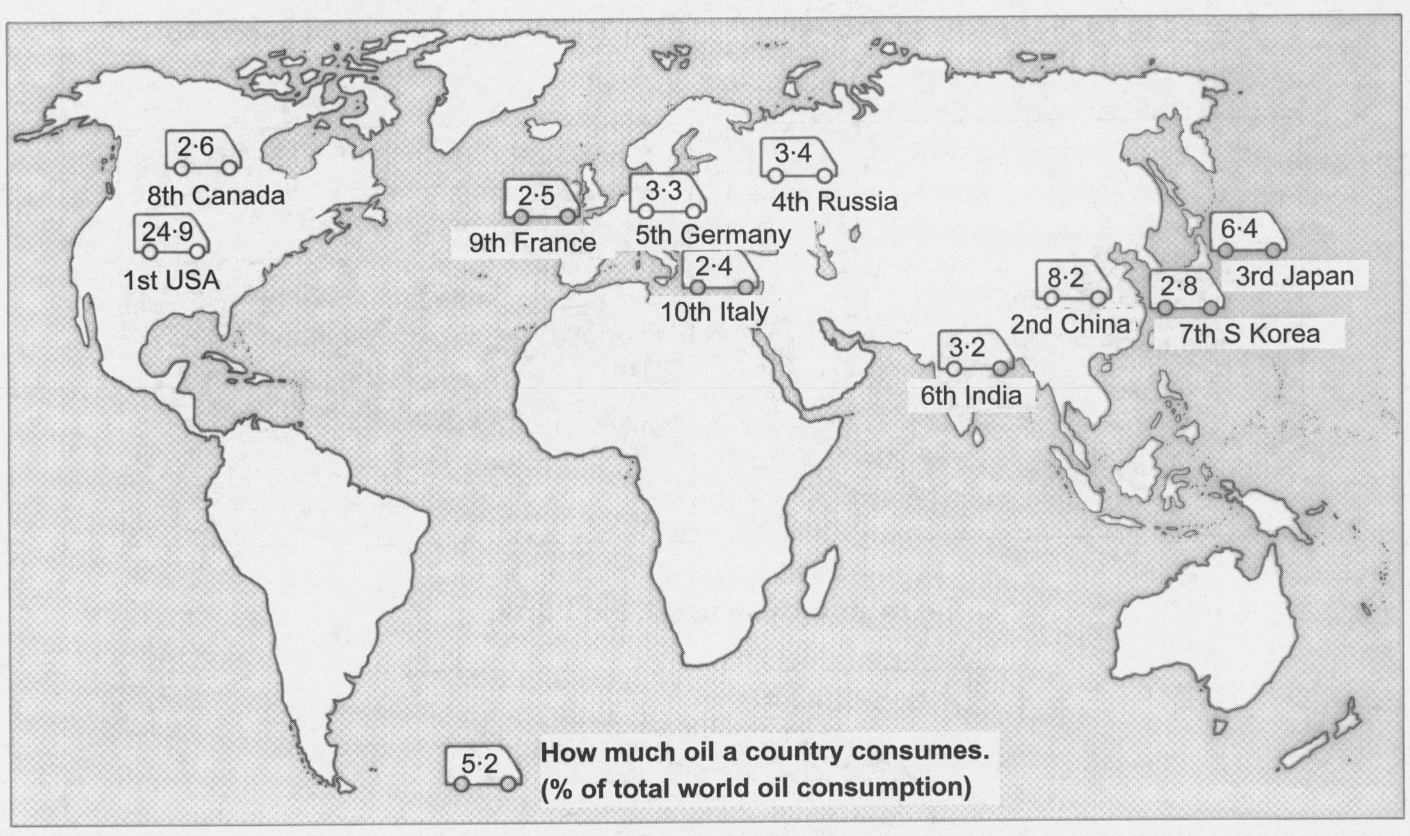

DO NOT WRITE IN THIS MARGIN

	KU	ES

Marks

Study Reference Diagram Q9.

Explain why certain areas such as the USA, Europe and Japan use such a great amount of the world's oil.

4

[Turn over

DO NOT WRITE IN THIS MARGIN

KU	ES

10. Reference Diagram Q10: Effects of Asian Tsunami, December 2004

Damage in Nam Khem village, Thailand

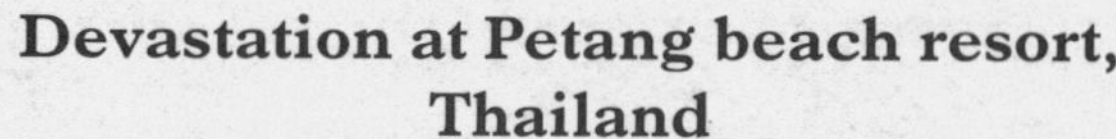

Devastation at Petang beach resort, Thailand

Farmland destroyed, Sri Lanka

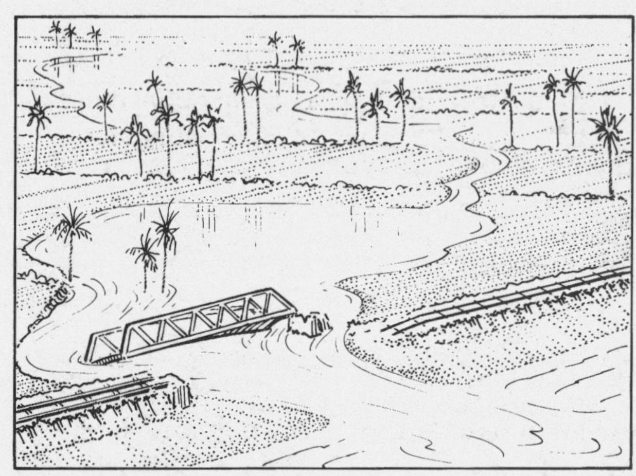

DO NOT WRITE IN THIS MARGIN

KU	ES

Marks

10. (continued)

Study Reference Diagram Q10.

> "Immediate help is essential but we also need long term aid for a full recovery."

Government spokesperson

For this type of natural disaster, **describe** what could be done to help these areas **in the longer term**.

____

____

____

____

____

____ 4

[*END OF QUESTION PAPER*]

[BLANK PAGE]

2007 | Credit

[BLANK PAGE]

C

1260/405

NATIONAL QUALIFICATIONS 2007

TUESDAY, 8 MAY
1.00 PM – 3.00 PM

GEOGRAPHY
STANDARD GRADE
Credit Level

All questions should be attempted.

Candidates should read the questions carefully. Answers should be clearly expressed and relevant.

Credit will always be given for appropriate sketch-maps and diagrams.

Write legibly and neatly, and leave a space of about one centimetre between the lines.

All maps and diagrams in this paper have been printed in black only: no other colours have been used.

PB 1260/405 6/19270

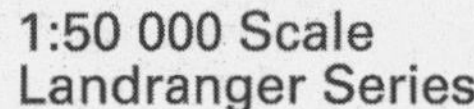

1:50 000 Scale
Landranger Series

Four colours should appear ab
Four colours should appear ab

2 centim

1 kilometre = 0·6214 mile

Extract No 1558/54

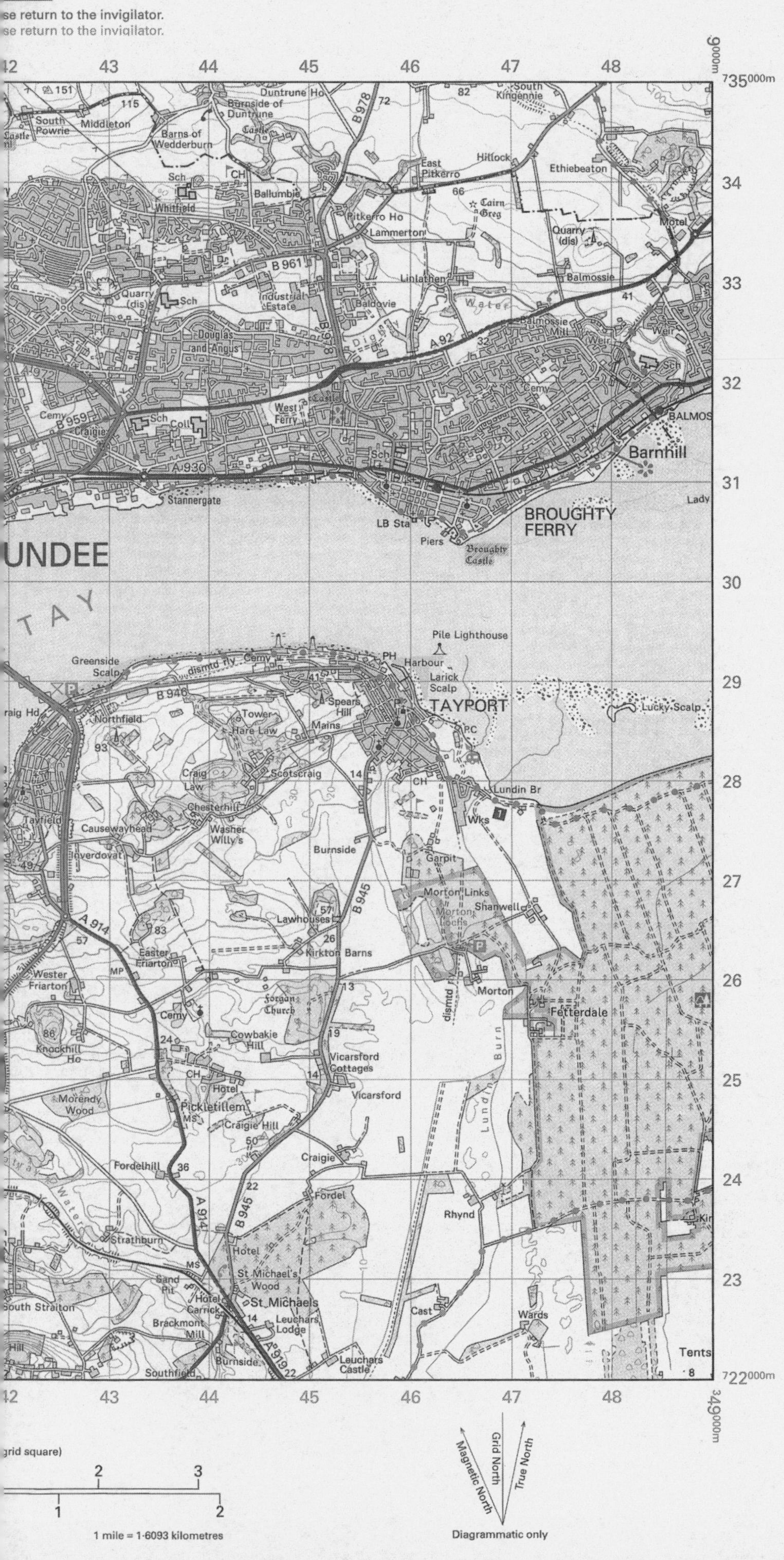

1. **Reference Diagram Q1A**

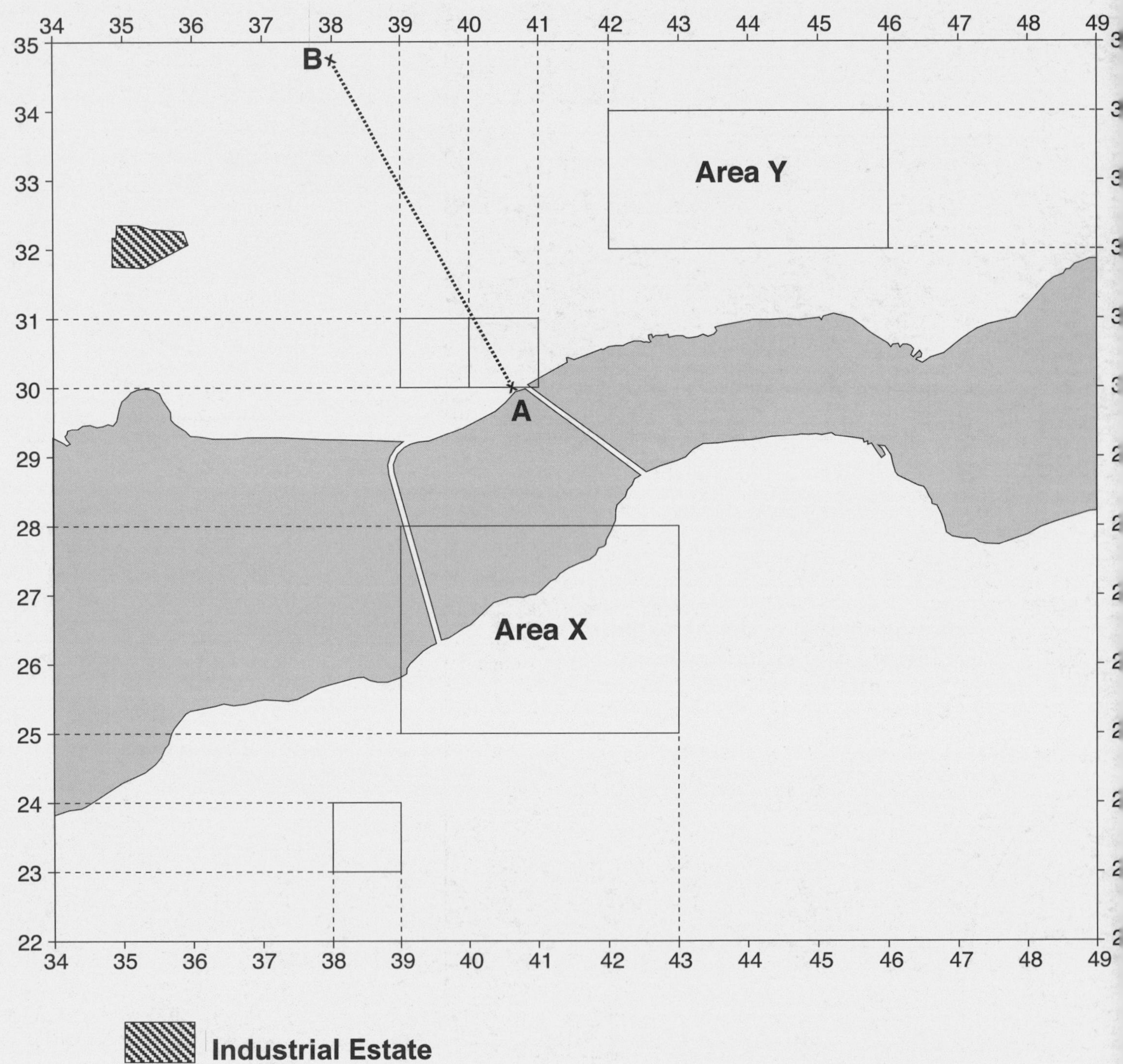

	Marks	
	KU	ES

1. (continued)

This question refers to the OS Map Extract (No 1558/54) of the Dundee area.

Reference Diagram Q1B: View SE from Dundee Law 392313

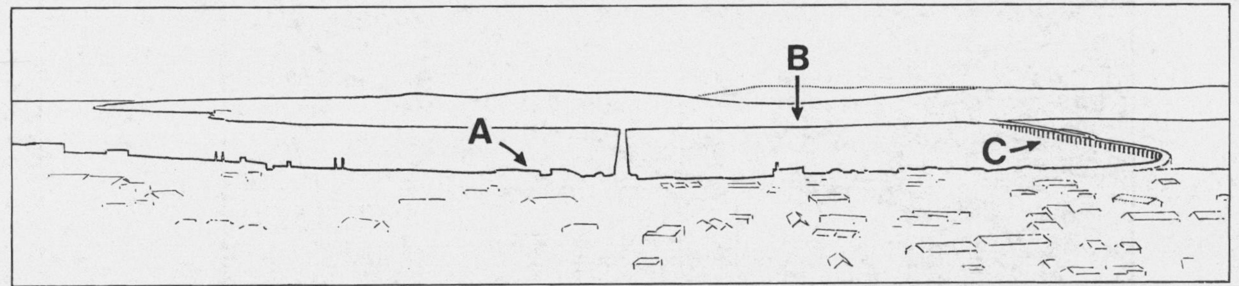

(*a*) Study Reference Diagram Q1B and the map extract.

Identify the **three** features A, B and C.

Choose from:

Railway Bridge; Tayport; Discovery Point; Road Bridge;

Docks; Newport on Tay. 3

(*b*) Find Area X on Reference Diagram Q1A (see *Page two*) and on the OS map extract.

Referring to map evidence, **explain** the way in which the **physical** landscape has affected land use in this area. 4

[Turn over

Marks | KU

1. (continued)

Reference Diagram Q1C: Area Y in the Year 1971

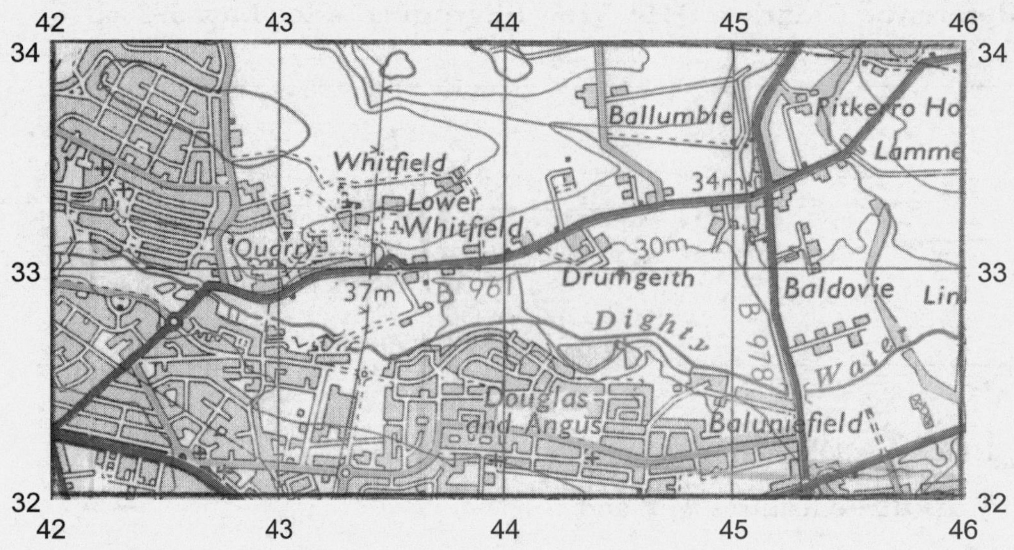

(*c*) Look at Reference Diagram Q1C.

Find Area Y on Reference Diagram Q1A and on the OS map extract.

Describe how the land use changes in the area since 1971 have **both** benefited **and** created problems for the area and its people.

(*d*) Mr Dick works in grid square 4030 and lives in a flat in grid square 3930. He is considering moving house to Gauldry 3823.

Do you think he should make this move?

Using map evidence, give reasons for your answer.

(*e*) Refer to Reference Diagram Q1A.

A group of students intends to gather information about differences in urban land use along transect AB (407300 to 380348).

Describe, in detail, the gathering techniques they might use.

Give reasons for your choice of techniques.

(*f*) **Explain** the location of the industrial estate at 3532. 4

Marks KU ES

2. Reference Diagram Q2: A Hanging Valley

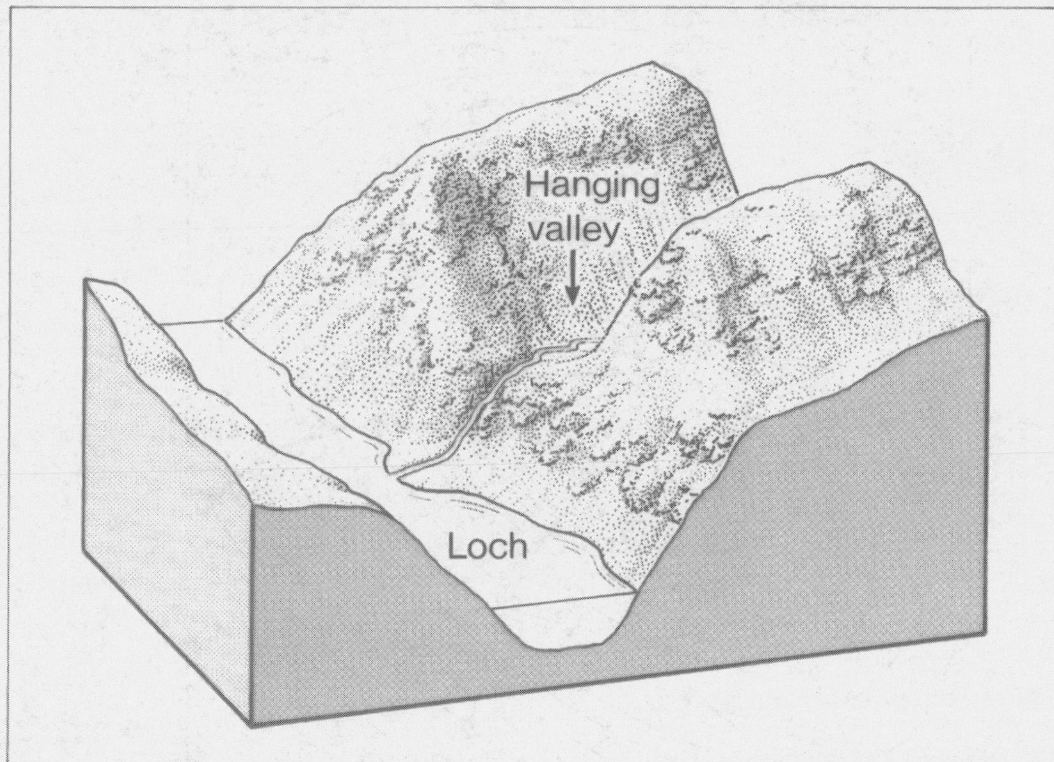

Look at Reference Diagram Q2.

Explain how a hanging valley is formed.

You may use diagram(s) to illustrate your answer. 4

[Turn over

Marks | KU | ES

3. **Reference Diagram Q3A: Synoptic Chart 12 noon, 18 November 2006**

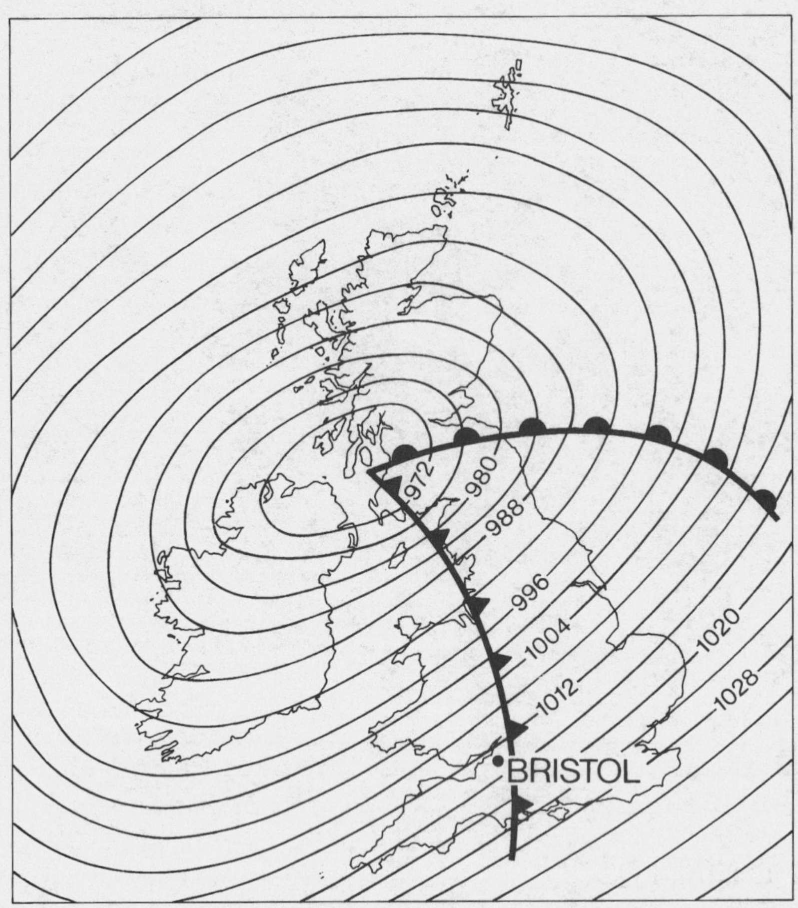

Reference Diagram Q3B: Two Sets of Weather Information

	Set X	**Set Y**
Temperature	5 °C	12 °C
Wind speed	35 knots	10 knots
Wind direction	SW	E
Precipitation	Heavy rain	Steady rain
Cloud amount	7 oktas	4 oktas
Cloud type	Cumulonimbus	Stratus

Look at Reference Diagrams Q3A and Q3B.

Which set of weather information, X or Y, is correct for Bristol?

Explain your choice in detail. **5**

Marks KU ES

4. Reference Diagram Q4: Desertification

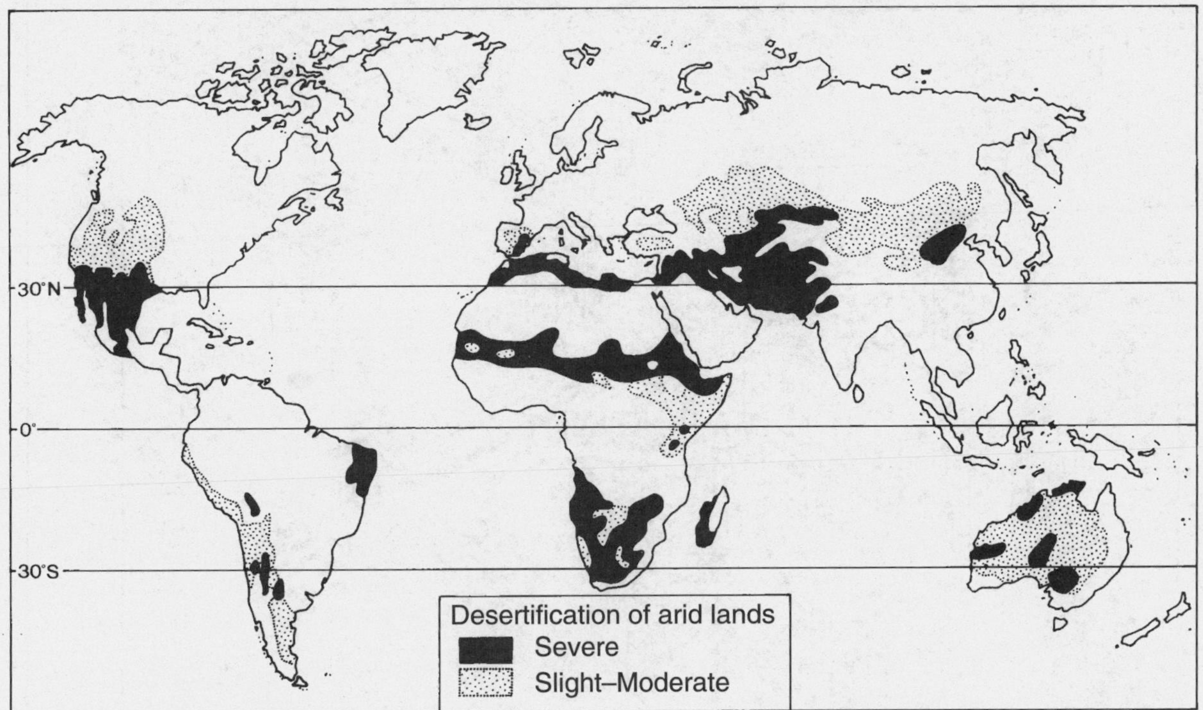

Physical Causes of Desertification
Unreliable rainfall
Wind
High temperatures

Human Causes of Desertification
Population increase
Overgrazing/overcropping
Removing trees for firewood

Look at Reference Diagram Q4.

(*a*) Desertification is a major problem in many areas of the world.

Choose **one** physical and **one** human cause and **explain** why each of them is a major reason for desertification. 4

(*b*) **Describe**, in detail, ways in which desertification can be overcome. 4

[Turn over

	Marks	
	KU	ES

5. Reference Diagram Q5: Central Business District of a Large City

Study Reference Diagram Q5.

In recent years many changes have taken place in the Central Business Districts of British cities.

Give reasons for these changes. 5

Marks

KU	ES

6. Reference Diagram Q6A: Inverlochlarig Sheep Farm, Perthshire

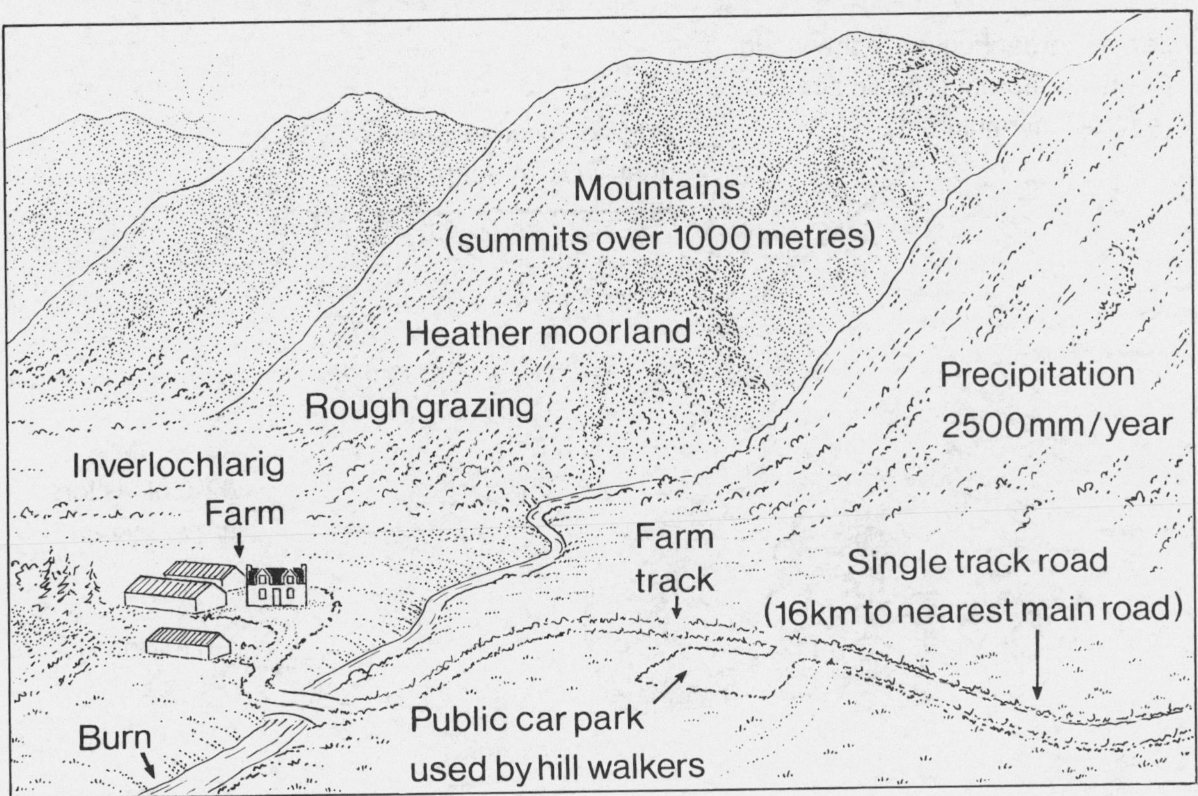

Reference Diagram Q6B

"I'm so fed up with ever increasing fuel costs, lower prices from animal sales and dealing with the EU that I wonder if it is worth carrying on."

Local farmer

Study Reference Diagrams Q6A and Q6B.

Human and physical factors both create problems for farmers in this type of environment.

Select **either** human **or** physical factors.

For the factors you have chosen **explain**, in detail, why these cause more problems for the farmer. 6

[Turn over

7. **Reference Diagram Q7A:**
The Eden Project—A Visitor Attraction in Cornwall

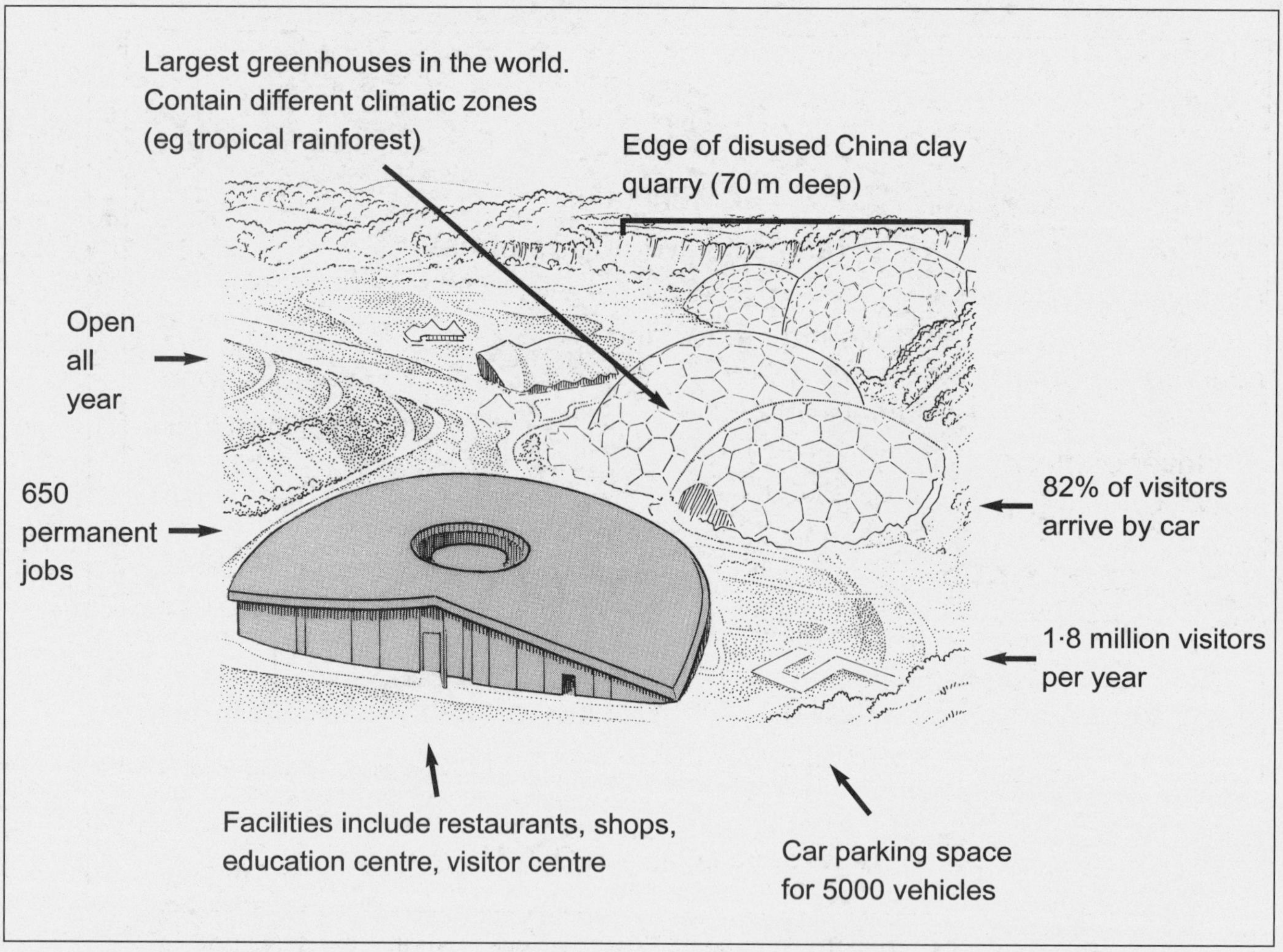

Largest greenhouses in the world.
Contain different climatic zones
(eg tropical rainforest)
Edge of disused China clay
quarry (70 m deep)
Open
all
year
650
permanent
jobs
82% of visitors
arrive by car
1·8 million visitors
per year
Facilities include restaurants, shops,
education centre, visitor centre
Car parking space
for 5000 vehicles

Reference Diagram Q7B: Location of the Eden Project

KEY
'A' CLASS ROAD
DUAL CARRIAGEWAY
MOTORWAY
COUNTY BOUNDARY
Bristol Channel
BARNSTAPLE
D E V O N
EXETER
M5
A30
A38
CORNWALL
NEWQUAY
PLYMOUTH
A391
EDEN
PROJECT
TRURO
ST. AUSTELL
FALMOUTH
PENZANCE
English Channel
N
0 10 20km

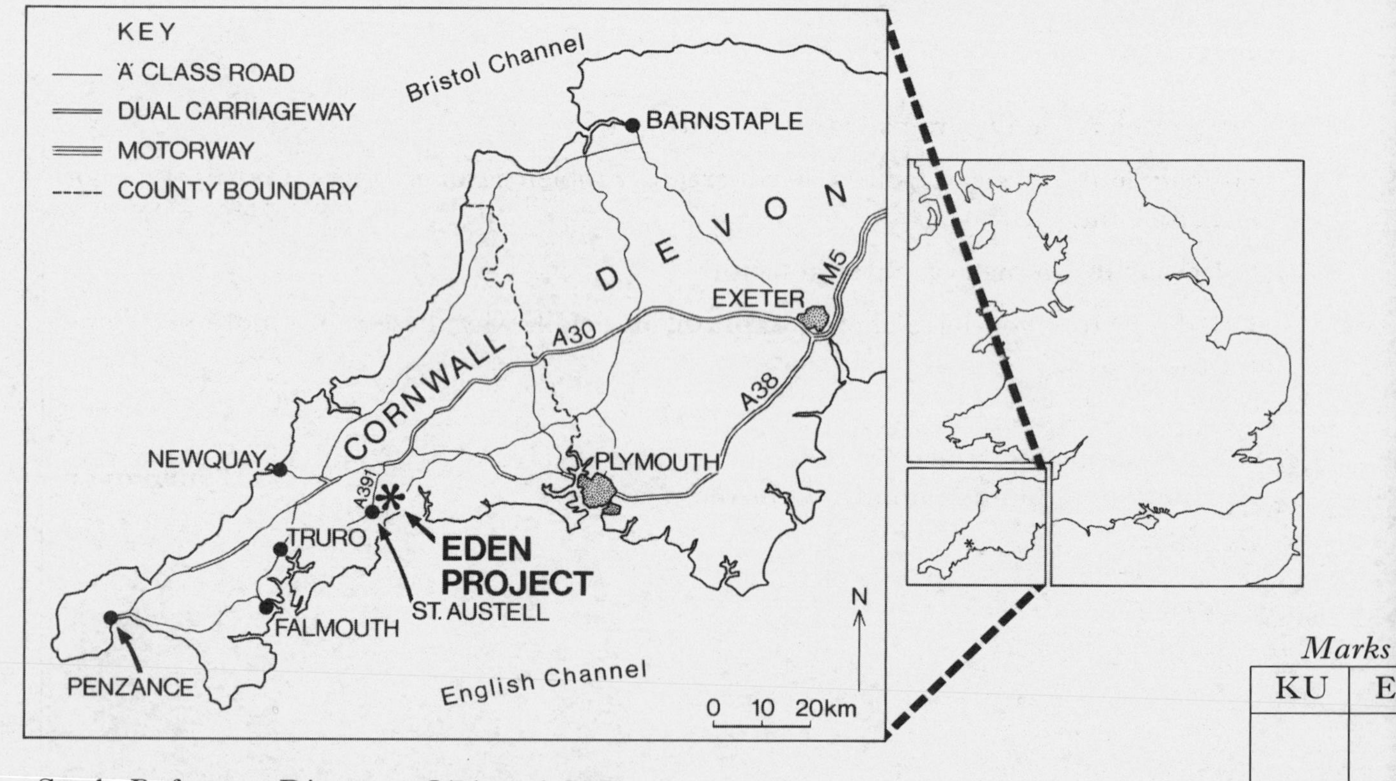

Marks	
KU	E

Study Reference Diagrams Q7A and Q7B.

Explain fully the advantages **and** disadvantages of this new visitor attraction to St Austell and the surrounding area.

8. **Reference Diagram Q8A: North America Population Distribution**

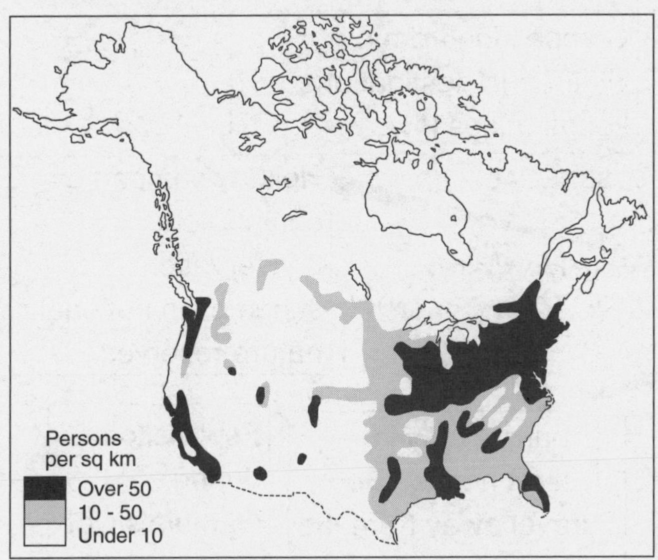

Reference Diagram Q8B: North America Relief

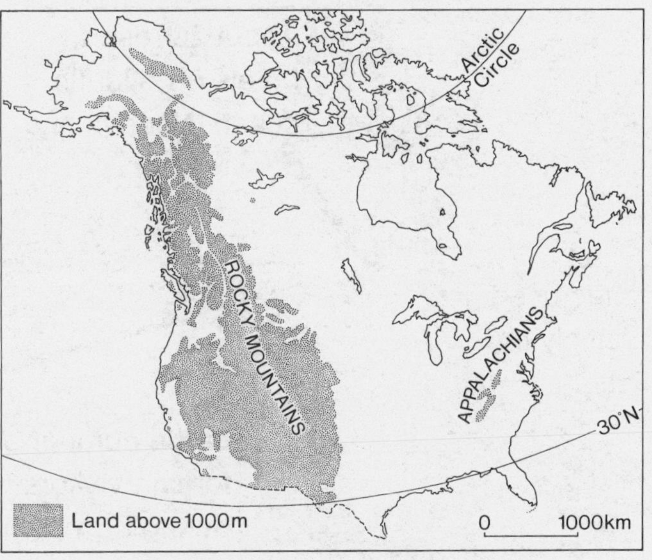

Reference Diagram Q8C: North America Annual Rainfall

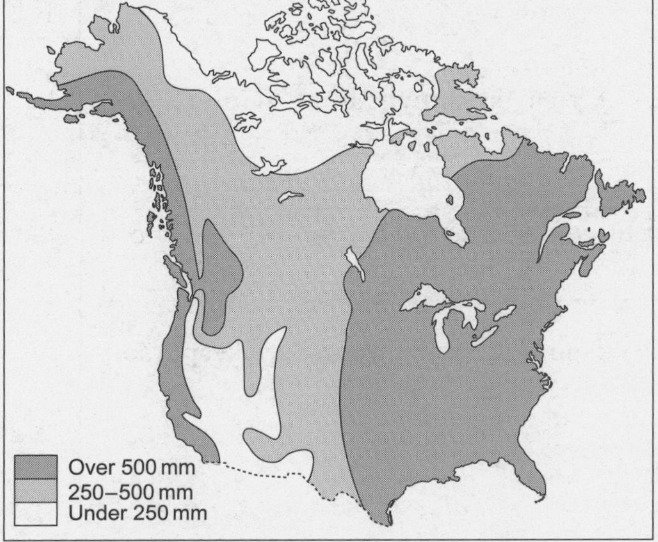

Reference Diagram Q8D: North America Power and Industry

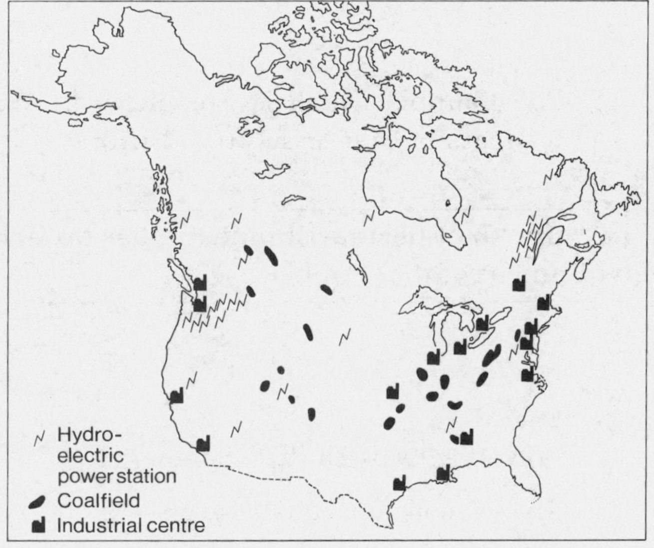

Marks	
KU	ES

Using information given in Reference Diagrams Q8A, B, C and D, **explain** the distribution of population in North America. **6** (ES)

[Turn over

9. Reference Diagram Q9A: Tourism in the Gambia (West Africa)

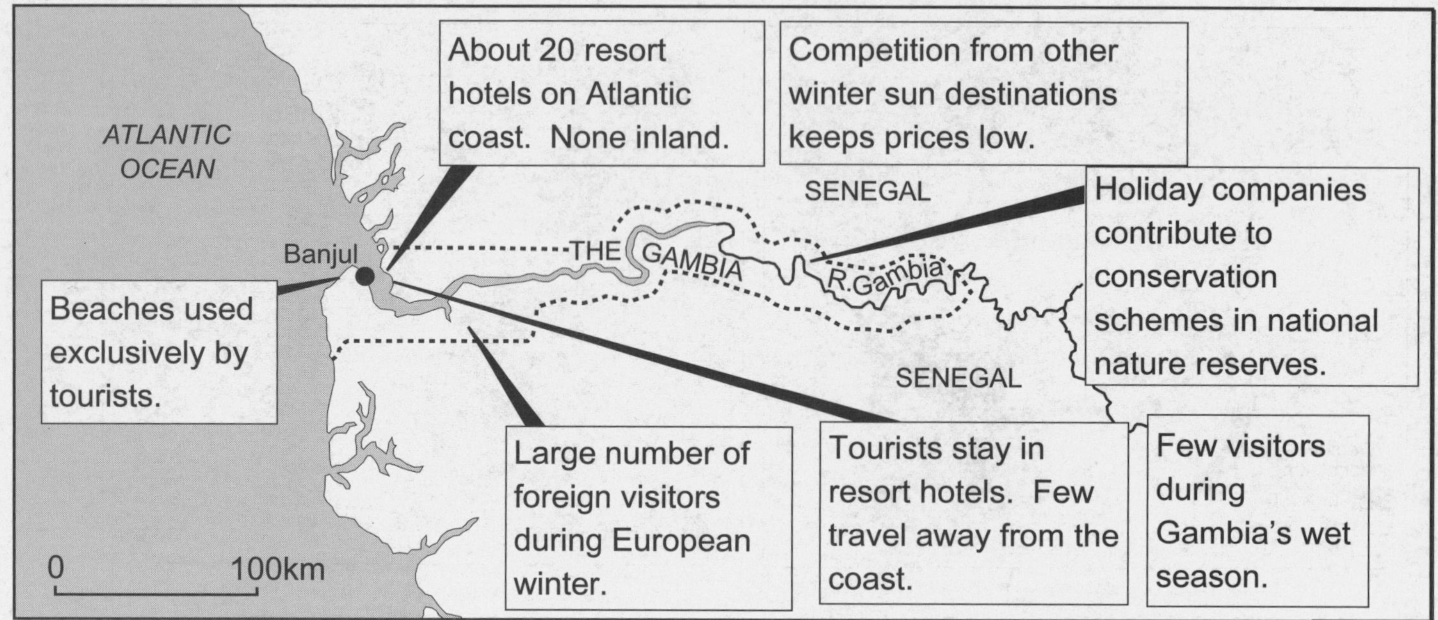

Marks	
KU	E

(*a*) The Gambia which is a country in West Africa is known as a "winter sun" destination for tourists from Europe.

"The growth of the tourist industry has brought huge benefits for the people and the environment of the Gambia."

Package holiday company spokesperson

Do you agree with this statement?

Give reasons for your answer.

	Marks	
	KU	ES

9. (continued)

Reference Diagram Q9B: Tourism Facts for The Gambia

- Population = 1 400 000
- Labour Force = 400 000
- Tourism employs 10 000 Gambians

- Tourism is the biggest foreign exchange earner in The Gambia
- GDP from Agriculture = 30% from Tourism = 25%
  from Fisheries = 30% from Others = 15%

- Most visitors come from Europe:
  from UK = 60% from Sweden = 7%
  from Netherlands = 12% from Others = 21%

(*b*) Study Reference Diagram Q9B.

Which processing techniques would be most effective to show the different information about tourism?

Explain your choice of techniques. 4

[Turn over for Question 10 on *Page fourteen*

Marks

KU	ES

10. **Reference Diagram Q10: Measures of Development**

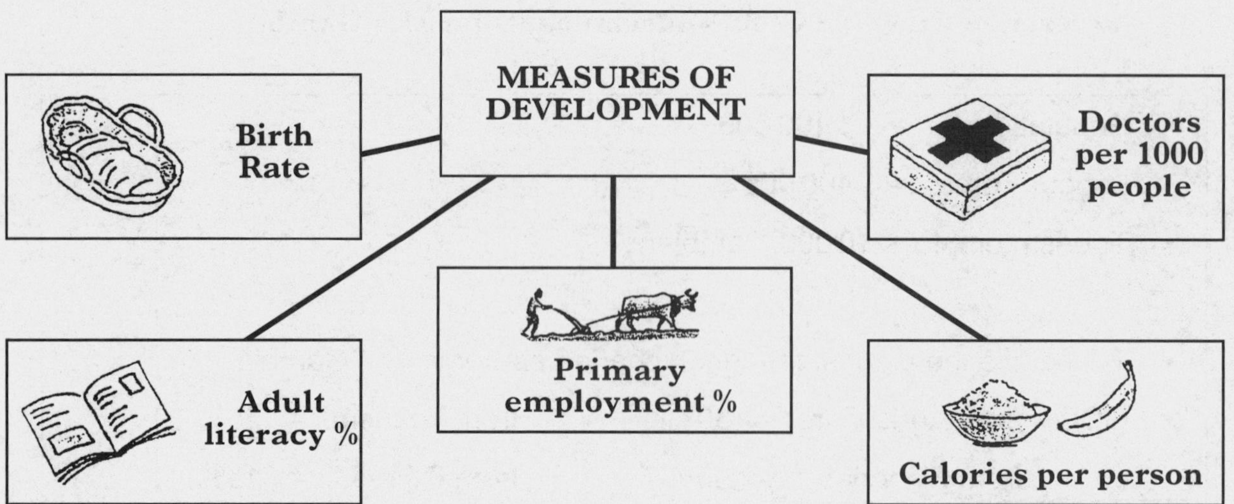

Study Reference Diagram Q10.

Choose **two** of the measures shown and **explain** why they are good indicators of the differences between ELDCs (economically less developed countries) and EMDCs (economically more developed countries). 6

[END OF QUESTION PAPER]

[BLANK PAGE]

[BLANK PAGE]

[BLANK PAGE]

[BLANK PAGE]

[BLANK PAGE]

Acknowledgements

Leckie and Leckie is grateful to the copyright holders, as credited, for permission to use their material:
This product includes mapping data reproduced by permission of Ordnance Survey on behalf of HMSO.

The following companies have very generously given permission to reproduce their copyright material free of charge:
Toyota PLC for a photograph (2004 Credit paper p 9).